Mastering Arabic 1

with 2 Audio CDs

Second Edition

Jane Wightwick &
Mahmoud Gaafar

HIPPOCRENE BOOKS, INC.
New York

to Leila

Hippocrene Books, Inc. edition, 2009.
Third printing, 2010.

First Published by Palgrave Macmillan
Published in North America under license from Macmillan Publishers Ltd, Houndmills, Basingstoke, Hants RG21 6XS, United Kingdom

For more information, contact:
HIPPOCRENE BOOKS, INC.
171 Madison Avenue
New York, NY 10016
www.hippocrenebooks.com

Cataloging-in-Publication data available from the Library of Congress.

ISBN 13: 978-0-7818-1238-2
ISBN 10: 0-7818-1238-0

Printed in the United States of America.

Mastering Arabic 1 Track Lists

CD 1 Units 1–9

Track	Title
	Unit 1
01	Introduction
02	Letters of the alphabet: group 1
03	Vowels
04	Exercise 2
05	Exercise 6
06	Shadda
07	Exercise 7
08	Conversation: Greetings
	Unit 2
09	Letters of the alphabet: group 2
10	Long vowels
11	Exercise 3
12	Exercise 4
13	Alif
14	Putting words together
15	Exercise 5
16	Simple sentences
17	Male and female
18	Conversation: Introductions
	Unit 3
19	Letters of the alphabet: group 3
20	Exercise 1
21	Exercise 2
22	Exercise 4
23	What's this?
24	The family
25	Conversation: Introducing your family
	Unit 4
26	Letters of the alphabet: group 4
27	Emphatic and non-emphatic sounds
28	Exercise 1
29	Jobs
30	Exercise 3
31	Making words plural
32	Conversation: Talking about what you do
	Unit 5
33	Letters of the alphabet: group 5
34	Exercise 1
35	Everyday objects
36	Describing things
37	Whose is it?
38	Conversation: Polite requests
	Unit 6
39	Letters of the alphabet: group 6
40	Exercise 1
41	Ghayn and ʿayn
42	Exercise 2
43	Sun letters
44	Exercise 6
45	Asking questions
46	Exercise 8
47	Where?
48	Conversation: Dialects
	Unit 7
49	The town
50	Exercise 4
51	Exercise 6
52	Exercise 7
53	Conversation: Describing your town or your room
	Unit 8
54	Exercise 1
55	Exercise 4
56	Conversation: Review
	Unit 9
57	The Middle East
58	Capital city
59	Geographical position
60	Exercise 5
61	Nationalities
62	Conversation: Talking about where you come from
63	Exercise 10

CD 2 Units 10–20

Track	Title
	Unit 10
01	Arabic numbers 1-10
02	Exercise 2
03	Counting things
04	How much?
05	In the market
06	Conversation: In the market
	Unit 11
07	Plural patterns 1 and 2
08	Exercise 3
09	What are these?
10	The party
11	Salwa in the party shop
12	Exercise 7
13	Conversation: Going shopping
	Unit 12
14	Ahmed Hamdi's alibi
15	Asking questions about the past
16	Zaynab's story
17	Joining sentences together
18	Exercise 8
	Unit 13
19	Plural patterns 3 and 4
20	Exercise 1
21	Numbers 11-100
22	What's the weather like?
23	Describing the weather
24	Conversation: Talking about a vacation
	Unit 14
25	Days of the week
26	Plural pattern 5
27	Exercise 4
28	What did the President do last week?
29	The cabinet
	Unit 15
30	Exercise 2
31	Exercise 10
32	Conversation: Review
	Unit 16
33	What's the time?
34	More about time
35	Exercise 3
36	Every day
37	Exercise 4
38	Negative statements
39	Asking questions about every day
40	At school
41	What does the class study?
42	Exercise 10
	Unit 17
43	At the grocer's
44	Describing packaging
45	Buying provisions
46	Exercise 3
47	Words for places
48	Waiter!
49	Conversation: At the restaurant
50	In the kitchen
51	Have you done it?
52	He didn't do it
	Unit 18
53	The biggest in the world
54	Exercise 3
55	Comparing past and present
56	How things used to be
	Unit 19
57	Months of the year
58	Exercise 1
59	In the future
60	The flying bicycle
61	Forms of the verb: VII, VIII, X
	Unit 20
62	Exercise 2
63	Exercise 6
64	Conversation: Review

Contents

Acknowledgements *ix*
Preface to the 2nd edition *x*
Introduction *xi*

1

Language units

Unit 1 ***Getting started*** *2*
Letters of the alphabet: group 1 (ب ت ث ن ي) *2*
Vowels *5*
Joining letters: group 1 *6*
Adding vowels to words *8*
Conversation sections *10*
Conversation: Greetings *11*
Vocabulary in Unit 1 *11*
Vocabulary learning *12*

Unit 2 ***Putting words together*** *13*
Letters of the alphabet: group 2 (ا د ذ ر ز و) *13*
Joining letters: group 2 *15*
Long vowels *17*
Putting words together *20*
Simple sentences *22*
Male and female *23*
Conversation: Introductions *24*
Vocabulary in Unit 2 *24*

Unit 3 ***The family*** *25*
Letters of the alphabet: group 3 (ج ح خ ه م) *25*
Joining letters: jīm, ḥā', khā' and mīm *27*
Joining hā' *29*
Feminine words *30*
What's this? *31*
The family *32*
Conversation: Introducing your family *36*
Vocabulary in Unit 3 *36*

Unit 4 ***Jobs*** *37*
Letters of the alphabet: group 4 (س ش ص ض) *37*
Joining letters: group 4 *39*

Jobs 42
Making words plural 44
Conversation: Talking about what you do 47
Structure notes: Case endings; the nominative case 48
Vocabulary in Unit 4 49

Unit 5 ***Describing things*** 50
Letters of the alphabet: group 5 (ف ق ك ل) 50
Joining letters: group 5 52
Everyday objects 54
Describing things 56
Whose is it? 59
Possessive endings 60
Structure notes: Indefinite and definite 62
Conversation: Polite requests 63
Vocabulary in Unit 5 64

Unit 6 ***Where is it?*** 65
Letters of the alphabet: group 6 (ط ظ ع غ) 65
Joining letters: group 6 69
Sun letters 72
Asking questions 74
Hamza 76
Where? 76
Keying Arabic 79
Conversation: dialects 79
Structure notes: The genitive case 80
Vocabulary in Unit 6 80

Unit 7 ***Describing places*** 81
Describing places 81
iḍāfa constructions 83
Group words 85
More about plurals 86
More about adjectives 86
Structure notes: Genitive with iḍāfa 88
Conversation: Describing your town 89
Vocabulary in Unit 7 89

Unit 8 ***Review*** 90
Conversation: Review 100

Unit 9 ***Countries and people*** 101
The Middle East 101
Capital city 102
Geographical position 103
Other countries of the world 105
Nationalities 106
Conversation: Talking about where you come from 111
Vocabulary in Unit 9 113

Unit 10 ***Counting things*** 115
Arabic numbers 1–10 115
Handwritten numbers 117
English words in Arabic 118
Counting things 119
How many? 121
How much? 123
In the market 125
What's it made of? 126
Describing what you have 126
Conversation: In the market 128
Structure notes: Case endings for the sound masculine plural 128
Vocabulary in Unit 10 129

Unit 11 ***Plurals and colours*** 131
Arabic roots 131
Plural patterns 1 and 2 133
What are these? 137
The party 140
Colours 142
Structure notes: The accusative case 144
Conversation: Going shopping 145
Vocabulary in Unit 11 145

Unit 12 ***What happened yesterday?*** 147
What happened yesterday? 147
Asking questions about the past 151
Questions with 'what?' 154
Verbs in the past 156
Joining sentences together 158
Using a dictionary 161
Structure notes: Plural and dual case endings 163
Vocabulary in Unit 12 164

Unit 13 ***Wish you were here*** *166*
Plural patterns 3 and 4 *166*
Numbers 11–19 *169*
Numbers 20–100 *171*
Numbers 11 upwards with a singular noun *172*
What's the weather like? *173*
Writing notes and postcards *176*
Past verbs in the plural *177*
Structure notes: Numbers *178*
Conversation: Talking about a vacation *179*
Vocabulary in Unit 13 *179*

Unit 14 ***All the President's men*** *181*
Days of the week *181*
Arabic words in English *182*
Plural pattern 5 *183*
What did the President do last week? *186*
Word order *188*
The cabinet *190*
Singular and plural verbs *193*
Structure notes: More about iḍāfa *195*
Vocabulary in Unit 14 *196*

Unit 15 ***Review*** *198*
Conversation: Review *206*
Vocabulary in Unit 15 *207*

Unit 16 ***Every day*** *208*
What's the time? *208*
Every day *212*
He and she *214*
Negative statements *216*
Asking questions about every day *217*
Present tense *218*
Education *219*
At school *219*
At university *222*
Vocabulary learning *222*
Structure notes: Present tense *223*
Vocabulary in Unit 16 *223*

Unit 17 ***Eating and drinking*** *225*
At the grocer's *225*

In the restaurant 229
Words for places 230
Waiter! 232
Conversation: In the restaurant 233
In the kitchen 234
Forms of the verb: II, III and IV 234
Have you done it? 237
He didn't do it 239
Vocabulary in Unit 17 241

Unit 18 ***Comparing things*** 244
The biggest in the world 244
At the car rental office 247
Comparing past and present 249
Was/were 251
Weak verbs 253
Forms of the verb: V and VI 255
Vocabulary in Unit 18 257

Unit 19 ***Future plans*** 260
Months of the year 260
In the future 261
An international tour 264
Forms of the verb: VII, VIII and X 267
The flying bicycle 267
Other features of verbs 269
Vocabulary in Unit 19 270

Unit 20 ***Review and advice on further study*** 272
Review 272
Advice on further study 278

2 **Reference material**
Appendix 1 ***The Arabic alphabet*** 281
Appendix 2 ***The Arabic verb*** 283
Appendix 3 ***Months of the year*** 286
Appendix 4 ***Broken plurals*** 286
Answers to exercises 287
English–Arabic glossary 345
Grammar index 370

Acknowledgements

We are lucky enough to have benefited from the expertise and experience of some of the foremost experts in teaching Arabic across the two editions of *Mastering Arabic*. For their useful comments on this revised edition we would like to thank Nadia Adbulaal of the University of Manchester, Kassem Wahba of Georgetown University, Ghinwa Ma'mari and her team at the School of African and Oriental Studies, London University, and Osman Nusairi for his careful proofreading. For suggestions on the first edition, our thanks go to Dr Said Badawi of the American University in Cairo and Dr Avi Shivtiel of Leeds University. The course is immeasurably better for all of their input.

We are also grateful to everyone at Palgrave Macmillan for their enthusiasm for this course, but specifically Dominic Knight, Helen Bugler and Isobel Munday who have supported us through both editions over two decades – a rare thing indeed in publishing these days.

The authors and publishers wish to thank the following who have kindly given permission for the use of copyright material: Otto Harrassowitz Verlag for material from Hans Wehr, *A Dictionary of Modern Arabic*, ed. J. Milton Cowan, 1991.

Preface to the second edition

When we first set out to write this course there was very little material available that combined modern language teaching methods with learning Arabic. *Mastering Arabic* was our attempt to provide a friendly and fun introduction for the general learner, and we are gratified that it has proved popular with a wide range of students over the years.

At the time of this second edition, the market for Arabic-teaching material has moved on and we have also learnt from our own subsequent experiences of teaching Arabic. We have tried to update and improve *Mastering Arabic* to keep it relevant and in the forefront, while not losing the essential elements that made it popular in the first place.

What's new in the second edition?

The second edition of *Mastering Arabic* has these additional features:

- Clearer, more modern page design and layout
- New 'Conversation' sections with accompanying audio, allowing learners to start talking right from the beginning
- New 'Grammar index' for easy reference
- More listening exercises to help with understanding spoken Arabic
- Transliteration of examples and end-of-unit vocabulary lists throughout the course to help with pronunciation and reading
- Some more advanced material moved to later units
- Additional explanations to support individual learning
- Individual amendments to take account of feedback received from both teachers and students of Arabic over the years.

As publishers as well as educators by trade, we wrote in the first edition that the writing experience had left us 'feeling far more sympathetic towards authors than before we started'. As well as writing this second edition we have also painstakingly laid out the pages using the kind of computer publishing software only dreamt about at the time of the first edition. We now also feel far more sympathetic towards typesetters!

Jane Wightwick and *Mahmoud Gaafar*

Introduction

Arabic is spoken in over twenty countries, from North-West Africa to the Arabian Gulf. This makes it one of the most widely-used languages in the world, and yet it is often regarded as obscure and mysterious. This perception is more often based on an over-emphasis on the difficulty of the Arabic script and the traditional nature of some of the learning material than it is on the complexity of the language itself. There is certainly no reason why the non-specialist should not be able to acquire a general, all-round knowledge of Arabic, and enjoy doing so.

Mastering Arabic will provide anyone working alone or within a group with a lively, clear and enjoyable introduction to Arabic. When you have mastered the basics of the language, then you can go on to study a particular area in more detail if you want.

Before we go on to explain how to use this book, you should be introduced to the different kinds of Arabic that are written and spoken. These fall into three main categories:

Modern Standard Arabic

Modern Standard Arabic (MSA) is the universal language of the Arab World, understood by all Arabic speakers. Almost all written material is in Modern Standard, as are formal and pan-Arab TV programmes, talks, etc.

Classical Arabic

This is the language of the Qur'an and classical literature. Its structure is similar to Modern Standard Arabic, but the style and much of the vocabulary is archaic. It is easier to begin by studying Modern Standard and then progress to classical texts, if that is what you wish to do.

Colloquial dialects

These are the spoken languages of the different regions of the Arab World. They are all more or less similar to the Modern Standard language. The colloquial dialects vary the most in everyday words and expressions, such as 'bread', 'how are you?', etc.

We have chosen to teach the Modern Standard in *Mastering Arabic* as is it a good starting point for beginners. Modern Standard is universally understood and is the best medium through which to master the Arabic script. However, whenever there are dialogues or situations where the colloquial language would naturally be used, we have tried to choose vocabulary and structures that are as close to the spoken form as possible. In this way, you will find that *Mastering Arabic* will enable you to understand Arabic in a variety of different situations and will act as an excellent base for expanding your knowledge of the written and spoken language.

How to use *Mastering Arabic*

This course has over two hours of accompanying audio and access to these recordings is essential, unless you are studying in a group where the tutor has the audio. Those parts of the book which are on the recording are marked with this symbol:

We are assuming that when you start this book you know absolutely no Arabic at all and may be working by yourself. The individual units vary in how they present the material, but the most important thing to remember is to try not to skip anything (except perhaps the 'Structure notes' – see below). There are over 200 exercises in the book, carefully designed to help you practise what you have learnt and to prepare you for what is coming. Work your way through these as they appear in the book and you will find that the language starts to fall into place and that words and phrases are revised. Above all, be patient and do not be tempted to cut corners.

Conversation sections

These sections are designed to introduce you to basic conversational Arabic in social and everyday situations so that you can get talking right from the start. They appear in all the units in the first half of the course, and then as appropriate in the later units.

Structure notes

These occur at the end of some units and contain useful additional information about Arabic grammar. They are not essential to your understanding of basic Arabic but will be helpful to you in recognising some of the finer points when you read or hear them.

Review units

These occur at three points in the course. They will be very useful to you for assessing how well you remember what you have learnt. If you find you have problems with a particular exercise, go back and review the section or sections that deal with that area.

So now you're ready to start learning with *Mastering Arabic*. We hope you enjoy the journey.

part 1

Language units

unit 1

Getting started

Letters of the alphabet: group 1

Many Arabic letters can be grouped together according to their shapes. Some letters share exactly the same shape but have a different number of dots above or below; other shapes vary slightly.

Look at this group of letters and listen to the recording:

	Name of letter	*Pronounced*
ب	bā'	'b' as in 'bat'
ت	tā'	't' as in 'tap'
ث	thā'	'th' as in 'thin'
ن	nūn	'n' as in 'nab'
ي	yā'	'y' as in 'yet'

You can see that bā', tā' and thā' share the same shape, but the position and the number of dots are different; whereas nūn has a slightly different shape, more circular and falling below the line, and yā' has a much curlier shape (but is connected with the other letters, as you will see later in Unit 1).

When Arabic is written by hand, the dots often become 'joined' for the sake of speed. Compare the printed and the handwritten letters below. The most common Arabic printed style is called *naskh,* and the most common handwriting style *riq'a*.

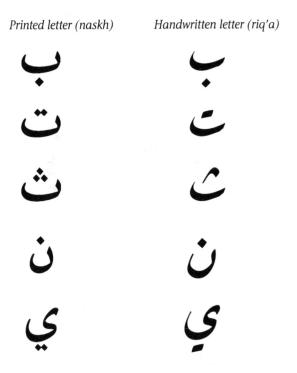

Printed letter (naskh)	*Handwritten letter (riq'a)*
ب	ب
ت	ت
ث	ث
ن	ن
ي	ي

Exercise 1

Look at the letters below and decide which each is:

Handwriting practice

(When practising handwriting, first trace the letters following the direction of the arrows, and then try writing them on lined paper.)

The Arabic script is written from *right* to *left*, so the letters should be formed starting from the *right*:

bā', tā', thā' 

nūn 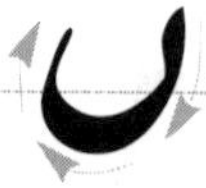

yā' 

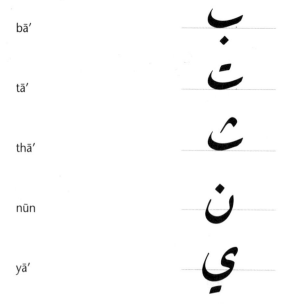

It's easier to finish the main shape first and then add the dots:

bā' ب

tā' ت

thā' ث

nūn ن

yā' ي

Tip: There are *no* capital letters in Arabic.

Vowels

Arabic script is similar to SMS messages in that both types of writing leave out many of the vowels. The short vowels in Arabic are written above and below the letters. If you read the Arabic press or pick up a novel you will rarely see these vowels, as they are not usually written. The reader is expected to deduce the meaning of the word from its pattern and the context.

This book will begin by showing all the short vowels and will gradually drop them as you become more proficient.

Look at these letters and listen to the recording:

بَ (ba) بِ (bi) بُ (bu)

From this you can see:

- A dash *above* the letter (ـَ) is pronounced as a short 'a' following the letter. This vowel is called fatha.
- A dash *below* the letter (ـِ) is pronounced as a short 'i' following the letter. This vowel is called kasra.
- A comma shape above the letter (ـُ) is pronounced as a short 'u' following the letter. This vowel is called ḍamma.

Exercise 2

Listen to the recording and write the correct vowels on these letters:

1 ب	4 ت	7 ب
2 ت	5 ي	8 ث
3 ث	6 ن	

Exercise 3

Now practise saying these letters with their vowels. Then check your answers in the answer section.

1 بِ	4 تُ	7 نُ
2 نَ	5 بَ	8 ثُ
3 يَ	6 تِ	

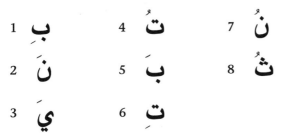

Joining letters: group 1

Written Arabic is 'joined up'. When letters come at the end of a word they look very much as they do when standing alone. However, when they come at the beginning or in the middle of a word they get 'shortened'.

Look at how these letters combine:

← (read from *right to left*)

ب + ث = بث

ت + ب = تب

ث + ب + ت = ثبت

Notice how the letter gets 'chopped' and loses its final flourish, or 'tail', when at the beginning or in the middle of a word, but still keeps its dots for recognition.

The letters nūn and yā' have exactly the same shape as the other letters in this group when they come at the beginning or in the middle of a word, but they retain their differences when at the end:

ب + ن = بن

ن + ي = ني

ب + ي + ت = بيت

ب + ن + ي = بني

ي + ب + ث = يبث

Handwriting practice

Notice how these letters are joined when written by hand:

ب + ث = بث

ب + ن = بن

ث + ب + ت = ثبت

ب + ن + ي = بني

It's easiest if you complete the main shape of the word and then go back to the right-hand side and add all the dots from right to left.

Exercise 4

Look at the newspaper headline. Two examples of the letters in group 1 are circled. How many others can you find?

Tip: When yā' is by itself or at the end of a word, you may see it without the two dots.

اتصالات ناجحة أعادت الأمور إلى

طبيعتها بين السعودية والمنظمة

Exercise 5

Write out these combinations of letters. The first is an example:

1 ت + ي + ن = تين

2 ن + ي = نبي

3 ت + ب + ن = تبن

4 ن + ب + ت = نبت

5 ي + ب + ن + ي = يبني

6 ب + ي + ت + ي =

Adding vowels to words

We can now add vowels to the combinations of letters to make words:

تُ (tu) + ب (b) = تُب (tub)

بِ (bi) + ن (n) = بِن (bin)

بِ (bi) + ن (n) + ت (t) = بِنْت (bint)

بَ (ba) + ي (y) + نَ (na) = بَيْنَ (bayna)

Sukūn

If there is a small circle (sukūn) above a letter (ـْ) this indicates that *no* vowel sound follows that letter – see bint and bayna above. Notice how the sukūn is not usually put above the *last* letter of a word.

Exercise 6

Listen to the recording and write the vowels on these words. Each word will be given twice.

ثبت	4	بيت	1
يثب	5	ثبتت	2
ثبن	6	تبن	3

Shadda

In addition to the three short vowels and the sukūn, there is another symbol: the shadda. This is a small *w* shape (ـّ) written above the letter to show that it is doubled. For example:

(bathth) بَثّ = (th) ث + (th) ث + (ba) بَ

(bunn) بُنّ = (n) ن + (n) ن + (bu) بُ

The sound of a letter is lengthened when there is a shadda. Take care to pronounce this, otherwise you may change the meaning of the word.

Listen to these examples and repeat them with the recording. Each example is given twice:

بُنّ	4	بَثّ	1
بَيِّن	5	ثَبَّتَ	*2
يَبُثُّ	6	ثَبَتَ	*3

**Compare the pronunciation of numbers 2 and 3.*

Notice that kasra is often written below the shadda (ـِّ) rather than below the letter itself – see example 5.

Exercise 7

Write these letter combinations and then try to pronounce them. Check your pronunciation with the recording or answer section.

1 بَ + ت + ت =

2 بَ + ي + يِ + ن =

3 تُ + ن + ن =

4 نَ + ي + ي =

Exercise 8

Say these words and then match their meanings with the English:

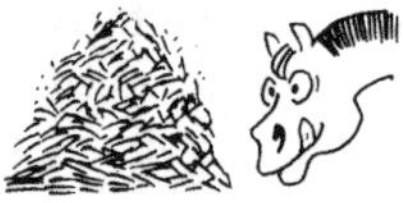

A تِبْن

B بَيْت

C بِنْت

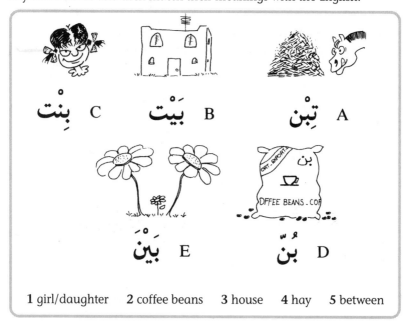

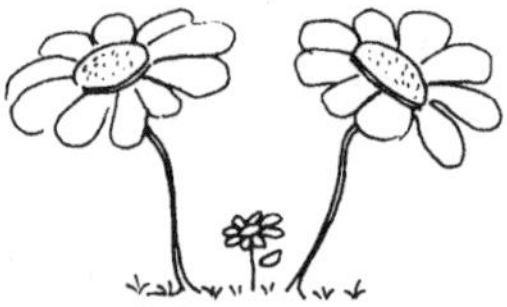

D بُنّ

E بَيْنَ

1 girl/daughter **2** coffee beans **3** house **4** hay **5** between

Conversation sections

These sections are designed to introduce you to basic conversational Arabic in social and everyday situations. They appear in all the units in the first half of the course, and then as appropriate in the later units. You'll find the conversational phrases on the recording, and you'll also be given the opportunity to take part in short dialogues with native speakers. Concentrate on speaking and listening in these sections. At first you may not be able to read all the Arabic script, but you will be able to recognise some of the letters and words.

Conversation

Greetings
One of the most important conversational skills initially in any language is to know how to greet people. Arabic greetings can be elaborate and prolonged, but some all-purpose expressions will get you by:

أهلاً (ahlan) Hello

أهلاً بِك/بِكِ (ahlan bik/biki) Hello to you *(talking to a male/female)*

صَباح الخَير (ṣabāḥ al-khayr) Good morning

صَباح النُّور (ṣabāḥ an-nūr) Good morning *(reply)*

مَساء الخَير (masā' al-khayr) Good evening/afternoon

مَساء النُّور (masā' an-nūr) Good evening/afternoon *(reply)*

مَعَ السَّلامة (maɛa s-salāma) Goodbye

Tip: The reply to a greeting often varies from the original, although it is also acceptable to use the original phrase in reply.

Vocabulary in Unit 1

بِنْت (bint) girl/daughter

بُنّ (bunn) coffee beans

بَيت (bayt) house

بَينَ (bayna) between

تِبن (tibn) hay

أهلاً (ahlan) Hello

أهلاً بِك/بِكِ (ahlan bik/biki) Hello to you

صَباح الخَير (ṣabāḥ al-khayr) Good morning

صَباح النُّور (ṣabāḥ an-nūr) Good morning (*reply*)

مَساء الخَير (masā' al-khayr) Good evening/afternoon

مَساء النُّور (masā' an-nūr) Good evening/afternoon (*reply*)

مَعَ السَّلامة (maɛa s-salāma) Goodbye

Vocabulary learning

Arabic presents some challenges to the beginner trying to learn vocabulary, as the words *and* the script are unfamiliar. However, you can use strategies to help you. One method recommended for learning vocabulary in new scripts is the use of flashcards, similar to the method used to teach young children how to read.

Try the following method to learn your vocabulary:

- Make a set of small cards, blank on both sides.
- Get five envelopes and mark them 'Day 1', 'Day 2', etc.
- Write each Arabic word, with vowels, on one side of a card and the English on the other:

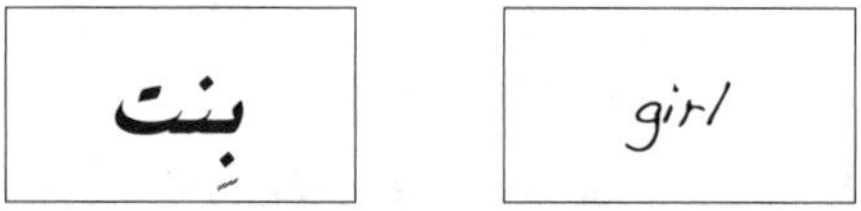

This is good handwriting practice and will also help you remember the word.

- Put all the cards in the envelope marked 'Day 1'.
- Each day, take the cards out of each envelope in turn starting with the highest-numbered envelope and working down to 'Day 1'. (The first day you'll only have cards in the 'Day 1' envelope, the next day you'll have 'Day 2' and 'Day 1', and so on until you have completed five days.)
- Put each card Arabic side up and say the Arabic aloud. Try to remember what it means. When you've finished, shuffle the cards and put them *English* side up, repeating the process.
- If you remember a word, it progresses to the next envelope; if you forget, it goes back to Day 1:

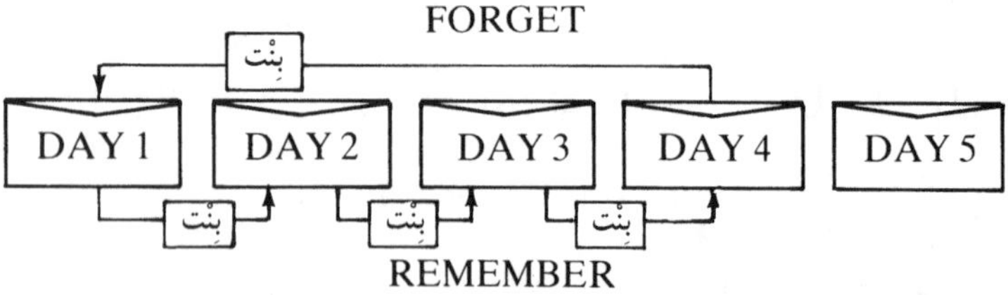

- If you can remember a word five days running you can throw the card away. (Or you can put it back in the Day 1 envelope *without* the vowels.) You can add up to 15 words a day to the Day 1 envelope.

unit 2

Putting words together

Letters of the alphabet: group 2

Look at the next group of letters and listen to the recording:

	Name of letter	*Pronounced*
ا	alif	(see pages 17 and 20)
د	dāl	'd' as in 'dad'
ذ	dhāl	'th' as in 'that'
ر	rā'	rolled 'r' as in Spanish 'arriva'
ز	zāy	'z' as in 'zone'
و	wāw	'w' as in 'wet'

You can see that the dāl and dhāl have the same basic shape, as do rā' and zāy. The only difference is that dhāl and zāy have the dot over the basic shape. Pay special attention to the position and shape of these four letters – dāl and dhāl sit *on* the line while rā' and zāy fall *under* the line.

Wāw and alif have very distinctive shapes, but their connection with the other letters in this group will become clear later in this unit.

As there are no dots to 'join up' in this group of letters, the handwritten versions tend to look very similar to the printed versions.

Exercise 1

Draw a line between the printed letters, their handwritten versions and the names of the letters, as in the example:

ر	و	alif
ذ	ا	dāl
و	ذ	zāy
ز	د	rā’
ا	ر	wāw
د	ز	dhāl

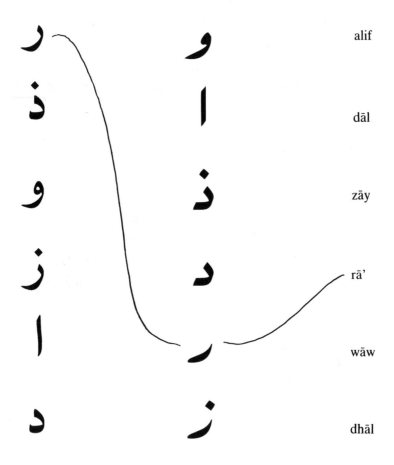

Handwriting practice

dāl, dhāl

rā', zāy

wāw

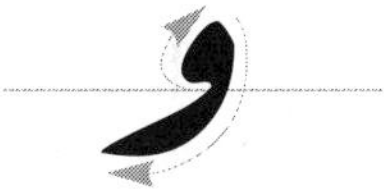

alif

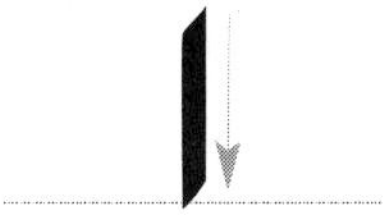

Remember, finish the shape first and then add any dots:

و ز ر ذ د ا

Joining letters: group 2

The similarity between the letters in group 2 becomes clear when we look at how they are joined to other letters. All of the six letters in this group are joined to the letter *before* but cannot be joined to the letter *after*. Look at how alif joins in these combinations:

ب + ا = با

ا + ب = اب

ب + ا + ب = باب

All the letters in this group have the same basic shape wherever they appear in a word, and *always* have a space after them because they do not join to the next letter.

ن + ا + ر = نار

ب + ر + د = برد

ز + ي + ن = زين

ا + ب + د + ا = ابدا

ذ + و + ب = ذوب

و + ز + ي + ر = وزير

The letters in group 2 are the only letters which cannot be joined to the letter following in a word. All other letters can be joined on either side.

Handwriting practice

Practise copying these words. Remember to write the whole word and then add the dots.

ابن ود دار ثوب نزور يبرد

Exercise 2

Fill in the missing letters or words to match the example:

1 بَ (ba) + ر (r) + د (d) = بَرْد (bard)

2 + + = وَرْد

3 + + = رَبْو

4 بَ + ذ + ر =

5 + + = بِرّ

6 بُ + ر + ر =

7 + + = ثَوْب

8 دَ + رَ + زَ =

Long vowels

In Unit 1 you met the three Arabic vowel signs: fatḥa (a), kasra (i) and ḍamma (u). These are all pronounced as short vowels. They can be made long by adding the three letters alif (ا), yā' (ي) and wāw (و).

Look at the following and listen to the recording:

(ba) بَ ⟶ (bā) بَا

(bi) بِ ⟶ (bī) بِي

(bu) بُ ⟶ (bū) بُو

From this you should be able to see that:

fatḥa + alif = ā (long 'a' as in h*ai*r or as in h*ea*rt)
kasra + yā' = ī (long 'i' as in m*ee*t)
ḍamma + wāw = ū (long 'u' as in b*oo*t)

Tip: In practice, the vowel signs are rarely written on long vowels as the extra letter already indicates the sound: با بو بي

Now listen to the pairs of words and repeat them after the recording. Listen carefully for the difference in the short and long vowels. Each pair is given twice:

1 نُذُر	2 بَرَّد	3 يَزِد
نُذُور	بَرَّاد	يَزِيد

It may have occurred to you that if the vowels signs are not usually included at all in written Arabic, then if you come across this word ...

زور

... how do you know whether to pronounce it

زُور (zūr) or ...

زَوْر (zawr) or ...

زَوَر (zawar) or even ...

زَوَّرَ (zawwara) or ...

زُوِّرَ (zuwwira)?

(All of these words exist!) The answer is that you do not know *automatically*. However, when you have learned more about the structure and vocabulary patterns in Arabic, you will usually be able to tell from the context.

Exercise 3

Listen to the recording and write the vowels on these words. Each word will be given twice.

1 وزير	3 دين
2 دين	4 بيت

5 يريد

6 بريد

7 بين

8 بين

9 زين

10 وارد

Exercise 4

Now try and write the eight words you hear, with their vowels. Each word will be given twice.

زبادي (zabādī) *yoghurt*

Alif

Alif is unique amongst Arabic letters because it does not have a definite sound. There are two main ways an alif is used:

1 To form the long vowel ā (see page 17).

2 To 'carry' a short vowel. If a word begins with a short vowel, the vowel sign cannot simply hang in the air before the next letter. So the vowel sign is placed above or under an alif, as in these examples:

أَب (ab) أُذ (udh) إِن (in)

The small 'c' shape (ء) that accompanies the vowel sign is known as hamza. (For more details about hamza, see Unit 6, page 76.)

Listen carefully to these words which begin with a vowel carried by an alif.

1 إِذْن

2 أُذْن

3 إِيران

4 أَنا

5 أَنْتَ

6 أَنْتِ

Putting words together

Look at the pictures and listen to the recording.

أَنْوَر

نور

أَنوَر وَنور

Tip: وَ (wa, 'and') is written joined to the word that follows:
أَنوَر وَنور (anwar wa-nūr, 'Anwar and Nour').

Exercise 5

Look at these pictures and read the names. Check your pronunciation with the recording or in the answer section.

نادِر ٥ زَيْد ٣ زَيْن ١

بَدْر ٦ زَيْنَب ٤ دِينا ٢

Now choose the correct description for each picture:

B

١ بدر وزين

٢ نادر وبدر

٣ زين ونادر

٤ زينب ودينا

A

١ زيد وبدر

٢ دينا ونادر

٣ زينب وزيد

٤ زينب وبدر

D

١ دينا وزين

٢ بدر ونادر

٣ زيد ودينا

٤ زين وزيد

C

١ دينا وزينب

٢ زيد وزينب

٣ زيد وزين

٤ دينا ونادر

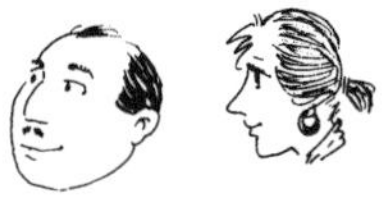

Simple sentences

Look at the picture and listen to the recording.

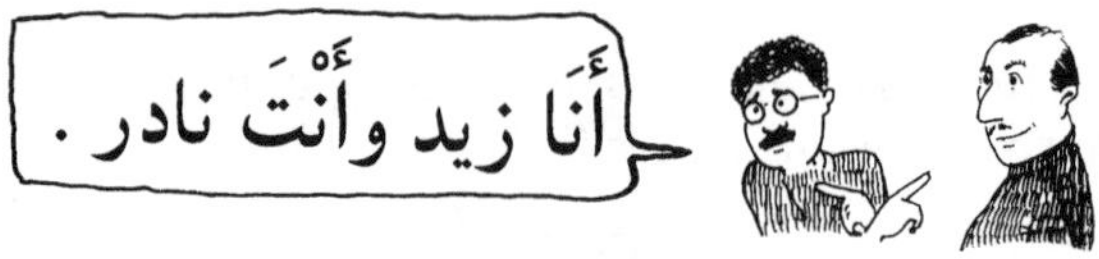

Many Arabic sentences do not need the verb 'to be' (am, is, are) in the present tense. This means that you can have a sentence with no verb at all. (Such sentences are called *nominal sentences*.)

أنا زيد.
I (am) Zaid.

أنت نادر.
You (are) Nadir.

Handwriting practice

Practise writing these sentences, firstly with the vowels and then without.

أَنا نادِر.   أنا نادر.

أَنتِ دِينا.   أنت دينا.

Exercise 6

Look at the pictures and make sentences for each bubble:

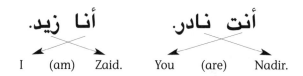

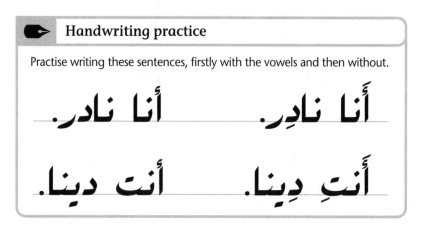

Male and female

Listen to this conversation:

← (read from right to left)

Look at the question (notice the reversed question mark).

وَأَنْتِ؟ And you?

أَنْتِ (anti) is used only to refer to a female. Arabic, like many other languages, makes a difference between male and female people and objects. It has two *genders*. So we have:

أَنا	(anā)	I *(male and female)*
أَنْتَ	(anta)	you *(male)*
أَنْتِ	(anti)	you *(female)*

Exercise 7

Fill in the missing words in these conversations:

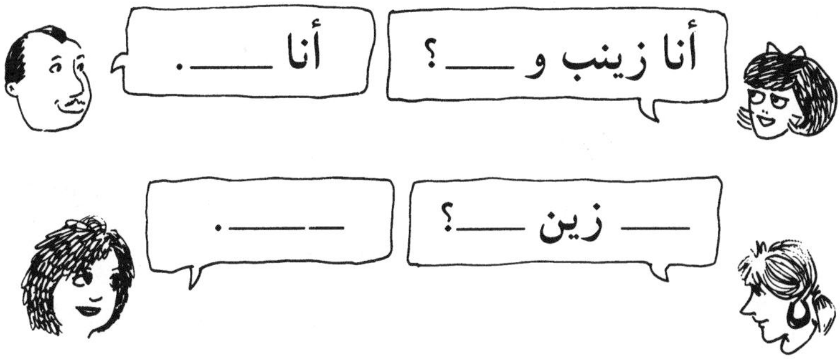

Conversation

Introductions

You learnt a few popular greetings in Unit 1, so now you're ready to introduce yourself. The simplest way to say your name is to use the phrase you've learnt in this unit: ana … (I'm …). You could then ask how someone is, or say you're pleased to meet him or her.

Listen to these conversations on your recording and then have a go at introducing yourself.

أهلاً. أنا توم، وأنت؟ (ahlan, anā Tom w-anti?) Hello, I'm Tom. And you?

أنا دينا. (anā dīnā) I'm Dina.

تشرّفنا يا دينا. (tasharrafnā yā dīnā) Pleased to meet you, Dina.

مَساء الخَير. أنا مدام لويس. (masā' al-khayr. anā madām lūwis) Good evening. I'm Mrs Lewis.

مَساء النور يا مدام لويس. كَيف الحال؟ (masā' an-nūr yā madām lūwis. kayf al-ḥāl?) Good evening, Mrs Lewis. How are you?

الحَمدُ للّه. (al-ḥamdu lillāh) Fine, thanks ('thanks be to God').

Notice the use of yā when addressing someone by name. This is common in some parts of the Arab world.

Vocabulary in Unit 2

أَنَا (anā) I

أَنْتَ (anta) you *(male)*

أَنْتِ (anti) you *(female)*

وَ (wa-) and

زَبادي (zabādī) yoghurt

تَشَرَّفْنا (tasharrafnā) pleased to meet you

كَيْفَ الحال؟ (kayf al-ḥāl) how are you?

الحَمدُ للّه (al-ḥamdu lillāh) fine, thanks

unit 3

The family

Letters of the alphabet: group 3

Look at the third group of letters and listen to the recording:

	Name of letter	*Pronounced*
ج	jīm	'j' as in French 'je'*
ح	ḥā'	Breathy, strong 'h'
خ	khā'	'ch' as in Scottish 'loch'
ه	hā'	'h' as in 'house'
م	mīm	'm' as in 'mastering'

*Also pronounced 'g' as in 'gate' in parts of Egypt.

There is an obvious similarity between the first three letters – jīm, khā' and ḥā'. The main letter has exactly the same basic shape: only the position of the dots will tell you which one it is.

The hā' and the mīm do not share their shapes with any other letters, but are included here for pronunciation and vocabulary reasons.

The pronunciation of ḥā' and khā' may be unfamiliar sounds to your ear. khā' is a sound similar to that made when clearing your throat. ḥā' is a breathy 'h' sometimes confused with hā' by beginners, so we will take extra care in showing you how to distinguish the two sounds.

Exercise 1

Listen to the recording and decide which is the first letter of each word. The first is an example. Each word is given twice.

ه	ح	خ	6	ه	(ح)	خ	1
ه	ح	خ	7	ه	ح	خ	2
ه	ح	خ	8	ه	ح	خ	3
ه	ح	خ	9	ه	ح	خ	4
ه	ح	خ	10	ه	ح	خ	5

Now replay the exercise, repeating the words after the recording.

Handwriting letters: group 3

Look at the handwritten versions of the letters in group 3:

Printed letter	*Handwritten letter*
ج	ج
ح	ح
خ	خ
ه	ه
م	م

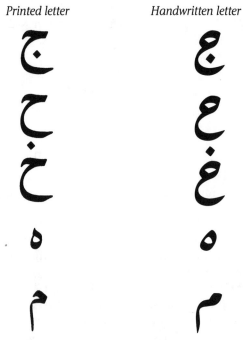

Notice how jīm, hā' and khā' have an additional upwards stroke in the handwritten version, producing an enclosed loop at the top of the letter.

The 'head' of the mīm is produced by turning your pen in a tight circle on the same spot.

Handwriting practice

jīm, ḥā', khā'

mīm

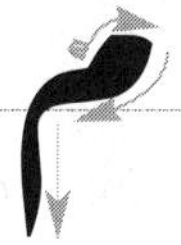

hā'

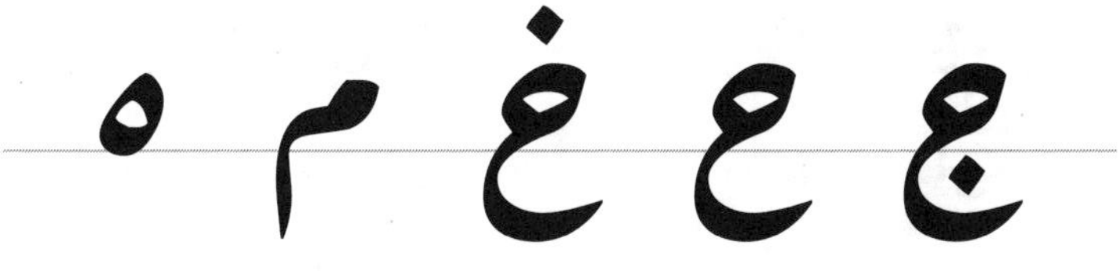

Joining letters: jīm, ḥā', khā' and mīm

When these four letters are at the beginning or in the middle of a word, the part of the letter which falls below the line (the 'tail') gets 'chopped'. Only when they occur at the end of a word do they keep their tails.

ج + ر + ب = جرب

ح + ر + م = حرم

أ + خ + ت = أخت

د + م + ج = دمج

م + ي + ز = ميز

أ + م = أم

Tip: sometimes you can see the mīm tucked in under the previous letter or over the following one. For example:

ح + م + د = حمد

م + ح + ا = محا

Exercise 2

Join the words with the correct combinations of letters, as in the example:

مِدْحَت	A	أَ + ح + م + د	1
أَخ	B	نَ + ج + ج + ا + ر	2
مَوج	C	ب + ح + ح + ا + ر	3
نَجّار	D	م + و + ج	4
نَجاح	E	م + د + ح + ت	5
بَحّار	F	أُ + خ + ت	6
أَحْمَد	G	أَ + خ	7
أُخْت	H	نَ + ج + ا + ح	8

Now try to pronounce the words. Check your answer with the recording or in the answer section. (See page 20 for an explanation of words that start with alif carrying a vowel.)

Joining hā'

Hā' changes its shape depending on how and where it is joined, so take extra care.

- If it is *not joined* to any other letter, it looks like this: ه
- If it is joined only to the letter *after* it, it looks like this: هـ
- If it is joined only to the letter *before* it, it looks like this: ـه
- If it is joined to letters on *both sides*, it looks like this: ـهـ or this: 
  (The second shape is more common in handwriting.)

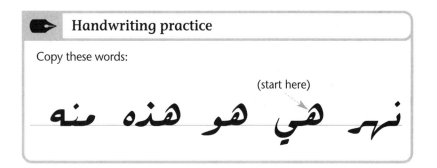

Handwriting practice

Copy these words:

(start here)

نهر هي هو هذه منه

Exercise 3

Handwrite these combinations of letters. Try them first on lined paper, then look at the answer section and study how the letters combine. After that, copy out the words several more times until you can write them all fluently.

1 ن + ح + ت

2 ب + ه + م

3 ج + م + د

4 ي + ت + ي + ه

5 ب + ح + ر

6 أ + م + ه

7 ه + ا + م + د

8 ن + ج + ز

Feminine words

You have already seen that there are two genders in Arabic. All nouns (people, objects, ideas, etc.) are either *masculine* (male) or *feminine* (female). Luckily it is fairly easy to tell which gender a particular word is.

There is a special feminine ending that is a 'bundled up' tā' (ت): ة . This is called tā' marbūṭa (literally *tied up* tā'). When the word is said by itself, the tā' marbūṭa is not usually pronounced:

مَدينَة (madīna) city　　　زَوْجَة (zawja) wife

There are two main categories of words which are feminine:

1 Female people or words that refer to females (girl, mother, etc.). Most countries are also considered female.
2 Singular words that end in tā' marbūṭa. (There are a few exceptions to this, but they are rare.)

A word could fall into both categories, e.g. زَوْجَة (zawja) wife.

There are a small number of feminine words that do not fall into either of these categories, often words connected with the natural world (wind, fire, etc.) or parts of the body (hand, leg, etc.). However, in general you can presume a word is masculine unless it falls into one of the two categories above.

Exercise 4

Listen to these words and decide if they are masculine or feminine.

خَيْمَة　بنت　بيت　دَجَاجَة

جَرِيدَة　زُجَاجَة　حِمَار　نَهْر

What's this? ما هذا؟

Listen to the recording and repeat the sentences:

1

2

(The vertical dash you can see above the hā' in هٰذا (hādhā) and هٰذه (hādhihi) is an alif. In a very few words, the alif is written above the letter rather than after it. This alif is pronounced as a long ā. Like the other vowel signs, it is not normally included in modern written Arabic.)

Masculine	*Feminine*
هذا بيت.	هذه جريدة.
This (is a) house.	This (is a) newspaper.

There is no need for the verb 'is' in this kind of sentence. Notice that there is also no direct equivalent of the English 'a' as in 'a house'.

Exercise 5

Make a sentence for each picture and then write it down.

1

2

3

هٰذا ____ .

4

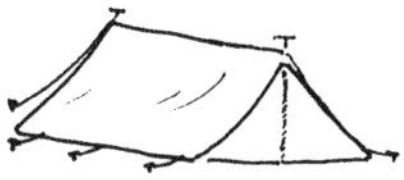

5

6

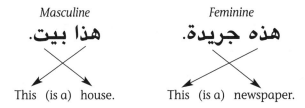

The family

Look at this family tree and read the names.

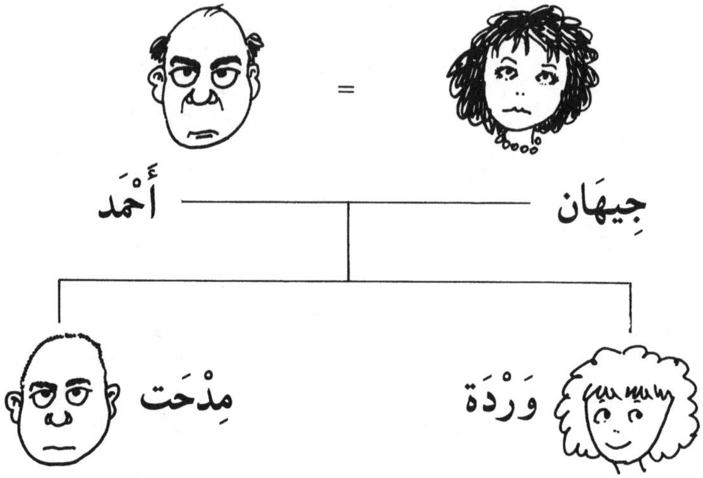

Listen to the recording, looking at the pictures and following the words:

If you take a noun (e.g. بنت bint, daughter/girl) and add '-ī' to the end, it then refers to 'my ...' (e.g. بنتي bintī, *my* daughter):

بنت + ي = بنتي

noun + '-ī' = my daughter

We could also put the noun directly in front of a name:

بنت + أحمد = بنت أحمد

noun + *name* = daughter *of* Ahmed, or Ahmed*'s* daughter

Putting two nouns together like this with a possessive meaning is known as idāfa.

When the *first* noun in idāfa ends in tā' marbūṭa (ة), you should pronounce the word with a 't' at the end:

زوجة أَحمد (zawjat aḥmad) wife of Ahmed/Ahmed's wife

خيمة مدحت (khaymat midḥat) Midḥat's tent

When letters are added to a word ending in tā' marbūṭa, it 'unties' and changes back to an ordinary tā'. This tā' is pronounced 't' in the normal way:

زوجة (zawja) wife زوجتي (zawjatī) my wife

Exercise 6

Now look back at the sentences on pages 32–3 and try to match the Arabic words with their translations:

mother	أُخت
father	بِنْت
son	أُمّ
daughter	زَوْج
wife	أَخ
husband	زَوْجَة
sister	اِبْن
brother	أَب

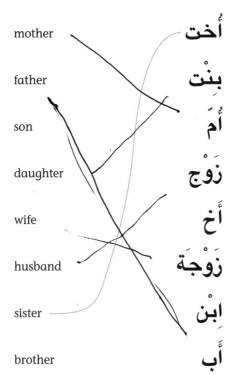

Exercise 7

Look at the family tree on page 32 and fill in the gaps in the sentences, as in the example.

1 مدحت هو ابن أحمد.

2 وردة هي ________ مدحت.

3 أحمد هو ________ جيهان.

4 وردة هي ________ جيهان.

5 جيهان هي ________ وردة.

6 جيهان هي ________ أحمد.

Exercise 8

Now make eight sentences about this family. The first is an example:

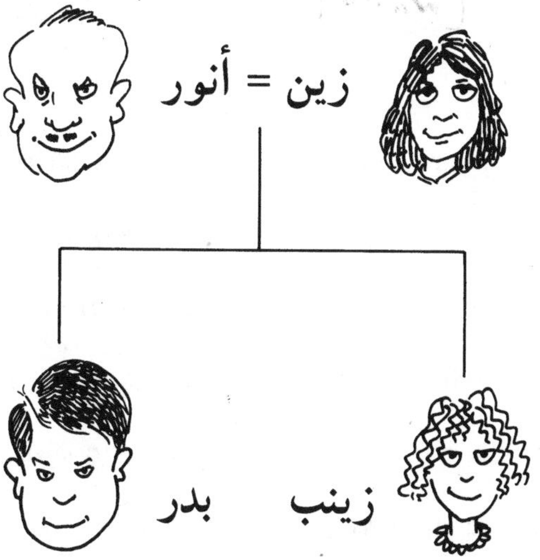

1 زينب هي بنت زين.

🔊 Conversation

Introducing your family

You can practise the words you've learnt in this unit to introduce *your* family. Just use the expression 'this is …': hādhā … for a male or hādhihi … for a female, followed by the family member and name:

مَن هذا؟ (man hādhā?) Who's this?

هذا زوجي جاك. (hādhā zawjī jāk) This is my husband, Jack.

تشرّفنا يا جاك. (tasharrafnā yā jāk) Pleased to meet you, Jack.

مَن هذه؟ (man hādhihi?) Who's this?

هذه بنتي لوسي. (hādhihi bintī lūsī) This is my daughter, Lucy.

تشرّفنا يا لوسي. (tasharrafnā yā lūsī) Pleased to meet you, Lucy.

Listen to these two conversations on the recording, then try to introduce members of *your* family. The recording will help you.

Vocabulary in Unit 3

أُمّ (umm) mother (walida) والِدة

أَب (ab) father (walid) والِد

اِبْن (ibn) son

بِنْت (bint) daughter/girl

أَخ (akh) brother

أُخْت (ukht) sister

زَوْج (zawj) husband

زَوْجَة (zawja) wife

هُوَ (huwa) he (and it, *masc.*)

هِيَ (hiya) she (and it, *fem.*)

هٰذا (hādhā) this *(masc.)*

هٰذِهِ (hādhihi) this *(fem.)*

زُجاجَة (zujāja) bottle

جَرِيدة (jarīda) newspaper

خَيْمَة (khayma) tent

نَهْر (nahr) river

حِمار (ḥimār) donkey

دَجاجَة (dajāja) hen/chicken

مَدِينة (madīna) city

مَن (man) who?

unit 4

Jobs

Letters of the alphabet: group 4

Listen to the recording, paying special attention to the pronunciation of the second pair of letters:

	Name of letter	*Pronounced*
س	sīn	's' as in 'sea'
ش	shīn	'sh' as in 'sheet'
ص	ṣād	strong, emphatic 's'
ض	ḍād	strong, emphatic 'd'

You can see that the letters sīn and shīn have the same basic shape, but shīn has three dots above. shīn and thā' are the only two letters in the Arabic alphabet that have three dots. Farsi (the language of Iran) has other letters with three dots above and below, and these are occasionally used for sounds that do not exist in Arabic (for example, p and v).

ṣād and ḍād have the same basic shape, but ḍād has one dot above. All the letters in group 4 have a similarly shaped tail.

Notice that when Arabic is written in English letters (*transliterated*), a dot is put under such letters as ṣād, ḍād and ḥā' to distinguish them from their more familiar equivalents.

Handwriting letters: group 4

Look at the handwritten versions of the letters in group 4:

Printed letter	*Handwritten letter*
س	س
ش	ش
ص	ص
ض	ض

You can see that the handwritten letters look similar to the printed versions except that the three dots on shīn have become joined, as they did with thā' (ث). The 'w' shape at the beginning of sīn and shīn can also become 'smoothed out' in handwriting, like this: ش س .

However, as a beginner, it's easier to stick to the more standard versions.

Handwriting practice

sīn, shīn

ṣād, ḍād

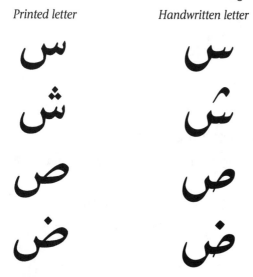

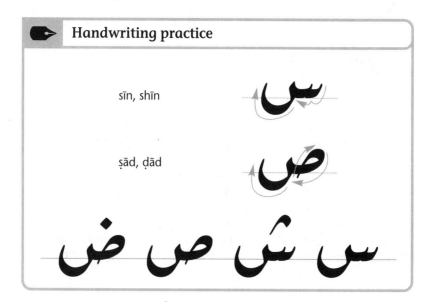

ض ص ش س

Joining letters: group 4

All of the letters in group 4 work on the same principle as the other letters which have tails (e.g., ح and م). The tail falling below the line gets 'chopped' when the letters are joined to another following. Only when they are standing by themselves or at the end of a word do they keep their tails.

1 ض + ر + ب = ضرب

2 م + ص + ر = مصر

3 ب + ي + ض = بيض egg

4 س + ي + د = سيد

5 ح + ش + م = حشم

6 ح + ر + س = حرس

Handwriting practice

ṣād, ḍād	– joined only to the letter after:	صـ...
	– joined on both sides	...ـصـ...
	– joined only to the letter before:	...ـص
sīn, shīn	– joined only to the letter after:	سـ...
	– joined on both sides:	...ـسـ...
	– joined only to the letter before:	...ـس

ṣād and ḍād are emphatic letters and have no direct equivalent in
English. The difference in the pronounciation of sīn and ṣād is similar to
the difference between the initial sounds of the English words 'sit' and
'sorry'; and dāl and ḍād similar to the difference between 'din' and 'dot'.

It is important to try to distinguish between emphatic and non-emphatic
letters, as it is between hā' (ه) and ḥā' (ح). Listen to these pairs of words
and repeat them after the recording. Each pair is given twice.

4 حَرَمَ	1 ضَرْب
هَرَمَ	دَرْب
5 صَارَ	2 حَزَمَ
سَارَ	هَزَمَ
6 ضَرَسَ	3 صَدَّ
دَرَسَ	سَدَّ

Exercise 1

Listen to the words on the recording and decide which is the first letter of
each. The words are given twice. The first answer is an example.

9 س ص	5 س ص	1 س ⃝ص
10 س ص	6 ه ح	2 د ض
11 ه ح	7 د ض	3 ه ح
12 س ص	8 د ض	4 د ض

Now check your answers and repeat the words after the recording.

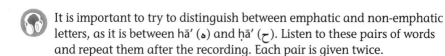

Exercise 2

All these Arabic words are similar to English. Can you match them to the pictures?

1 بَاص

2 بِيتْزَا

3 شُورْت

4 تَنِس

5 بُورجَر

6 سِينِمَا

A

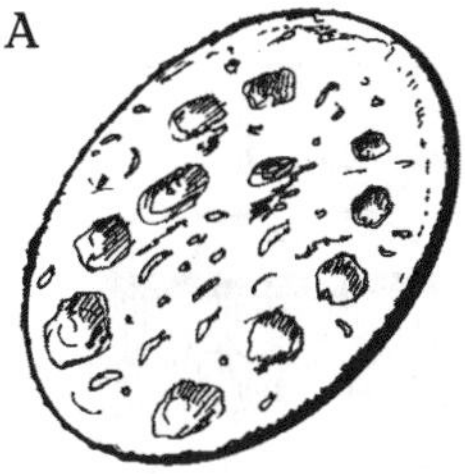

B

C

D

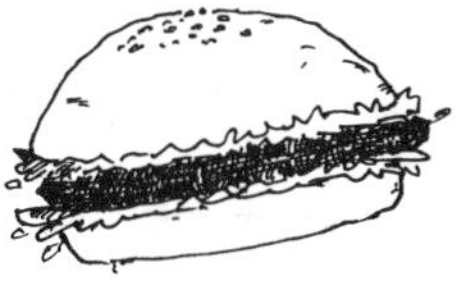

E

F

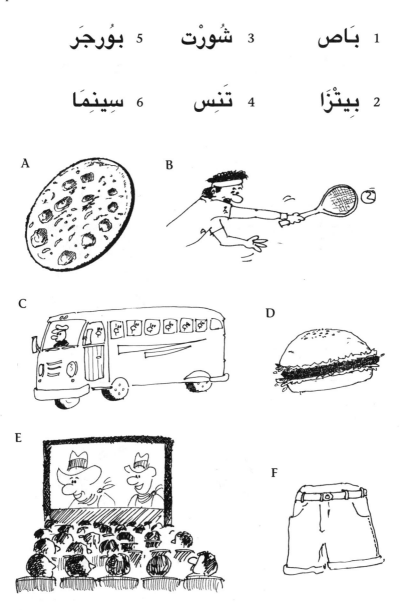

Handwriting practice

Practise writing these words from Exercise 2:

باص شورت تنس بيتزا بورجر

Jobs

Listen to the recording and look at the pictures:

1

هو مُدَرِّس.

2

هي مُدَرِّسة.

3

هو مُراسِل.

4

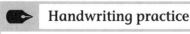

هي مُراسِلة.

A word referring to a single male (*masculine singular*) can be made to refer to a single female (*feminine singular*) by adding a fatḥa (ـَ) and a tā' marbūṭa (ة): مدرّس (mudarris) male teacher, مدرّسة (mudarrisa) female teacher; مراسل (murāsil) male correspondent, مراسلة (murāsila) female correspondent.

Exercise 3

Here are some more jobs. Look at the list and listen to the recording.

خَبَّاز	baker
مُحَاسِب	accountant
مُمَرِّضَة	nurse *(fem.)*
مُهَنْدِس	engineer
نَجَّار	carpenter

Now make one sentence for each picture. The first is an example:

1 هي ممرّضة.

2

3

4

5

6

Making words plural

Look at the pictures and listen to the recording:

1

هُمْ مُدَرِّسُون .

2

هُنَّ مُدَرِّسَات .

3

هُمْ مُحَاسِبُون .

4

هُنَّ مُحَاسِبَات .

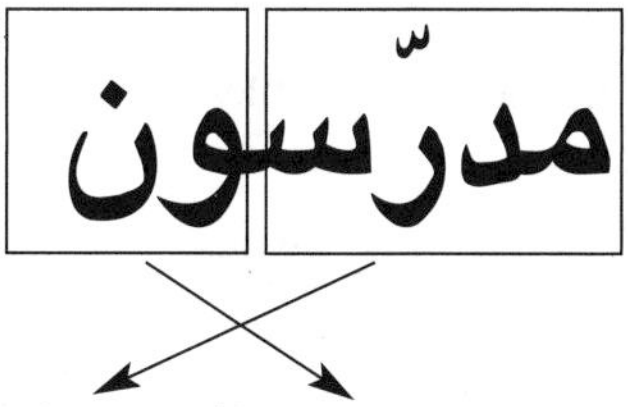

masculine singular + ūn = *masculine plural*

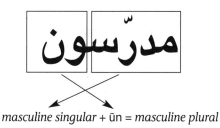

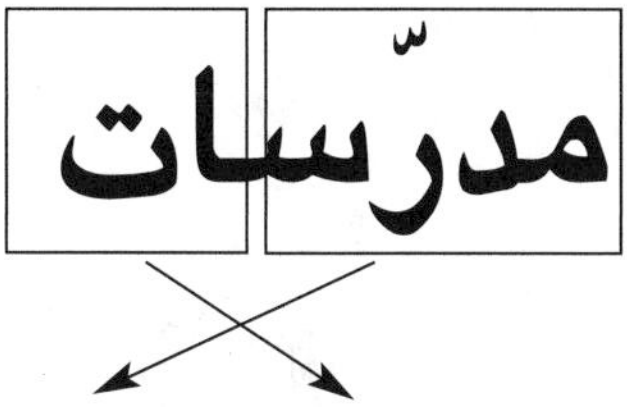

masculine singular + āt = *feminine plural*

These plurals are known as the *sound masculine plural* and the *sound feminine plural* ('sound' here means 'complete' and does not refer to the pronunciation). All the jobs in this chapter can be made plural by adding the endings shown above.

Notice that although there is only one word for 'we', نحن (naḥnu), the word for 'they' is هم (hum) for the masculine plural and هنّ (hunna) for the feminine plural:

هم مدرّسون. (hum mudarrisūn) They are *(male)* teachers.

هنّ مدرّسات. (hunna mudarrisāt) They are *(female)* teachers.

The feminine plural is not as common as the masculine plural as all members of a group must be female for it to be used. If the group is mixed, the masculine is always used. (Spoken dialects often use the masculine plural only whatever the gender of the group.)

Exercise 4

Look again at the words listed in Exercise 3. Write the masculine and feminine plurals for these words.

Exercise 5

Now write the words in the speech bubbles and underneath the pictures, as in the example.

1 هنّ ______________________

2 ______________________

3 ______________________

4 ______________________

____________________ 6   ____________________ 5

Conversation

Talking about what you do

If you want to ask someone what they do for a living you can ask:

ما عملك؟ (mā ʿamalak/-ik?) What's your job? *(to a man/woman)*

أنا مدرّس/ممرّضة. (ānā mudarris/mumarriḍa) I'm a teacher/a nurse.

ʿamal means 'work' or 'job' and the ending -ak or -ik means 'your' (-ka and -ki in more formal Arabic). You could also ask where someone works:

أين عملك؟ (ayna ʿamalak/-ik?) Where's your job?

في لندن/في بيروت. (fī lundun/fī bayrūt) In London/In Beirut.

If you're studying at university or school you may want to say:

أنا طالب/طالبة. (ānā ṭālib/ṭāliba) I'm a student *(male/female).*

أنا تلميذ/تلميذة. (ānā tilmīdh/tilmīdha) I'm a pupil *(male/female).*

A good expression to express interest or admiration is:

ما شاء الله! (mā shā'a allāh) Wonderful!

Listen to the conversation and then take one of the roles yourself.

Structure notes

The structure note sections are intended to give more details about the structure of the Arabic language. They will be useful mainly for recognition purposes and should not be slavishly learnt. If you require a more general understanding of Arabic, you can quickly skim through these sections or even skip them altogether.

Case endings

Arabic nouns and adjectives have *case endings* – grammatical endings that can be added to the end of nouns. However, unlike many languages, for example German, these endings are rarely pronounced and for practical purposes do not exist in spoken dialects. So learners of Arabic (and native speakers) can get by without a detailed knowledge of these endings.

The sort of situations in which you are likely to meet the full endings are readings of classical literature (particularly the Qur'ān), and more formal radio and TV broadcasts, especially if the speaker wishes to show his or her 'grammatical correctness'. You will rarely find them written in modern newspapers or literature.

Having said that, there are some occasions in Modern Standard Arabic when the endings affect the spelling and pronounciation and so some knowledge of how they work is desirable.

The nominative case (ar-rafع)

There are three cases. The first is the *nominative*. The easiest way to explain this case is to say that you can assume a noun is nominative unless there is a reason for it *not* to be. Almost all of the nouns you have met in the book so far have been in the nominative case.

If we take the noun بنت (bint), girl/daughter, and add the full ending for the nominative case we have:

بنتٌ (pronounced 'bint<u>un</u>')

The ending (ـٌ) is written above the final letter like the vowels, and is pronounced 'un'. So the sentence هذا بَيت (hādhā bayt), This is a house, would be هذا بَيتٌ (hādhā baytun) if fully pronounced.

Look at these other nouns you know with their full endings:

نَجّارٌ (najjārun) carpenter

زُجاجةٌ (zujājatun*) bottle

مُمَرِّضاتٌ (mumarriḍatun*) nurses

* the tā' marbūta is pronounced 'at' when a case ending is added to the noun.

The sound masculine plural is an exception and has a different ending:

مُدَرِّسونَ (mudarrisūn(a))

Here, the whole of the part underlined can be considered as the nominative case ending, but only the final 'a' is not usually pronounced in Modern Standard Arabic.

Optional exercise
Go back to Exercise 3 and say the sentences again, this time pronouncing the full endings on the words.

Vocabulary in Unit 4

نَحْنُ (naḥnu) we

هُمْ (hum) they *(masc.)*

هُنَّ (hunna) they *(fem.)*

مُدَرِّس (mudarris) teacher

مُحَاسِب (muḥāsib) accountant

خَبَّاز (khabbāz) baker

مُمَرِّضة (mumarriḍa) nurse

مُهَنْدِس (muhandis) engineer

نَجَّار (najjār) carpenter

مُراسِل (murāsil) correspondent

طالِب (ṭālib) student

تِلْميذ (tilmīdh) pupil

تَنِس (tanis) tennis

باص (bāṣ) bus

سينِما (sīnimā) cinema

بيتزا (bītzā) pizza

شورت (shūrt) shorts

بورجَر (būrgar) burger

ما عَمَلك؟ (mā ɛamalak/-ik?) What's your job?

أيْنَ عَمَلك؟ (ayna ɛamalak/-ik?) Where's your job?

ما شاءَ الله! (mā shā'a allāh) Wonderful!

unit 5 Describing things

Letters of the alphabet: group 5

Listen to the recording and look at the letters:

	Name of letter	*Pronounced*
ف	fā'	'f' as in 'foot'
ق	qāf	*see below*
ك	kāf	'k' as in 'kettle'
ل	lām	'l' as in 'lamb'

The fā' and qāf have similar shapes, but the tail of the qāf is rounder and falls below the line (a little like the difference between ب and ن).

The tail of the lām must also fall below the line and not sit on it like an English 'l'. Both lām and kāf have distinctive shapes which are not shared with any other letter.

Pronunciation of qāf

It takes practice to pronounce qāf properly. You should say a 'q' from the back of your throat. In Modern Standard Arabic, care must be taken to distinguish the pronunciation of kāf and qāf (listen again to the recording).

However, spoken dialects tend to pronounce the qāf either as a 'g' as in 'gate' or as a *glottal stop*. (A glottal stop is the sort of sound produced when you pronounce 'bottle' with a Cockney accent, or in 'Estuary English', dropping the 'tt'.) This book will pronounce the qāf in the classical way, but be prepared to hear the same words pronounced with a 'g' or a glottal stop by native speakers.

Exercise 1

Listen to these pairs of words. All the words begin with either qāf or kāf. Decide if each pair of words begins with the same or different letters. Each pair is given twice. The first answer is an example.

1	same	different	**5**	same	different
2	same	different	**6**	same	different
3	same	different	**7**	same	different
4	same	different	**8**	same	different

Handwriting letters: group 5

Look at the letters in group 5 handwritten:

Printed letter *Handwritten letter*

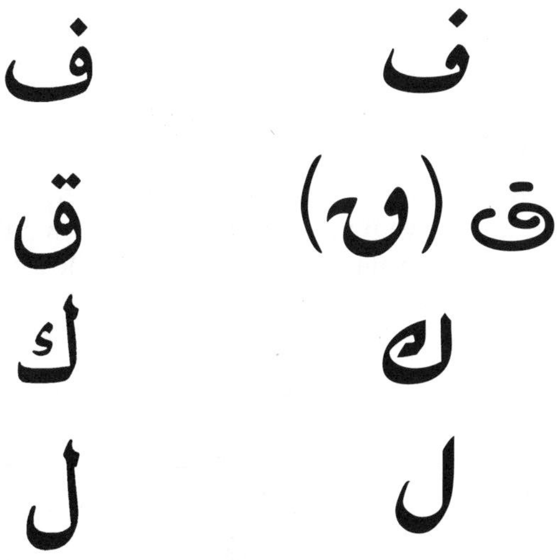

Notice how the 'hamza' shape in the middle of the kāf becomes 'joined' to the rest of the letter for the sake of speed in the handwritten version. The alternative handwritten version of qāf should be noted for recognition purposes, although it is generally easier for beginners to write the more standard version.

Handwriting practice

fā’

qāf

kāf

lām

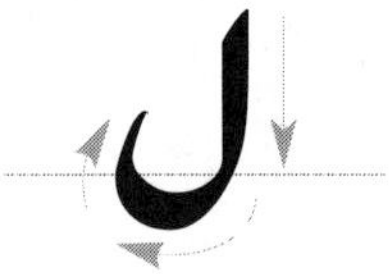

Joining letters: group 5

fā’, qāf and lām all lose their tails when they are joined to the following letter. This leaves fā’ and qāf with the same shape at the beginning or in the middle of a word. The only difference is that fā’ has one dot above and qāf two:

ف + ر + ق = فرق

ق + ر + ن = قرن

ق + ف + ل قفل

ل + ف + ق = لفق

م + ل + ل = ملل

It is important to remember that lām can be joined on *both sides*, as beginners often confuse this letter with alif, which can be joined only to the letter before:

ج + ا + ب = جاب

ج + ل + ب = جلب

kāf, like hā' (ه), changes its shape depending on how it is joined:

- If it stands on its own or is at the end of a word, it looks like this: ك
- If it stands at the beginning or in the middle of a word, it looks like this: كـ

Exercise 2

Look at this newspaper headline. It contains 2 kāfs and 5 qāfs. Can you find and circle them?

كلمات رئيس مصر الصادقة

تعكس عمق علاقات الشعبين الشقيقين

Handwriting practice

When a kāf is written at the beginning or in the middle of a word, the main shape of the word is often completed first without the downwards stroke of the kāf, which is added with the dots:

stage 1: ٮلٮ

stage 2: كلب

Compare this with the way most people would write the English word 'tin':

stage 1: lın

stage 2: tin

Now practise copying these words:

كلب كتاب ركب بنتك مكسور

Everyday objects

Look at these pictures and listen to the recording:

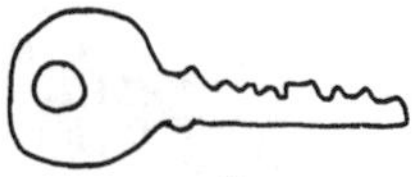
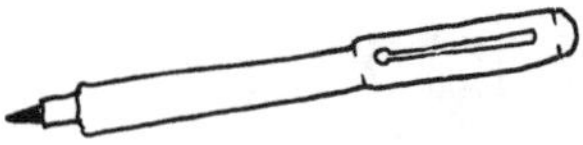

1 كِتَاب

2 مِفْتَاح

3 قَلَم

4 حَقِيبَة

5 قَمِيص

6 كَلْب

7 دَرَّاجَة

8 سَيَّارَة

9 خَاتِم

Exercise 3

Now make a sentence for each picture, as in the example:

1 هٰذا كِتابٌ.

Signs and crosswords

If an English word is written vertically instead of horizontally, as in a crossword or a shop sign, then the same basic letters are used:

(horizontal) accountant

(vertical) a
c
c
o
u
n
t
a
n
t

However, because of the way Arabic letters are joined, vertical words have to be written using the separate, isolated letters:

محاسب *(horizontal)*

م *(vertical)*
ح
ا
س
ب

Crosswords are compiled entirely in separate letters.

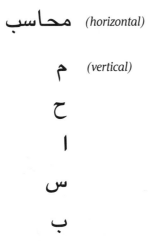

Exercise 4

Look at the picture clues and complete the crossword. One clue is completed for you.

أُفُقِيّ ←

1 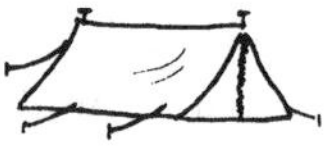

2 

4 

رَأْسِيّ ↓

1 

2 

3 

Describing things

Look at these pairs of descriptive words *(adjectives)* and listen to the recording.

1 جَدِيد 

2 قَدِيم 

3 مَكْسُور 

4 سَلِيم 

5 خَفِيف 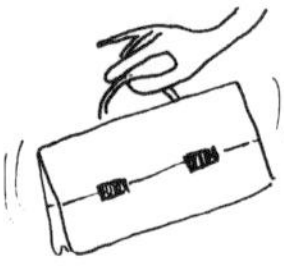

6 ثَقِيل 

7 قَبِيح 

8 جَمِيل 

9 أَسْوَد 

10 أَبْيَض 

Now listen to these sentences:

القَلَم سلَيم.

الحَقيبة خَفيفة.

هذا القلم مكسور.

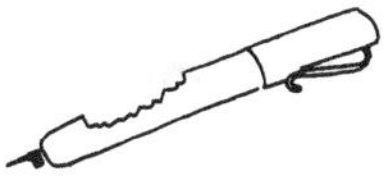

هذه الحقيبة ثَقيلة.

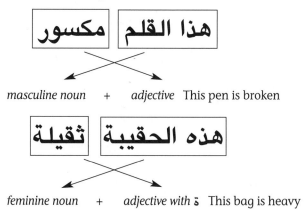

القلم = ال | قلم

الـ (al) the + قلم (qalam) pen = القلم (al-qalam) *the* pen

الـ (al) is the same for all nouns, whether masculine, feminine or plural, and is written as part of the word that follows. Adding hādha or hādhihi directly in front of al changes the meaning from *the* to *this*, for example from القلم (al-qalam) *the* pen, to هذا القلم (hādhal-qalam) *this* pen.

Tip: In spoken dialects الـ can be pronounced al, il or el.

مكسور	هذا القلم

masculine noun + *adjective* This pen is broken

ثقيلة	هذه الحقيبة

feminine noun + *adjective with* ة This bag is heavy

An adjective must have the feminine ending (ة, a) if the noun it is describing is feminine. In other words, the adjective *agrees with* the noun.

> Note the difference between:
>
> هذا قلم. This is a pen.
>
> هذا القلم ... This pen ...

Exercise 5

Match the opposite pairs of adjectives:

جميل	سليم
ثقيل	قديم
أبيض	قبيح
مكسور	خفيف
جديد	أسود

Now pronounce the adjectives out loud.

Exercise 6

Fill in the gaps in these descriptions, using the English prompts in brackets. Remember to add the feminine ending ة a to the adjective if necessary.

1 هذا القميص ________ (white).

2 وهذا ________ (shirt) أسود.

3 ________ (This) البنت جميلة.

4 ________ (And this) البنت ________ (ugly).

5 ________ (This) السيّارة ________ (old).

6 ________ ________ ________ (And this car is new).

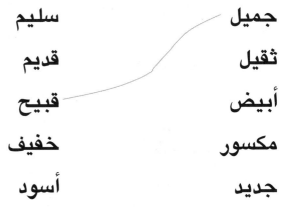

Whose is it?

Listen to these two exchanges:

1

2

Tip: 2 fatḥas followed by alif (اً) is pronounced an: شكراً (shukran) thank you.

Now listen to these descriptions:

هذا كتاب البنت وكتابُها جديد وأبيض.

هذا كتاب الولد وكتابُه قديم وأسود.

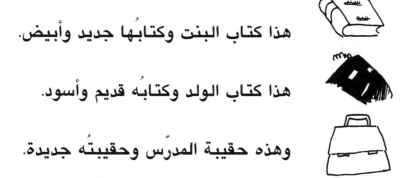

وهذه حقيبة المدرّس وحقيبتُه جديدة.

Tip: قديم (qadīm, old) can only be used with objects, not people.

Possessive endings

You have now met the following endings which describe possession:

my *(masculine & feminine)*	-ī	كتابِي (kitābī) my book
your *(masculine)*	-(u)ka*	كتابَك (kitābuka) your book
your *(feminine)*	-(u)ki*	كتابِك (kitābuki) your book
his	-(u)hu*	كتابُه (kitābuhu) his book
her	-(u)hā	كتابَها (kitābuhā) her book

* *Tip:* In spoken dialects these endings are usually simplified to -ak, -ik and -uh: kitābak, kitābik, kitābuh.

These endings are known as *attached pronouns* since they are 'attached' to the end of the word. Remember that when you add an ending to a word which finishes in tā' marbūṭa, the tā' unties and is pronounced:

حقيبة (ḥaqība) حقيبتَك (ḥaqībatuka)

Exercise 7

Complete the conversation and fill in the missing words in the description:

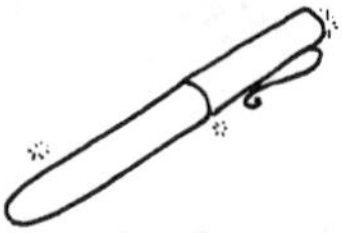

هذا ___ الوَلَد وقلمهُ ___ و___ .

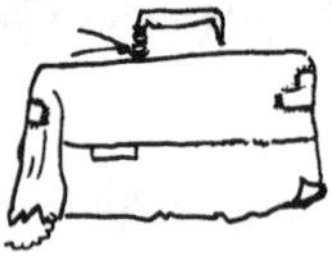

و___ حقيبة ___ و___ ___ .

Exercise 8

Read the description of Jihan's dog. Then look at the pictures of Jihan and her friend Mohammed, together with some of their possessions.

هذا كلب جيهان وهو أبيض.

كلبها قبيح وثقيل.

Now make similar descriptions of Jihan's and Mohammed's other possessions.

Tip: Do not use أبيض (abyaḍ, white) or أسود (aswad, black) to describe feminine objects, as they have a special feminine form which you will learn in Unit 11. Stick to using these colours with masculine objects for the moment.

Exercise 9

Try to describe some of your possessions, using the sentences you produced in Exercise 8 as models.

Structure notes

Indefinite and definite

When you add ﺍﻟ (al, the) to an indefinite noun, you make it definite. The case ending you met in Unit 4 changes slightly:

بِنتٌ (bint_un_) a girl/daughter *(indefinite)*

اَلْبِنتُ (al-bint_u_) the girl/daughter *(definite)*

The indefinite case ending -un becomes -u when the noun is definite.

Nouns which have possessive endings are also definite, and this accounts for the 'u' which appears before the attached pronouns:

بِنتُكَ (bint_u_ka) your *(masculine)* daughter

بِنتُكِ (bint_u_ki) your *(feminine)* daughter

بِنتُهُ (bint_u_hu) his daughter

بِنتُها (bint_u_hā) her daughter

But notice that when you add ي (ī , my), the case ending is not included.

Look at these sentences you have met in this unit with the full case endings added. Notice that the adjectives as well as the nouns carry the case endings.

اَلسَّيَّارةُ جَدِيدةٌ. (as-sayyāratu jadīdatun) The car is new.

بِنْتُكَ جَمِيلةٌ. (bintuka jamīlatun) Your daughter is beautiful.

اَلكِتابُ قَدِيمٌ (al-kitābu qadīmun) The book is old.

Elision of ﺍﻟ

When the word before ﺍﻟ (al, the) begins with a vowel, the 'a' of 'al' is dropped and the sound is elided:

اَلْحَقِيبَة   (al-ḥaqība) the bag

هذه الْحَقِيبَة   (hādhihi l-ḥaqība) this bag (*not* hādhihi al-ḥaqība)

Conversation

Polite requests
It is useful at an early stage of learning a language to master a few phrases so that you can ask politely for what you want. These can come in handy in stores or when you want someone to pass you something.

ممكن ...؟ (mumkin ...?) May I have ...? (literally 'possible?')

ممكن كتابي من فضلك؟ (mumkin kitābī min faḍlak?)

May I have my book, please? *(said to a male)*

ممكن القميص الأبيض من فضلك؟ (mumkin al-qamīṣ al-abyaḍ min faḍlik?)

May I have the white shirt, please? *(said to a female)*

أريد ... (urīd ...) I'd like ...

أريد حقيبة جديدة. (urīd ḥaqība jadīda) I'd like a new bag.

أريد بيتزا من فضلك. (urīd pītzā min faḍlak) I'd like pizza, please.

When the item is handed over, you may hear:

تفضّل (tafaḍḍal) Here you are. *(said to a male)*

تفضّلي (tafaḍḍalī) Here you are. *(said to a female)*

And don't forget to say 'thank you': شكرًا (shukran).

Listen to the request phrases on the recording with some examples, and then try asking for the following items:

بورجر (būrgar) a burger

هذه الزجاجة (hādhihi z-zujāja) this bottle

قلمك (qalamak) your pen

القميص الأسود (al-qamīṣ al-aswad) the black shirt

مفتاحي (miftāḥī) my key

Vocabulary in Unit 5

قَلَم (qalam) pen

مِفْتَاح (miftāḥ) key

كِتَاب (kitāb) book

قَمِيص (qamīṣ) shirt

كَلْب (kalb) dog

حَقِيبة (ḥaqība) bag

خَاتِم (khātim) ring

سَيَّارة (sayyāra) car

دَرَّاجة (darrāja) bicycle

وَلَد (walad) boy

شُكْراً (shukran) thank you

أَسْوَد (aswad) black

أَبْيَض (abyaḍ) white

مُمكِن؟ (mumkin) may I have?

مَكْسُور (maksūr) broken

سَلِيم (salīm) whole/unbroken

جَدِيد (jadīd) new

قَدِيم (qadīm) old

خَفِيف (khafīf) light (weight)

ثَقِيل (thaqīl) heavy

جَمِيل (jamīl) beautiful

قَبِيح (qabīḥ) ugly

...كَ (-ka) your *(masc.)*

...كِ (-ki) your *(fem.)*

...هُ (-hu) his

...هَا (-hā) her

...ي (-ī) my

أُرِيد (urīd) I'd like

مِن فَضْلك (min faḍlak/min faḍlik) please *(to a male/female)*

تَفَضَّل/تَفَضَّلي (tafaḍḍal/tafaḍḍalī) here you are *(to a male/female)*

unit 6

Where is it?

Letters of the alphabet: group 6

This is the final group of letters. All of these sounds are less familiar to a Western ear, so listen carefully to the recording:

	Name of letter	*Pronounced*
ط	ṭā'	Strong, emphatic 't'
ظ	ẓā'	Strong, emphatic 'z'
ع	ع ayn	Guttural 'ah' (see below)
غ	ghayn	a gargling sound similar to a French 'r'

You can see that the ṭā' and ẓā' share the same basic shape, and عayn and ghayn also share the same basic shape. A single dot distinguishes each pair.

Emphatic letters

Altogether there are four emphatic letters which you should take care to distinguish from their non-emphatic equivalents. Listen to the recording and repeat the letters in the table on page 66.

Non-emphatic letter		*Emphatic letter*	
ت	tā’	ط	ṭā’
ذ	dhāl	ظ	ẓā’
س	sīn	ص	ṣād
د	dāl	ض	ḍād

Remember that when Arabic is written in English letters (transliterated), a dot is put under the emphatic letter to distinguish it.

Exercise 1

Listen to the words on the recording and decide which of the letters in the table above each word begins with. The first is an example. Each word will be given twice.

1 ط	5
2	6
3	7
4	8

Now check your answers and repeat the words after the recording.

ghayn **and** ɛayn

These two letters, especially ɛayn, represent unfamiliar sounds and take practice to pronounce. However, you will develop a feel for them and will gradually find them easier to say and recognise.

- ghayn (غ) is pronounced like the French ‘gr’ as in ‘gratin’, and is similar to the noise you make when you gargle.

– عayn (ع) is produced by tightening your throat and making an 'ah' sound by pushing out air from your lungs – easier said than done! Imagine you are at the dentist and the drill touches a nerve. Beginners often fail to hear عayn as a letter at all, but to native speakers it is no different from any other letter and leaving it out could lead to blank looks. عayn does not have a near equivalent in English and so the Arabic letter itself is used in the transliteration.

Repeat the six words that you hear on the recording. They all contain the letter ghayn.

Now repeat the next six words, which all contain the letter عayn.

Exercise 2

Listen to the eight words on the recording. Decide if the word begins with a عayn or not. The first is an example. Each word is repeated.

1 ✔	3	5	7
2	4	6	8

Handwriting practice

ṭā', ẓā'

عayn, ghayn

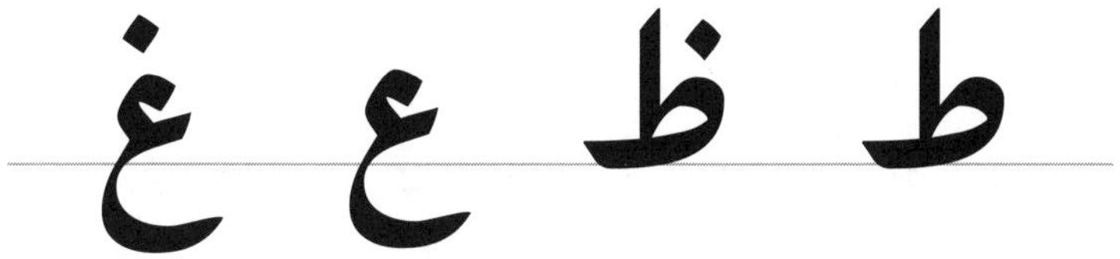

Exercise 3

You have now met all 28 Arabic letters. Look at the following table of all the letters in *alphabetical order*. Fill in the missing letters in either their printed or handwritten versions.

Name of letter	*Printed version*	*Handwritten version*
alif	ا	ا
bā'	ب	ب
tā'	ت	
thā'		ث
jīm	ج	
ḥā'	ح	
khā'		خ
dāl	د	
dhāl		ذ
rā'		ر
zāy	ز	
sīn		س
shīn	ش	
ṣād	ص	
ḍād		ض
ṭā'	ط	
ẓā'	ظ	
ɛayn		ع
ghayn	غ	
fā'		ف
qāf	ق	

kāf	ك	
lām		ل
mīm	م	
nūn	ن	
hā'		ه
wāw	و	
yā'		ي

Joining letters: group 6

ṭā' **and** ẓā'

These two letters have the same shape, wherever they appear in a word:

و + س + ط = وسط

ط + ي + ر = طير

ن + ظ + ر = نظر

Exercise 4

Match the Arabic newspaper titles with their English equivalents:

A

B

C

D

1 *Al Ahram* **2** *Al-Qabas* **3** *Ashsharq Al-Awsat* **4** *Al Wafd*

Handwriting practice

ṭā' and ẓā' are formed a bit like ṣād and ḍād, except there is no 'kink' after the loop:

– joined only to the letter after: طـ...

– joined on both sides: ...ـطـ...

– joined only to the letter before: ...ـط

The downwards stroke and dot are usually added after the whole shape of the word is complete:

stage 1: ٮطر

stage 2: نظر

Practise copying these words:

طير وسط نظر محطة طوكيو

ʿayn **and** ghayn

Like hā' (ه), these two letters change their shapes depending on where they appear in a word.

- Joined only to the following letter they look like this: ...عـ (like the isolated version without its tail)
- Joined on both sides they look like this: ...ـعـ...
- Joined only to the letter before they look like this: ...ـع

Look carefully at how these letters combine:

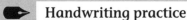

غ + ي + ر = غير

م + و + ع + د = موعد

ص + غ + ي + ر = صغير

ش + ا + ر + ع = شارع

م + ص + ن + ع = مصنع

ن + ع + م = نعم

Notice especially that ع‍ayn and ghayn each look very different at the end of a word, depending on whether or not they are joined to the previous letter (see the fourth and fifth examples above).

Handwriting practice

– Joined only to the letter after: عـ...

– Joined on both sides: ...ـعـ...

– Joined only to the letter before: ...ـع

Practise copying these words:

عاطف صغير بالغ جامع شارع

Exercise 5

Handwrite these combinations of letters, as in the example:

1 ع + ل + ي = علي

2 ج + م + ع =

3 غ + ط + س =

4 ظ + ل + م = ظلم   Injustice

5 ط + ي + ن =

6 ن + ع + م =

Sun letters

Listen to these two sentences:

> **القميص أبيض.** (al-qamīṣ abyaḍ) The shirt is white.
>
> **السيّارة جديدة.** (as-sayyāra jadīda) The car is new.

Notice that القميص is pronounced al-qamīṣ, but السيّارة is pronounced as-sayyāra. This is because when الـ (al-, the) is added to words beginning with particular letters, the lām is pronounced like the first letter of that word and not as a lām. The letter 'takes over' (*assimilates*) the 'l' sound of the lām. When this assimilation happens, the first letter of the word sounds as though it is pronounced twice: as-sayyāra.

Letters like sīn, which assimilate the lām of al-, are known as 'sun letters' since the Arabic word shams,'sun', starts with shīn – one of the assimilating letters. The others are 'moon letters'. All sun letters are pronounced with your tongue at the top of your mouth, just behind your teeth. This is the same position as lām. Half the letters of the alphabet are sun letters. All of the letters in group 4 (sīn, shīn, ṣād and ḍād) are sun letters, and none of the letters in group 3 (jīm, ḥā',khā', mīm and hā').

Exercise 6

Listen to these words pronounced with الـ and decide which of the letters in groups 1, 2, 5 and 6 are sun letters. The first is an example. Each word will be given twice:

Word	*Initial letter*	*Sun letter?*
البنت	ب	✗
التبن		
الثوب		
النهر		
الياسمين		
الدجاجة		
الذباب		
الراديو		
الزجاجة		
الولد		
الفيلم		
القميص		
الكتاب		
الليمون		
الطين		
الظاهر		
العرب		
الغرب		

Asking questions

 Look at these objects and listen to the recording:

1 مَائِدَة   2 كُرْسِيّ   3 سَرِير   4 بَاب

mahedu   *Kesei*   *snrrer*   *beb*

5 تِلِيفِزْيُون   6 شُبّاك   7 صُورَة   8 خَزَانَة

telenbo rafec   *Shubak Nafecthu*   *sowa*   *Lrzapu*

Exercise 7

Fill in the missing words in the sentences and match them to the correct
pictures, as in the example.

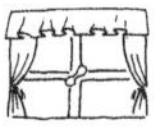

1 __هذا__ كرسيّ .

2 _____ خزانة .

3 _____ مائدة .

4 _____ باب .

5 _____ شبّاك .

6 _____ تليفزيون .

7 _____ سرير .

8 _____ .

a

b

c

d

e

f

g

h

Yes/no questions

You can form a question in Arabic to which the answer is either 'yes' (نعم, naعm) or 'no' (لا, lā) by adding the question marker هل (hal) in front of a sentence:

هذا نهر. (hādhā nahr) This is a river.

هل هذا نهر؟ (hal hādhā nahr) Is this a river?

هذه بنتها. (hādhihi bintuhā) This is her daughter.

هل هذه بنتها؟ (hal hādhihi bintuhā) Is this her daughter?

Exercise 8

Listen to these two exchanges:

هل هذا كرسي؟ (hal hādhā kursī?)

لا، هو سرير. (lā, huwa sarīr.)

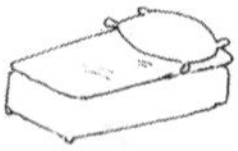

هل هذه صورة؟ (hal hādhihi ṣūra?)

نعم، هي صورة. (naعm, hiya ṣūra.)

Note the shape of the Arabic question mark (؟) and comma (،). Now say and write one question and its answer for each picture, following the prompts.

1 خزانة ؟

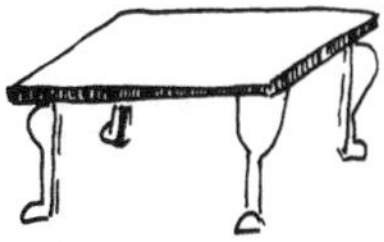

2 كتاب ؟

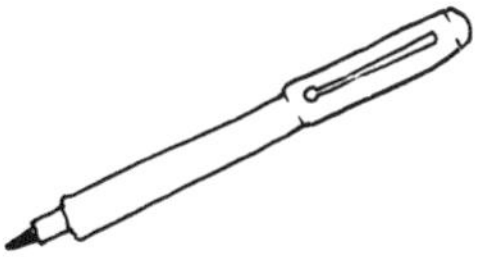

3 مفتاح ؟

4 كلب ؟

5 درّاجة ؟

6 شبّاك ؟

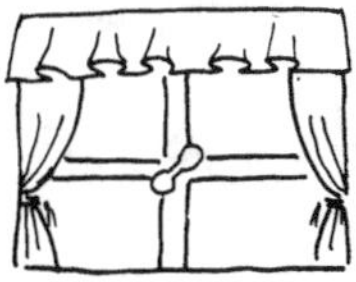

Hamza

The hamza shape that you have seen sitting on an alif in words such as أمّ (umm, mother) or أب (ab, father) can also be found written in other ways. One of these is on a yā' letter shape with no dots, as in مائدة (mā'ida, table). Hamza is pronounced as a short pause when it falls in the middle of a word. There are detailed rules concerning how to write hamza, but it is best at first to learn each word as it appears.

Where? أَيْنَ؟

Listen to the recording and look at the pictures:

1 أَيْنَ الكلب؟

هو تَحْتَ المائدة.

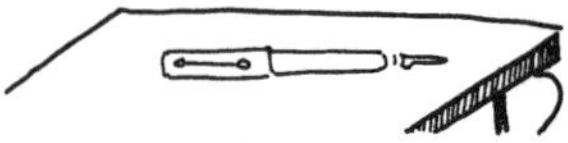

2 أَيْنَ القلم؟

هو عَلَى المائدة.

3 أَيْنَ الولد؟

هو بين المائدة و الكرسي.

4 أَيْنَ البنت؟

هي في الخزانة.

5 أَيْنَ الصورة؟

هي فَوْقَ المائدة.

6 أَيْنَ الكلب؟

هو بجانِب الكرسي.

فَوقَ (fawqa) عَلَى (ɛalā*) في (fī)

تَحْتَ (taḥta) بِجانِب (bi-jānib) بَيْنَ (bayna)

*Note: على (ɛalā, on) finishes with a yā' with no dots and yet is pronounced ā. Some words that end in ā are written with a yā' instead of an alif. This makes no difference to the pronunciation and is only ever found at the end of a word. This yā' is known as alif maqṣūra.

Exercise 9

Fill in the gaps in these sentences:

1 الزجاجة ____ المائدة .

2 الجريدة ____ الكرسيّ .

3 ____ ____ الخيمة و ____ .

4 الصورة ____ ____ .

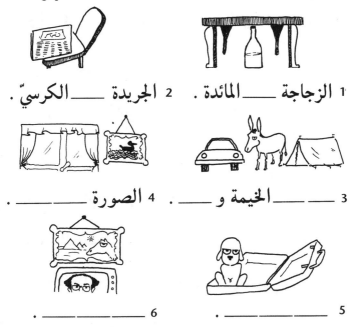

5 ____________ .

6 ____________ .

Exercise 10

Now look at this bedroom and answer the questions, as in the example.

1 هل الكرسيّ بجانب المائدة؟

نعم، هو بجانب المائدة.

2 أيْن التليفزيون؟

3 أيْن المائدة؟

4 هل الصورة بجانب الشبّاك؟

5 أين الخزانة؟

6 هل التليفزيون تحت الشبّاك؟

7 أين السرير؟

8 هل الباب بجانب المائدة؟

9 أين الحقيبة؟

10 هل المائدة بين الكرسيّ والخزانة؟

Keying Arabic

Keying Arabic is much simpler than handwriting in that the computer automatically joins the letters. An Arabic keyboard will show mainly separate letters (ب ق ح , etc.). All you need to do is key the individual letters in a word and the computer will figure out how to join them. The *previous* character is altered, depending on the next one keyed. For example, the word حقيبة, bag, is five keystrokes. As you key each character, you will see the one *before* alter to the correct form:

keystroke 1: ح → *screen 1:* ح
keystroke 2: ق → *screen 2:* حق
keystroke 3: ي → *screen 3:* حقي
keystroke 4: ب → *screen 4:* حقيب
keystroke 5: ة → *screen 5:* حقيبة

When you key a space, the computer knows that this word is finished and the process begins again with the next word.

Conversation

Dialects

So far you have met some simple Modern Standard Arabic (MSA) phrases for greetings, for introducing yourself and your family, and for asking for things. These phrases will be understood throughout the Arab world. However, spoken dialects will vary from one region to another.

MSA is the foundation that underpins all these dialects, and through MSA you will understand the principles that guide the Arabic language. However, there are some variations for basic words used in dialect and it is worth recognising the most common. Two of these are the question words 'what?' and 'where?'

	What's your name?	*Where's the door?*
MSA	ما اسمك؟ (mā ismak)	أين الباب؟ (ayna l-bāb)
Egyptian	اسمك ايه؟ (ismak eh)	فين الباب؟ (fayn il-bāb)
Levant/Gulf	شو اسمك؟ (shū ismak)	وين الباب؟ (wayn il-bāb)

Listen to the phrases in dialect on the recording and see if you can hear the differences.

Structure notes

The genitive case

Nouns that follow positional words, such as في (in) or على (on), are in the *genitive* case. This case is formed in a similar way to the nominative (see Unit 4), but using kasra, not ḍamma:

	Nominative	*Genitive*
Indefinite	بنتٌ (bintun)	بنتٍ (bintin)
Definite	البنتُ (al-bintu)	البنتِ (al-binti)

So the sentence ...

الصورة فوق السرير. (aṣ-ṣūra fawqa s-sarīr) The picture is above the bed.

... would be pronounced as follows, if fully vowelled:

اَلصُّورَةُ فَوْقَ السَّرِيرِ. (aṣ-ṣūratu fawqa s-sarīri)

The noun الصورة (picture) is in the nominative and السرير (bed) is in the genitive as it follows the positional word فوق (above).

Vocabulary in Unit 6

فِي (fī) in

عَلَى (ɛalā) on

فَوْقَ (fawqa) above

تَحْتَ (taḥta) below

بِجانِب (bijānib) beside

بَيْنَ (bayna) between

هَل...؟ (hal) question marker

نَعَم (naɛm) yes

لا (lā) no

ما اِسْمك؟ (mā ismak/-ik) what's your name? *(to a male/female)*

أَيْنَ...؟ (ayna) where?

مائِدة (mā'ida) table

كُرْسيّ (kursī) chair

سَرير (sarīr) bed

باب (bāb) door

تِلِيفِزْيُون (tilīfizyūn) television

شُبّاك (shubbāk) window

صُورَة (ṣūra) picture

خَزانَة (khazāna) cupboard

نَهْر (nahr) river

unit 7 Describing places

Describing places

The town المدينة (al-madīna)

Look at this picture of a town (madīna) and look at the labels, listening to the recording.

Exercise 1

Who works where? Match the jobs with the places.

A	ممرّضة	1	مَدْرَسَة
B	مهندس	2	مُسْتَشفى
C	مدرِّس	3	بَنْك
D	محاسب	4	مَصْنَع

Now write sentences, as in the example:

1 بدر/محاسب بدر محاسب وهو في البنك.

2 زينب/ممرّضة

3 زين/مدرّسة

4 أحمد/مهندس

What's the town like?

Listen to the description of the town on page 81, following the text below.

هذه صورة مَدينَة، وهُنَاك نهر في المدينة، وبجانب النهر هُنَاك شارِع.

في وسط الصورة هُنَاك بنك وبجانب البنك هُنَاك مدرسة. المدرسة بين البنك والمستشفى.

وعلى يمين البنك هُنَاك مصنع أسود وقبيح، وهو مصنع السيّارات، ولكن ليس هُنَاك سيّارات في الشارع. أمام البنك هُنَاك شجر جميل، ولكن ليس هُنَاك شجر أمام المصنع.

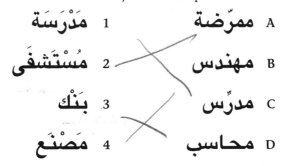

على يَمين ... (ɛalā l-yamīn) on the right of ...

على يَسار ... (ɛalā l-yasār) on the left of ...

أَمام ... (amām) in front of ...

في وَسَط ... (fī wasaṭ) in the middle of ...

هُنَاك (hunāka) there is/there are

لَيس هُنَاك (laysa hunāka) there isn't/there aren't

ولكن (wa-lākin) but

وراء behind

هُنَاك شجر أمام البنك.
There are trees in front of the bank.

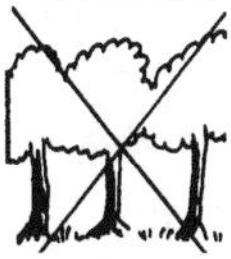

لَيس هُنَاك شجر أمام المصنع.
There aren't any trees in front of the factory.

هُنَاك شجر أمام البنك ولكن
لَيس هُنَاك شجر أمام المصنع.
There are trees in front of the bank but
there aren't any trees in front of the factory.

Iḍāfa constructions

Notice these phrases from the description of the town:

صورة مدينة (ṣūrat madīna) picture of a town

مصنع السيّارات (maṣnaɛ as-sayyārāt) car factory ('factory of the cars')

Putting two or more nouns directly together in this way is known as iḍāfa ('addition'). You have also met examples of iḍāfa in Units 3 and 4: بنت أحمد (bint aḥmad), Ahmad's daughter; حقيبة الولد (ḥaqībat al-walad), the boy's bag. Arabic uses iḍāfa to describe a close relationship, where English might use a possessive 's, of ('a bottle *of* water') or a compound ('clothes store').

The ta' marbūta is always pronounced on the first noun in an iḍāfa. Only the last noun in an iḍāfa can have al- (the). Whether or not the last noun has al- depends on the meaning. Look at the examples below:

بيت مدرس (bayt mudarris) *a* teacher's house

بيت المدرّس (bayt al-mudarris) *the* teacher's house

زُجاجة عصير (zujājat ɛaṣīr) *a* bottle of juice

زُجاجة العصير (zujājat al-ɛaṣīr) *the* bottle of juice

An iḍāfa can consist of more than two nouns:

باب بيت المدرّس (bāb bayt al-mudarris) the door of the teacher's house

اِبن أمير الكُويت (ibn amīr al-kuwayt) the son of the Emir of Kuwait

Exercise 2

Decide whether these sentences about the town on page 81 are true or false.

1 هُناك نهر في المدينة. ☐

2 هُناك شارع بجانب النهر. ☐

3 ليس هُناك بنك في الصورة. ☐

4 هُناك مصنع على يمين البنك. ☐

5 هُناك مستشفى بين البنك والمصنع. ☐

6 هُناك ممرضة أمام المستشفى. ☐

7 المصنع هو مصنع السيّارات. ☐

8 في وسط الصورة هُناك مستشفى. ☐

9 ليس هُناك شجر أمام المستشفى. ☐

10 المصنع أبيض وجميل. ☐

Exercise 3

Make sentences for each picture, as in the example:

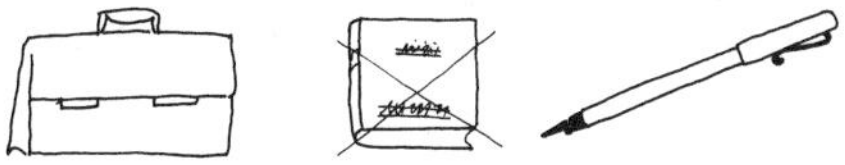

هناك قلم في الحقيبة
ولكن ليس هناك كتاب.

1

2

3

4

Group words

Some words have a plural meaning, even though they are grammatically singular. For example:

شجر (shajar) trees   دجاج (dajāj) poultry (hens)

These words are group words (*collective nouns*). Most of these words refer to plants or animals that are naturally found together in groups. If a tā' marbūṭa is added to the word, then it refers to only one of the group.

شجر (shajar) trees	شجرة (shajara) a tree
دجاج (dajāj) poultry (hens)	دجاجة (dajāja) a hen

group word + ة = *one of group*

Exercise 4

Here are some more collective nouns. Listen to the words and then make them refer to just one of the group, as in the example.

1 تين (tīn) figs: تينة (tīna) a fig
2 وَرْد (ward) roses
3 حَمام (ḥamām) pigeons
4 ذُباب (dhabāb) flies
5 لَوْز (lawz) almonds
6 بَطّيخ (baṭṭīkh) water melons

More about plurals

You have seen in Unit 4 how many words which refer to people can be made plural by adding certain endings. Remind yourself of the singular and plural for 'teacher':

	Singular	*Plural*
Masculine	مُدرّس (mudarris)	مُدرّسون (mudarrisūn)
Feminine	مَدرّسة (mudarrisa)	مُدرّسات (mudarrisāt)

The sound masculine plural (-ūn) is only used as a plural for words referring to *male people*. The sound feminine plural (-āt) is used as a plural for words referring to female people, and also as the plural of a number of other words which are not people (and which may be masculine or feminine in the singular). Here are some words you already know that can be made plural using the sound feminine plural:

	Singular	*Plural*
car	سيّارة (sayyāra)	سيّارات (sayyārāt)
bicycle	درّاجة (darrāja)	درّاجات (darrājāt)
television	تليفزيون (tilīfizyūn)	تليفزيونات (tilīfizyūnāt)

Notice that you must remove the tā' marbūṭa before adding the sound feminine plural (-āt). There are no rules to tell you which words can be made plural using the sound feminine plural, but many long words and words derived from other languages (for example, tilīfizyūn) can be made plural by adding this ending.

More about adjectives

In the description of the town you met this sentence:

على يمين البنك هُناك مصنع أسود وقبيح.

On the right of the bank, there's a black and ugly factory.

Notice that the two adjectives come *after* the noun (and not before, as they would in English). The use of و (wa, and) to separate the adjectives is optional. If you are referring to a specific factory, then you must add الـ (al, the) to the adjectives as well as the noun:

مصنع أسود قبيح	(masnaع aswad qabīḥ) *a* black ugly factory
المصنع الأسود القبيح	(al-masnaع al-aswad al-qabīḥ) *the* black ugly factory

You also add الـ to the adjective if the noun has a possessive ending:

حقيبتي الجديدة	(ḥaqībatī al-jadīda) my new bag
كلبه الأبيض الثقيل	(kalbuhu al-abyaḍ ath-thaqīl) his white heavy dog

The presence and position of الـ can change the meaning, and you must take care where you place it when describing things:

البنت جميلة.	(al-bint jamīla.) The girl is beautiful.
البنت الجميلة	(al-bint al-jamīl) the beautiful girl
بنت جميلة	(bint jamīla) a beautiful girl

Exercise 5

Put these sentences in the right order. The first is an example.

المصنع	هناك	أمام	سيّارة	جديدة	1

هناك سيّارة جديدة أمام المصنع.

على	قلم	المائدة	هناك	مكسور	2
سيّارتي	أنا	الجديدة	الجميلة	في	3
هناك	المستشفى	بجانب	ليس	شجر	4
مدرّس	المدرسة	هناك	جديد	في	5
محاسب	البنك	أحمد	في	الجديد	6

Exercise 6

Listen to these six new adjectives:

كَبير (kabīr) big

صَغير (ṣaghīr) small

طَويل (ṭawīl) long/tall (for people)

قَصير (qaṣīr) short

ضَعيف (ḍaعīf) weak

قَويّ (qawīy) strong

Now say and write a sentence for each, as in the example:

Exercise 7

Listen to the recording and draw a picture of the description you hear. Play the recording through once without stopping, and then play it again, stopping and repeating it as many times as you like until you have finished the drawing.

Structure notes

Genitive with iḍāfa

The second word in an iḍāfa construction (see pages 83–4) is always in the genitive case:

صورةُ مدينةٍ (ṣūratu madīnat<u>in</u>) a picture of a town

حقيبةُ الولدِ (ḥaqībatu l-walad<u>i</u>) the boy's bag

Conversation

Describing your town or your room
Alternative phrases for 'hunāka' and 'laysa hunāka' commonly used in colloquial Arabic are 'fīh' and 'mā fīh' (also pronounced 'mā fīhsh'). Listen to the example sentences on your recording and then try to make some similar descriptions about your town or room.

فيه مدرسة كبيرة في المدينة. ما فيه مستشفى. (fīh madrasa kabīra fī l-madīna. mā fīh mustashfā.) There's a big school in the town. There isn't a hospital.

فيه صورة جميلة في غُرفتي. ما فيه تليفزيون. (fīh ṣūra jamīla fī ghurfatī. mā fīh tilīfizyūn.) There's a beautiful picture in my room. There isn't a television.

Vocabulary in Unit 7

مَدينة (madīna) town
بَنك (bank) bank
مَدرسة (madrasa) school
شَجَر (shajar) trees
أمَام (amāma) in front of
هُنَاك (hunāka) there is/are
لَيس هُنَاك (laysa hunāka) there isn't/aren't
مَصْنَع (maṣnaع) factory
مُستشفَى (mustashfā) hospital
شَارِع (shāriع) street
غُرفة (ghurfa) room
ولَكِن (wa-lākin) but
تين (tīn) figs
لَوْز (lawz) almonds
بَطّيخ (baṭṭīkh) water melons
وَرْد (ward) roses
حَمام (hamām) pigeons
ذُباب (dhubāb) flies
كَبير (kabīr) big
صَغير (saghīr) small
طَويل (ṭawīl) long/tall
قَصير (qaṣīr) short
ضَعيف (daعīf) weak
قَويّ (qawīy) strong
عَلى يمين... (عalā yamīn) on the right of ...
عَلى يسار... (عalā yasār) on the left of ...
في وَسَط... (fī wasaṭ) in the middle of ...

unit **8** Review

Exercise 1

Handwrite these combinations of letters.

1 م + ص + ر = مِصْر

2 ع + م + ا + ن = عُمان

3 د + م + ش + ق = دِمَشْـق

4 م + س + ق + ط = مَسْقَط

5 ل + ب + ن + ا + ن = لُبْنان

6 ب + ي + ر + و + ت = بَيروت

7 ب + غ + د + ا + د = بَغْداد

 Now listen to the recording and add the vowels to the words you have written.

Exercise 2

Complete the table opposite, as in the examples:

word with ال	sun letter	first letter of word	word
اَلْبَيْت (al-bayt)	no	ب	بيت
اَلنَّهْر (an-nahr)	yes	ن	نهر
الخيمة	no	خ	خيمة
الذباب	yes	ذ	ذباب
الزجاجة	yes	ز	زجاجة
الوردة	no	و	وردة
المصنع	no	م	مصنع
الكتاب	no	ك	كتاب
السيارة	yes	س	سيّارة
الدرّاجة	yes	د	درّاجة
القميص	no	ق	قميص
الحقيبة	no	ح	حقيبة
الشبّاك	yes	ش	شبّاك
الصورة	yes	ص	صورة

Exercise 3

Write the names in the correct rows, as in the examples:

مدحت	نور	جيهان	أحمد
حسين	أنور	زيد	زينب
دينا	محمّد	زين	بدر

male   أحمد   ، بدر ، محمّد ، زيـد ، أنور ، مدحت
جيهان

female   جيهان   ، دينا   زينب

both   نور   زين

Exercise 4

Listen to the description of the family on the recording and fill in the names on the family tree.

جيهان   حسين

أحمد   دينا   زينب

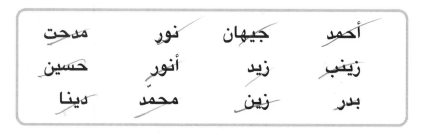

Now draw a family tree for yourself and describe it in a similar way.

Exercise 5

Find the professions in the word square. (The words run either top to bottom or right to left.)

ق	ا	ف	و	ن
م	ث	ظ	م	ي
م	ص	ش	ه	ح
ر	ا	ج	ن	س
ض	ذ	ض	د	ق
ة	م	ت	س	ش
ي	د	خ	ط	ر
و	ر	ب	ه	ن
ب	س	ا	ح	م
ا	ل	ز	ج	و
خ	ط	ت	م	ش

Now write out all the plurals for the words, as in the example:

Masculine sing.	*Masculine pl.*	*Feminine sing.*	*Feminine pl.*
مدرّس	مدرّسون	مدرّسة	مدرّسات

Exercise 6

Find the odd word out in these groups of words. The first is an example.

1 حمار كلب جريدة حمامة دجاجة

2 أنا أنتَ هم نحن هل

3 بدر زينب أحمد مدحت أنور

4 هناك في بين فوق بجانب

5 مدرِّس نجّار مصنع خبّاز محاسب

6 تين ذباب بطيخ لوز

7 كبير صغير ثقيل خفيف كتاب

8 أمّ أب باب أخ بنت

Exercise 7

Write a sentence for each picture, as in the example.

1 هذه سيّارة.

2

3

4

5

6

7

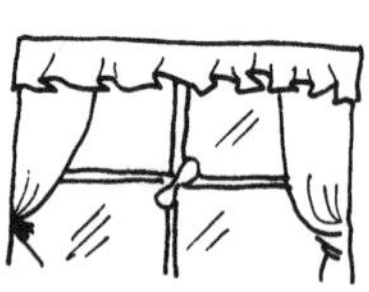

8

9

10

11

12

Exercise 9

Match the opposite pairs of adjectives, as in the example:

مكسور	طويل	قبيح	قصير	جديد
قويّ	قديم	ثقيل	كبير	سليم	صغير
أسود	ضعيف	جميل	خفيف	أبيض

Now choose one of the adjectives to fit into each *gap* in the description of the picture. Remember to add tā' marbūṭa and/or al- if necessary. You can use an adjective more than once.

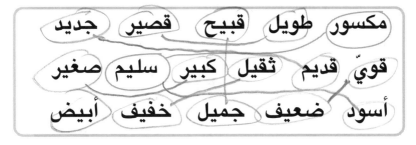

هذه صورة بيت جميل، وعلى يمين البيت هناك شجرة

______ . لون (colour) هذا البيت الجميل ______ ،

ولكن الباب ______ . أمام البيت هناك سيّارة

______ ولكن على يسار السيّارة هناك درّاجة

______ ، والدرّاجة أمام الشجرة ______ . وهناك

دجاجة ______ تحت السيّارة. على يمين الصورة

هناك حمار ______ ، وبين الحمار ______

والسيارة هناك كلب ______ و ______ .

Exercise 10

Now make questions and answers about the picture in Exercise 9 ı the prompts given, as in the example:

مار / قبيح

الحمار قبيح؟ لا، هو جميل.

2 يارة / أمام / بيت

3 ب / جميل

4 اجة / سليم

5 جاجة / على / سيّارة

6 اب / البيت / الأبيض

7 شجرة/الصغيرة / على يسار / بيت

8 ب / بين / حمار / سيّارة

Exercise 11

Look again at these characters you met in Unit 2.

دينا زيد زينب نادر بدر

Now say and write sentences to match the pictures, as in the (s.

هذا كلب زينب.
هذا كلبها.

هذه حقيبة زيد.
هذه حقيبته.

1

2

3

4

Conversation

Review

Review some of the conversational Arabic you've learned so far by taking part in these two conversations.

Prepare your part first by looking at the guide below. You can look back at the conversation boxes in Units 1–7 if you want to remind yourself of the conversational phrases.

Conversation 1

– مساء الخير. (masā al-khayr)

Reply.

– ما اسمك؟ (mā ismak)

Say 'I'm ...'.

– ومن هذا؟ (wa man hādhā?)

Introduce a male member of your family.

– تشرفنا (tasharrafna)

Conversation 2

– أهلا! (ahlan)

Say 'Hello to you, Dina'.

– كيف الحال؟ (kayf al-hāl?)

Reply.

– هل هذا قلمك؟ (hal hādhā qalamak?)

Say 'No, that's my sister's pen. My pen is black.'

– أين أختك؟ (ayna uhktak?)

Say 'in the house'.

– تفضل. (tafaḍḍal)

Thank Dina and say goodbye.

Now say your part in the pauses on the recording. You could also vary the conversations, changing the person you introduce or the item you are describing. You could also practise with a native speaker, another learner or a teacher if this is possible.

unit

9 Countries and people

The Middle East الشّرْق الأوْسَط

Look at this map of the Middle East (الشّرْق الأوْسَط, ash-sharq al-awsaṭ) and then listen to the names of the countries. They are keyed by number and written out below the map.

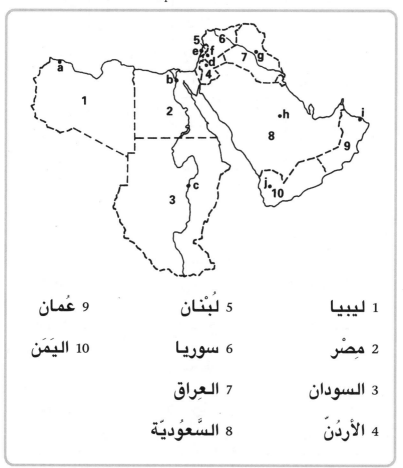

1 ليبيا

2 مِصْر

3 السودان

4 الأردُنّ

5 لُبْنان

6 سوريا

7 العِراق

8 السَّعوديّة

9 عُمان

10 اليَمَن

Exercise 1

Can you find the other nine countries in the word square? Find the country and circle it, as in the example.

ب	ث	م	ا	ه	ر	ض	ن	ف	ت
ا	ق	ص	ل	ظ	و	س	ل	ش	ز
ه	ز	ر	س	ر	ض	ص	ي	ي	ن
ق	ا	ر	ع	ل	ا	ز	ب	ذ	ت
ش	ب	خ	و	ا	ن	م	ي	ل	ا
س	ح	ن	د	ر	ا	ل	ا	ب	ج
غ	ع	ا	ي	ث	ت	ج	ل	ن	ف
ي	و	غ	ق	ي	ح	و	س	ا	ن
ف	ت	ث	م	ه	ض	ش	و	ن	ز
ا	ي	ر	و	س	ز	ت	د	ذ	ز
س	ع	ن	ب	ا	خ	ن	ا	م	ع
ق	ش	ث	ذ	ز	غ	ج	ن	م	ر

Capital city عاصِمة

Now listen to these capital cities, looking at the map on page 101.

a طَرابْلُس

b القاهِرة

c الخَرْطوم

d عَمَّان

e بَيرُوت

f دِمَشْق

g بَغْداد

h الرِّياض

i مَسْقَط

j صَنْعَاء

Notice that without the vowels the word عمان could be عُمان (ɛumān), the country Oman, or عَمّان (ɛammān), the capital of Jordan, Amman. Watch carefully for the context to tell you which is being referred to.

Exercise 2

Answer these questions referring to the map. The first is an example. Remember that towns and cities are almost always feminine (see Unit 3).

1 هل القَاهِرة في اليمن؟

لا، هي في مصر.

2 هل بَغْداد في لبنان؟

3 هل الرياض في السُعودِيّة؟

4 أين عَمَّان؟

5 هل الأردن بين السُعودِيّة وسوريا؟

6 أين مَسْقَط؟

7 هل اليمن تحت السُعودِيّة؟

8 هل العراق بجانب السودان؟

Exercise 3

Now write ten sentences describing the countries and capital cities shown on the map. The first is an example:

1 القاهرة في مصر وهي عاصمة مصر.

Geographical position

Look at the compass with the Arabic for the different directions.

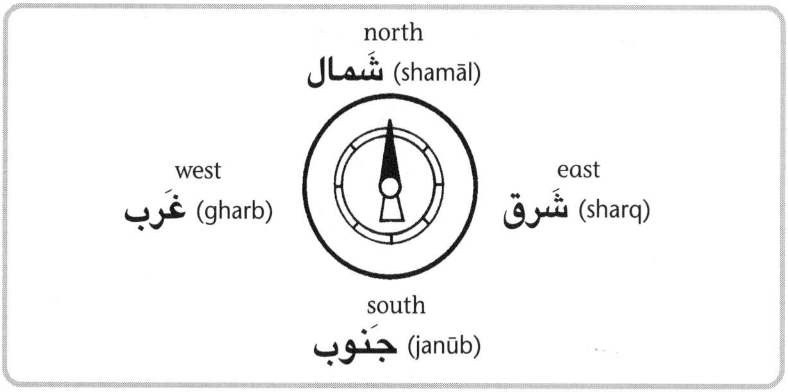

Now listen to these descriptions:

مسقط في شمال عُمان.

بيروت في غرب لبنان.

دمشق في جنوب سورية.

بغداد في شرق العراق.

Notice that in Arabic you use the iḍāfa construction (see page 83) to describe geographical position, putting the position (شمال (shamāl), north) directly in front of the place (عمان (ɛumān), Oman) with the meaning 'the north *of* Oman': مسقط في شمال عمان (musqaṭ fī shamāl ɛumān) Musqat is in the north of Oman.

Exercise 4

Look at this map of Egypt and the four towns marked on it.

Now fill in the gaps in these sentences:

١   أسوان في غَرب ___ مصر.

٢   سيوة في شَمال ___ غَرب.

٣   الإسكندرية هي ___ شمال ___ مصر.

٤   بور سعيد هي ___ شَمال ___ شَرق.

Other countries of the world

Many Arabic names for countries are similar to the English. Names of foreign countries often end in a long ā sound. You will find that you will become better at picking out these foreign names as you become more aware of patterns in the Arabic language.

Exercise 5

Try to read the names of the countries in Arabic and then see whether you can match them to their English equivalents, as in the example.

أَمريكا	1	A China
الصِّين	2	B Spain
روسْيا	3	C America
اليابان	4	D Italy
انجلترَا	5	E Japan
فَرنسا	6	F Russia
ألمانيا	7	G England
أسبانيا	8	H France
إيطاليا	9	I Germany

 Now check your pronunciation of the Arabic with the recording.

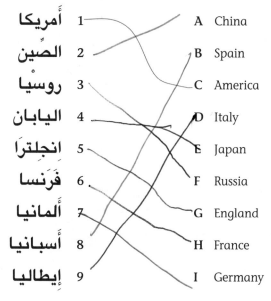

Nationalities

Listen to the recording and look at the pictures.

1 هو مِنْ أين ؟

هو من مسقط .

هو عُمانِيّ .

2 هو مِنْ أين ؟

هو من الرياض .

هو سعودِيّ .

3 هي من أين ؟

هي من أسوان .

هي مصرِيَّة .

4 هُمْ من أين ؟

هُمْ من طُوكْيُو .

هم يَابَانِيُّون .

5 هُنَّ من أين ؟

هُنَّ من طَرَابْلُس .

هنّ لِيبِيَّات .

مصر + يّ = مصريّ

country (miṣr) + (īy) = nationality (miṣrīy)

Nisba adjective

Adjectives describing nationality are made by adding -īy to the noun, in this case the country. This ending has come into English through words adopted from Arabic, such as Kuwaiti, Saudi, Omani, Yemeni, etc.

The -īy adjectival ending is known as نسبة (nisba). Nisba is used to describe nationality, but is also commonly employed to make many other nouns into adjectives, for example turning بيت (bayt), house, into بيتيّ (baytīy), domestic, or شمال (shamāl), north, into شماليّ (shamālīy), northern. Nisba adjectives are a very useful way of expanding your vocabulary quite easily.

There are a few things to remember when adding the nisba ending:

1 If the noun ends in tā' marbūṭa (ة), ā or yā, you need to remove this before adding the nisba ending:

سوريا (sūriyā) Syria	➛	سوريّ (sūrīy) Syrian
أمريكا (amrīkā) America	➛	أمريكيّ (amrīkīy) American
ليبيا (lībyā) Libya	➛	ليبيّ (lībīy) Libyan
مهنة (mihna) profession	➛	مهنيّ (mihnīy) professional
موسيقى (mūsīkā) music	➛	موسيقيّ (mūsīkī) musical

2 If a country starts with al-, remove this before adding the nisba ending:

السودان (as-sūdān) Sudan	➛	سودانيّ (sūdānī) Sudanese
اليابان (al-yābān) Japan	➛	يابانيّ (yābānī) Japanese

3 One nationality is unusual. Take a special note of it:

انجلترا (injiltarā) England	➛	انجليزيّ (injilīzī) English

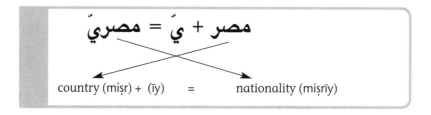

Exercise 6

Complete the following table, filling in the missing country or nationality.

Country الدَّوْلَة	*Nationality* الجِنْسيَّة
الأردن	________
________	عِراقيّ
اليابان	________
أمريكا	________
أسبانيا	________
________	رُوسيّ
الصّين	________
________	عُمانيّ
إيطاليا	________
________	سوريّ
لُبنان	________
________	مِصْريّ
ليبيا	________
فرنسا	________
ألمانيا	________
________	انجليزي

Exercise 7

Make sentences about where these people come from, as in the example.

1

هو من الأردنّ.

هو أردنيّ.

2

3

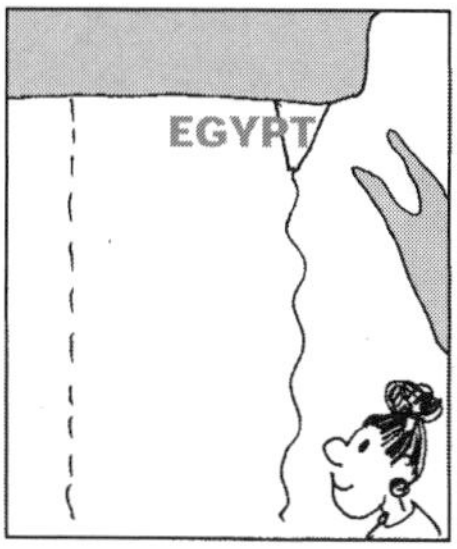

4

5

6

7

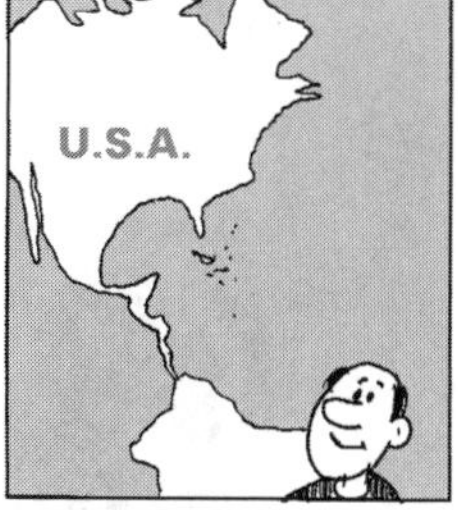

8

Plural of nisba

As with many of the jobs you met in Unit 4, nationalities and other nisba adjectives can generally be made feminine by adding tā' marbūṭa, and plural by using the sound masculine plural (-ūn) or the sound feminine plural (-āt):

	Masc. sing.	*Fem. sing.*	*Masc. plural*	*Fem. plural*
Egyptian	مصري (miṣrīy)	مصرية (miṣrīya)	مصريون (miṣrīyūn)	مصريات (miṣrīyāt)
French	فرنسي (faransīy)	فرنسية (faransīya)	فرنسيون (faransīyūn)	فرنسيات (faransīyāt)

There are a few exceptions. In these cases the masculine plural is made by *removing* the nisba ending (-īy). The feminine plural is not affected.

	Masc. sing.	*Fem. sing.*	*Masc. plural*	*Fem. plural*
Arab	عربي (ɛarabīy)	عربية (ɛarabīya)	عرب (ɛarab)	عربيات (ɛarabīyāt)
English	انجليزي (injilīzīy)	انجليزية (injilīzīya)	انجليز (injilīz)	انجليزيات (injilīzīyāt)
Russian	روسي (rūsīy)	روسية (rūsīya)	روس (rūs)	روسيات (rūsīyāt)

Exercise 8

Say and write sentences, as in the example:

هو من أمريكا. هو أمريكيّ.

Exercise 9

Make these sentences and questions plural, as in the example:

1 هو يَمَنيّ.

هم يمنيّون.

2 هي ألمانيّة.

3 هو اِنجليزيّ.

4 هي لبنانيّة.

5 هل هي سَعُوديّة؟

6 هل هو روسيّ؟

Conversation

Talking about where you come from

If you want to ask someone where he or she comes from, you can use this question, which literally means 'you from where?':

أنت من أين؟ (anta/anti min ayn?) Where are you from? *(masc./fem.)*

A more formal question would be:

ما جنسيتك؟ (mā jinsīyatak/-ik?) What's your nationality? *(masc./fem.)*

The answer could be:

أنا من لبنان. (ānā min lubnān) I'm from Lebanon.

Or:

أنا لبنانيّ/لبنانيّة. (ānā lubnānīy/lubnānīya) I'm Lebanese. *(masc./fem.)*

You could also be asked:

من أية مدينة؟ (min ayyat madīna?) From which town?

هل هي في الشمال؟ (hal hiya fī sh-shamāl?) Is that in the north?

Now have a go on the recording at answering questions about where *you* come from. The recording will help you.

Exercise 10

Look at the immigration form and listen to the conversation on the recording. Listen once without writing; then listen again, filling in the missing information on the form. (*Note:* مِهنة mihna = profession.)

الاِسم ...... أحمد حسين ......

الجِنسيّة ......

المِهنة ......

اسم الزوجة ......

جنسية الزوجة ......

مهنة الزوجة ......

Now read this description of Ahmed and Dina:

أحمد حسين مهندس في الرّياض. أحمد سعودي، ولكن زوجته دينا مصريّة. دينا مُدَرّسة في الرّياض.

From the following completed form, write a similar description for Mohammad and Zaynab.

الاِسم ...... محمد نور ......

الجِنسيّة ... سوري ......

المِهنة .... محاسب (في دمشق) ......

اسم الزوجة .. زينب الشريف ......

جنسية الزوجة .. يمنيّة ......

مهنة الزوجة .... ممرّضة ......

Vocabulary in Unit 9

اَلشَّرْق الأَوْسَط (ash-sharq al-awsaṭ) The Middle East

لِيبْيا / لِيبِي (lībyā/lībīy) Libya/Libyan

مِصْر / مِصْرِيّ (miṣr/miṣrīy) Egypt/Egyptian

السُّودان / سُودَانيّ (as-sūdān/sūdānīy) Sudan/Sudanese

لُبْنان / لُبْنانيّ (lubnān/lubnānīy) Lebanon/Lebanese

سورِيا* / سوريّ (sūriya/sūrīy) Syria/Syrian (*also written as سورية)

العِرَاق / عِراقيّ (al-ɛirāq/ɛirāqīy) Iraq/Iraqi

الأُرْدُنّ / أُرْدُنيّ (al-urdunn/urdunnīy) Jordan/Jordanian

السَّعودية / سَعوديّ (as saɛūdiyya/saɛūdīy) Saudi (Arabia)/Saudi

عُمان / عُمانيّ (ɛumān/ɛumānīy) Oman/Omani

اليَمَن / يَمَنيّ (al-yaman/yamanīy) Yemen/Yemeni

أمْريكا / أمْريكيّ (amrīkā/amrīkīy) America/American

الصِّين / صِينيّ (aṣ-ṣīn/ṣīnīy) China/Chinese

رُوسيا / روسيّ (rūsya/rūsīy) Russia/Russian

اليابان / يابانيّ (al-yābān/yābānīy) Japan/Japanese

اِنجِلْترا* / اِنْجِليزيّ (injiltarā/injilīzīy) England/English (*also انكلترا)

فَرَنسا / فَرَنسيّ (faransā/faransīy) France/French

أَلمَانيا / أَلمَانيّ (almānyā/almānīy) Germany/German

أَسْبَانيا / أَسْبَانيّ (asbānyā/asbānīy) Spain/Spanish

إيطَاليا / إيطاليّ (ītālyā/ītālīy) Italy/Italian

عَاصِمة (ɛāṣima) capital (city)

دَولَة (dawla) country, state

جِنْسيَّة (jinsiyya) nationality

اِسْم (ism) name

مِهنة (mihna) profession

شَمَال (shamāl) north

جَنُوب (janūb) south

غَرْب (gharb) west

شَرْق (sharq) east

مِنْ (min) from

unit 10

Counting things

Arabic numbers 1–10

European languages adopted Arabic numerals in the Middle Ages to replace the very clumsy Roman numerals. Although Arabic and English figures are basically the same numbers, the shape varies somewhat. Compare the Arabic figures 1 to 10 with their English equivalents.

Arabic	*English*
١	1
٢	2
٣	3
٤	4
٥	5
٦	6
٧	7
٨	8
٩	9
١٠	10

You can see obvious similarities between the 1 and the 9 in both languages. There is also a theory that the Arabic ٢ and ٣ were turned on their side to produce the English 2 and 3:

Look at the Arabic numbers written out below and repeat them after the recording. Each number is given twice:

١	وَاحِد	(wāḥid)	٦	سِتَّة	(sitta)
٢	اِثْنَان	(ithnān)	٧	سَبْعة	(sabع a)
٣	ثَلاثَة	(thalātha)	٨	ثَمَانية	(thamānya)
٤	أَرْبَعَة	(arbaعa)	٩	تِسْعَة	(tisعa)
٥	خَمْسَة	(khamsa)	١٠	عَشَرَة	(عashara)

Direction of Arabic numbers

One unusual feature of Arabic numbers is that they are written from left to right, the same direction as English numbers. (Look at the Arabic ١٠ and the English 10.) This is the opposite direction to the rest of the Arabic script. You may see Arabs writing numbers backwards (as if you wrote 12387 starting with the 7 and finishing with the 1). However, writing numbers backwards is a difficult art to master and it is common to leave a space and start the numbers from the left:

Arabic script ←	*Arabic number* →	*Arabic script* ←
مُدرِّسات في المَدْرَسة.	١٠	هناك
teachers in the school	10	there are

Exercise 1

Match the numbers with the words, as in the example.

1	٦	خمسة
2	٩	ثلاثة
3	٨	سبعة
4	٣	تسعة
5	١٠	واحد
6	٤	ستة
7	١	ثمانية
8	٥	اثنان
9	٢	عشرة
10	٨	أربعة

Now write the vowels on the words.

Handwritten numbers

Most Arabic handwritten numbers look similar to the printed ones. The main difference is that the ٢ (2) is usually handwritten as ۲ (see the 'Handwriting practice' panel).

Tip: Watch out for the handwritten ٣ (3). Sometimes the wavy shape at the top becomes smoothed out for the sake of speed, making it look more like a printed ٢. Remember this, especially when reading handwritten prices.

Handwriting practice

Practise writing the numbers, starting at the dot.

٩ ٨ ٧ ٦ ٥ ٤ ٣ ۲ ١

Now write out these numbers by hand: 57, 102, 956, 340, 788.

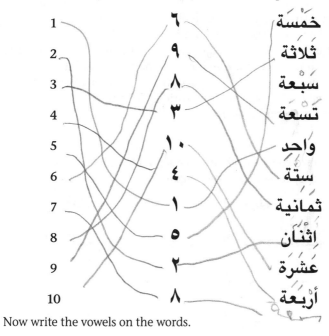

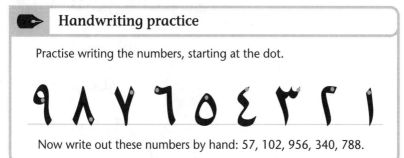

English words in Arabic

If English took its numbers from Arabic, then Arabic has taken quite a few words in return. For example, a frequently used word for 'bank' is بَنك. The word used for the Egyptian and British currency 'Pound' is جنيه (pronounced junayh or gunayh), originating from the English word 'guinea'.

Some of the adopted words also have alternative words with Arabic roots (another word for 'bank' is مصرف (maṣraf), meaning 'place to change/cash money'). The word used varies from country to country, and also sometimes from spoken to written.

Exercise 2

Read these Arabic words, which are all adopted from European languages, and try to work out their meaning:

١ فيلم

٢ تِليفون

٣ طَماطِم

٤ بَطاطِس

٥ سيجَارة

٦ كِيلو

٧ ديموقْراطيّة

٨ بَرْلَمان

٩ ميدالْية

١٠ مَلْيون

Now check your pronunciation with the recording.

Exercise 3

Four of the words in Exercise 2 can be made plural using the sound feminine plural ending -āt (see page 86). Write them out again in the plural, as in the example:

١ تِليفون – تِليفونات

٢ ديموقْراطيّة

٣ بَرْلَمان

٤ ميدالْية

Counting things

Look at the following and listen to the recording:

مدرّسة

مدرّس

مدرّستان

مدرّسان

٣ مدرِّسات

٣ مدرِّسين

The dual

Notice how Arabic uses the plural for 'three teachers', but not for 'two teachers'. This is because there is a special dual ending, ان (-ān), which is added to the *singular*: مدرّسان (mudarrisān) two teachers. There is no need to also use the number 2, ithnān, as the dual ending already gives you this information. So 'two dogs' would be كلبان (kalbān), 'two girls' بنتان (bintān), etc. An alternative form of the dual ending is -ayn (kalbayn, bintayn), which is more common in spoken dialects.

When the dual ending is added to feminine words ending in tā' marbūṭa, this unties and so must be pronounced:

Feminine singular	*Feminine dual*
مدرّسة (mudarrisa) teacher	مدرّستان/تين (mudarrisatān/-tayn)
سيّارة (sayyāra) car	سيّارتان/تين (sayyāratān/-tayn)

Plural with numbers

1 The masculine plural مدرّسون (mudarrisūn) becomes مدرّسين (mudarrisīn) when it follows a number. The -īn ending is an alternative sound masculine plural that is sometimes used in Modern Standard Arabic (see 'Structure notes' at the end of this unit for further explanation). Spoken dialects tend to use -īn almost exclusively, so as a beginner you can do the same.

2 You may see the numbers with or without the final tā' marbūṭa, e.g. 'three' as ثلاث (thalāth) or ثلاثة (thalātha). Strictly speaking, a *masculine* noun should be preceded by the number *including* tā' marbūṭa and a feminine noun by the number *without* tā' marbūṭa, the opposite to what you might expect:

ثلاثة مدرّسين (thalaathat mudarrisīn) three *(male)* teachers

ثلاث مدرّسات (thalaath mudarrisāt) three *(female)* teachers

This use of tā' marbūṭa with the masculine is an unusual feature that even native speakers can overlook. Spoken dialects tend to simplify the rules, keeping the tā' marbūṭa when the number is pronounced by itself, but dropping it when there is a noun following the number. As a beginner, you can do the same while being aware of the more formal rules.

Exercise 4

Say and write these words in the dual, as in the example. What do they mean?

١ كتاب – كتابان/ين 2 books

٢ مِفتاح ....

٣ مَدرَسة ....

٤ نَهر ....

٥ جَريدة ....

٦ دَولة ....

Exercise 5

Look at the pictures and say how many there are, as in the example.

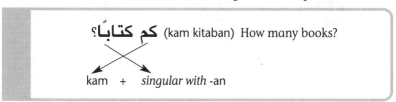

How many? كَم؟

'How many?' is كَم؟ (kam?). In Arabic, this is followed by a *singular* word:

كم درّاجة؟ (kam darrāja) How many bicycles?

kam + *singular*

In addition, if the word following kam does *not* end in tā' marbūṭa (i.e. almost all masculine nouns), an extra ending is added: اً, pronounced -an.

كم كتاباً؟ (kam kitaban) How many books?

kam + *singular with* -an

Exercise 6

Ask and answer six questions about this picture, as in the example.

هناك كَم سيّارة في الصورة؟ How many cars are there in the picture?

هناك خمس سيّارات. There are five cars.

How much? بِكَم؟

There are many currencies used throughout the Arab world. Here are the most common, together with some of the countries that use them:

جُنَيْه	(junayh)	Pound (Egypt)
ريال	(riyāl)	Riyal (Saudi, Qatar)
دينار	(dīnār)	Dinar (Kuwait, Bahrain, Iraq, Jordan)
ليرة	(līra)	Lira (Lebanon)
دِرْهَم	(dirham)	Dirham (United Arab Emirates)

Look at the fruit stall and the vocabulary list. Take note of how much each type of fruit costs.

بَطاطِس	(baṭāṭis)	potatoes
بُرتُقال	(burtuqāl)	oranges
مَوز	(mawz)	bananas
طَماطِم	(ṭamāṭim)	tomatoes
تُفّاح	(tuffāḥ)	apples
مَنجة	(manga)	mangoes

Now listen to this conversation between the stall holder and a customer:

بِـ + كَم؟ = بِكَم؟

'with' + 'how many?' = how much?

When you answer the question بِكَم (bikam), 'how much?', you should also put بِـ (bi), 'with', in front of the amount:

بكم كيلو الموز؟ (bikam kīlo l-mawz?)
How much is a kilo of bananas?

كيلو الموز بخمسة جنيهات. (kīlo l-mawz <u>bi</u>-khamsa junayhat.)
A kilo of bananas is five pounds.

Tip: Remember how to say 'please': من فضلك, pronounced fully as min faḍluka/faḍluki (*to a man/woman*), but often simplified in spoken Arabic to min faḍlak/faḍlik.

Exercise 7

Now make up similar conversations about the other fruit on the stall. For example:

– بكم كيلو المنجة من فضلك؟

– كيلو المنجة بعشرة جنيهات.

In the market في السوق

Here are a few typical souvenirs you might want to buy from the local market. Listen to the words on the recording.

صَنْدَل	(ṣandal)	sandals
طَبلة	(ṭabla)	drum
قِلادة	(qilāda)	necklace
سَلّة	(salla)	basket
تي-شيرت	(tī shīrt)	T-shirt
طَبَق	(ṭabaq)	plate

Exercise 8

Ask about the price of each of the above items, as in the example.

بكم الصندل من فضلك؟

What's it made of?

You can describe the material something is made of by putting the material directly after the item:

صَنْدَل جِلد	(ṣandal jild)	leather sandals
قِلادة فِضّة	(qilādat fiḍḍa)	a silver necklace

Exercise 9

Choose a suitable material for each item. (There may be more than one possible material.)

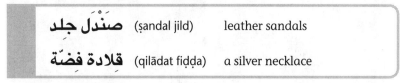

خَشَب (khashab) wood
قُطن (quṭn) cotton
جِلد (jild) leather
زُجاج (zujāj) glass
حَرير (ḥarīr) silk
فِضّة (fiḍḍa) silver
ذَهَب (dhahab) gold
نُحاس (nuḥās) copper

Now make requests using أُريد (urīd, I'd like ...), for example:

أريد قلادة ذهب/فضّة من فضلك. I'd like a gold/silver necklace, please.

Describing what you have

Arabic does not generally use a verb to express the meaning of the English 'have/has'. Instead a number of prepositions are used. لِـ (li, to), عِندَ (ʿinda, at) and مَعَ (maʿa, with) are three of the most common prepositions used in this way. The preposition is followed by the possessor, as in the following examples:

لمحمد سيّارة جديدة. (li-muḥammad sayyāra jadīda.)
Mohammad has a new car. ('to Mohammad a new car')

عند سارة قلادة ذهب. (ɛinda sāra qilādat dhahab.)
Sarah has a gold necklace. ('at Sarah a gold necklace')

القلم مع أختي. (al-qalam maɛa ukhtī.)
My sister has the pen. ('the pen is with my sister')

لِـ (li) is written as part of the word that follows. If it is put before al-, the combination becomes للـ... (lil-):

للمُحاسِب كمبيوتر قديم. (lil-muḥāsib kompyūtir qadīm.)
The accountant has an old computer.

You can also use these prepositions with the attached pronouns (see Unit 5):

لي أخ في البرازيل. (lī akh fī l-barāzīl.)
I have a brother in Brazil.

عندها كلب صغير. (ɛindahā kalb ṣaghīr.)
She has a small dog.

معك كبريت؟ (maɛak kibrīt?)
Do you have any matches?

Plural attached pronouns

The most common plural attached pronouns are كم (-kum) your *(plural)*, نا (-nā) our, and هم (-hum) their. These can be attached to nouns or prepositions in the same way as the singular pronouns.

هل عندكم برتقال؟ (hal ɛindakum burtuqāl?) Do you *(pl.)* have any oranges?

بيتنا كبير ولكن بيتهم أكبر. (baytnā kabīr walākin bayt-hum akbar) Our house is large but their house is larger.

عندهم طبق نحاس جميل. (ɛindahum ṭabaq nuḥās jamīl) They have a beautiful copper plate.

Conversation

In the market

Put all you've learnt in this unit to good use in the market. You're going to buy some jewellery. You'll need to think about how to say the following in Arabic:

– Good evening.

– I'd like a silver ring, please.

– How much is the ring?

– Here you are. Seven pounds.

– Do you have a bag*?

– Thank you. Goodbye.

Now join in the conversation on the recording, saying your part in the pauses.

**Tip*: A bag to take away purchases is كيس (kīs).
حقيبة (ḥaqība) = handbag, suitcase, etc.

Structure notes

Case endings for the sound masculine plural

The sound masculine plural does not have the same case endings as other nouns. The nominative is mudarris<u>ūn</u>, but the genitive is mudarris<u>īn</u>.

The numbers 3 to 10 are always followed by a plural noun in the *genitive*. This is what causes the sound masculine plural ending to change from -ūn to -īn.

هناك محاسبون في البنك. (hunāka muḥāsib<u>ūn</u> fī l-bank)
There are accountants in the bank.

هناك ستّة محاسبين في البنك. (hunāka sitta muḥāsib<u>īn</u> fī l-bank)
There are six accountants in the bank.

This change is one of the few instances when a case ending affects the spelling, so it is important to know when it is used.

Vocabulary in Unit 10

وَاحِد (wāhid) one

اِثْنَان (ithnān) two

ثَلاثَة (thalātha) three

أرْبَعَة (arbaعa) four

خَمْسَة (khamsa) five

سِتَّة (sitta) six

سَبْعَة (sabعa) seven

ثَمَانِيَة (thamānya) eight

تِسْعَة (tisعa) nine

عَشَرَة (عashara) ten

كَمْ؟ (kam) how many?

بِكَمْ؟ (bikam) how much?

جُنَيه (junayh) Pound

رِيَال (riyāl) Riyal

دِينَار (dīnār) Dinar

لِيرَة (līra) Lira

دِرْهَم (dirham) Dirham

طَمَاطِم (tamātim) tomatoes

بَطَاطِس (baṭāṭis) potatoes

مَنْجَة (manga) mangoes

تُفَّاح (tuffāh) apples

بُرْتُقَال (burtuqāl) oranges

مَوْز (mawz) bananas

ذَهَب (dhahab) gold

فِضّة (fiḍḍa) silver

نُحاس (nuḥās) copper

خَشَب (khashab) wood

قُطن (qutn) cotton

جِلد (jild) leather

زُجَاج (zujāj) glass

حَرِير (harīr) silk

فيلم (fīlm) film

تِليفون (tilīfūn) telephone

سيجَارة (sījāra) cigarette

كيلو (kīlū) kilo

ميدالْية (mīdālya) medal

مَليون (malyūn) million

بَرْلَمان (barlamān) parliament

ديموقراطيّة (dīmūqrāṭīyya) democracy

سوق (sūq) market

صَنْدَل (ṣandal) sandals

طَبلة (ṭabla) drum

قِلادة (qilāda) necklace

سَلّة (salla) basket

تي–شيرت (tī shīrt) T-shirt

طَبَق (ṭabaq) plate

كُمبيوتر (kumbyūtir) computer

كِبريت (kibrīt) matches

unit 11 Plurals and colours

Arabic roots المَصدَر

Look at the following words with their translations:

كتاب	a book
مَكْتَب	an office/a desk
كِتابَة	writing
كَتَبَ	(he) wrote
كاتِب	writer/clerk
يَكْتُب	(he) writes
مَكْتُوب	(something) written down; a letter (correspondence)
كُتَيِّب	a booklet
مَكْتَبَة	a library/bookshop

All these words have a connection with writing. Can you find the three letters that occur in all these words?

You should be able to pick out quite easily the three common letters:

ك	kāf
ت	tā'
ب	bā'

Notice how the letters always appear in the same order. The bā' does not come before the tā' in any of the words, nor the kāf after the tā', etc. So we can say that if the sequence of letters ك/ت/ب (reading from right to left) appears in a word, the word will have something to do with the meaning of 'writing'. These three letters are the root (المصدر, al-maṣdar) connected with writing.

The eight words above are made up of the three root letters, with different long and short vowels between them and sometimes with extra letters added onto the beginning and/or the end of the root letters:

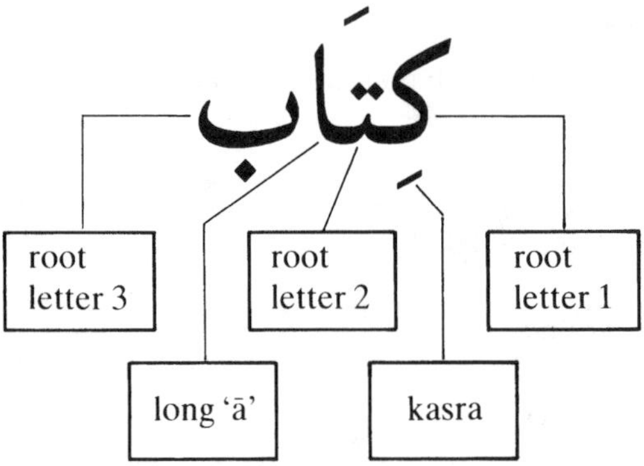

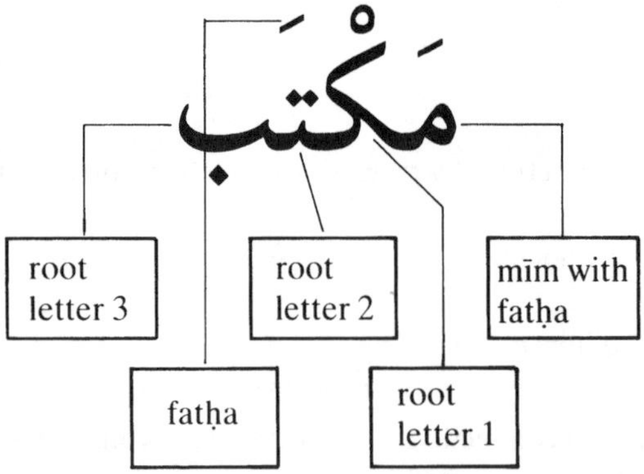

The great majority of Arabic words are formed around a sequence of three root letters, and learning to recognise these will help you enormously with learning the language.

You can often (but not always) find the root of a word by ignoring the vowels (long and short) and removing the extra letters at the beginning and end. As you learn more about the structure of Arabic, you will learn to recognise these extra letters. For the moment, it is enough to know that mīm is a common extra letter on the front of a sequence (*prefix*) and tā' marbūta is a common extra letter on the end (*suffix*).

Exercise 1

Try to write the three root letters for these words which you already know, as in the example. The left-hand column tells you the general meaning of this root.

General meaning	*Root*	*Word*
calculating	ح/س/ب	محاسب
bigness	/ /	كبير
carving (wood)	/ /	نجّار
opening	/ /	مفتاح
sealing (a letter)	/ /	خاتم
moving along	/ /	درّاجة
producing	/ /	مصنع
falling sick	/ /	ممرّضة
studying	/ /	مُدرّس + مَدْرَسة

Plural patterns 1 and 2

You already know two ways of making words plural:

1 *Sound masculine plural*. This can be used only with some words that refer to male people:

مدرّس (mudarris) ← مدرّسون/مدرّسين (mudarrisūn/mudarrisīn)

2 *Sound feminine plural*. This can be used with most words that refer to female people, and with some other masculine and feminine words:

ممرّضة (mumarriḍa) ← ممرّضات (mumarriḍāt)

سيّارة (sayyāra) ← سيّارات (sayyārāt)

تليفون (tilīfūn) ← تليفونات (tilīfūnāt)

However, many Arabic words cannot be made plural in either of these ways. They are made plural by following different patterns which you will learn in the next few chapters.

Look at the pictures and listen to the recording:

١ قلم أَقْلام ٢ ولد أَوْلاد

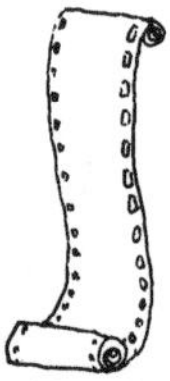

٣ فيلم أَفْلام ٤ بيت بُيُوت

٥ بنك بُنُوك

Plural pattern 1

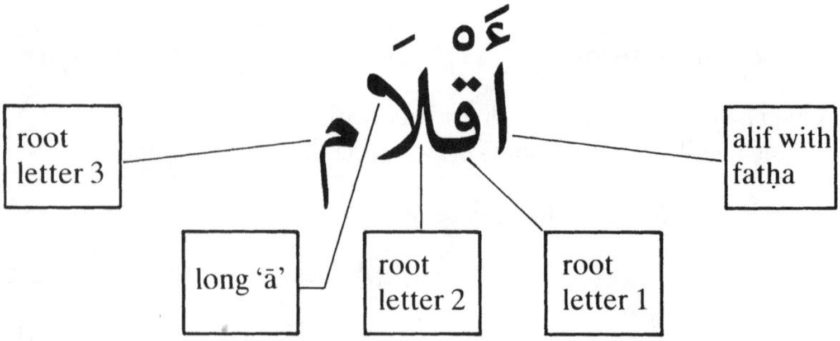

Plural pattern 2

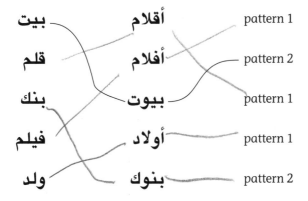

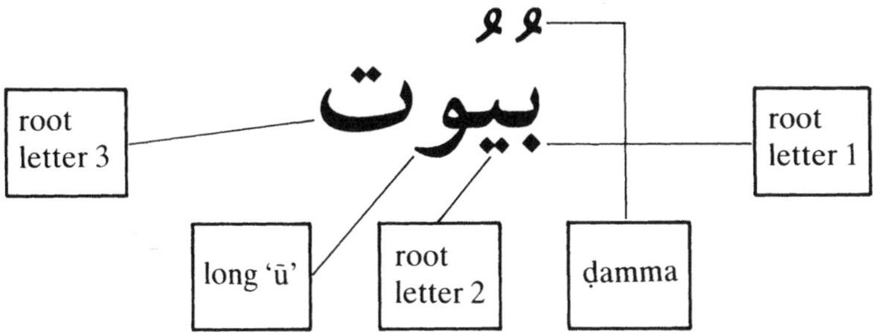

Exercise 2

Match the singular and plural words, as in the example.

بيت	أقلام	pattern 1
قلم	أفلام	pattern 2
بنك	بيوت	pattern 1
فيلم	أولاد	pattern 1
ولد	بنوك	pattern 2

Now write the vowels on the words.

Broken plurals

Notice that although the vowels on the singular words may vary, they are always the same in the plural pattern. These plural patterns are known as *broken plurals* because the word is 'broken apart' and different long and short vowels are arranged around the root letters.

The two patterns you have met in this unit are examples of broken plurals. Arabic will also often fit *loan words* originated from other languages, such as 'film' and 'bank', into the broken plural patterns if they have three *consonants* (i.e. letters that are not vowels).

There are about a dozen significant different broken plural patterns, seven or eight of these being the most common. You will gradually be introduced to the different patterns.

Exercise 3

The following words also make their plurals according to pattern 1. Write out their plurals, as in the example.

Plural	*Singular*
ألوان	لَوْن (lawn) colour
أطباق	طَبَق (ṭabaq) plate
أصحاب	صَاحِب (ṣāḥib) friend/owner
أشكال	شَكل (shakl) shape
أوقات	وَقْت (waqt) time
أسواق	سُوق (sūq*) market
أكواب	كُوب (kūb*) cup/beaker

*In these cases, و is the 2nd root letter.

These words fit into pattern 2. Write out their plurals.

Plural	*Singular*
سُيوف	سَيْف (sayf) sword
	قَلْب (qalb) heart
	مَلِك (malik) king
	شَمعة (shamɛa) candle
	شَيْخ (shaykh) sheikh

Now check your answers with the recording or in the answer section.

Vocabulary learning

From now on, try to learn each word with its plural. If you are using the card system (see Unit 1), write the plural below the singular:

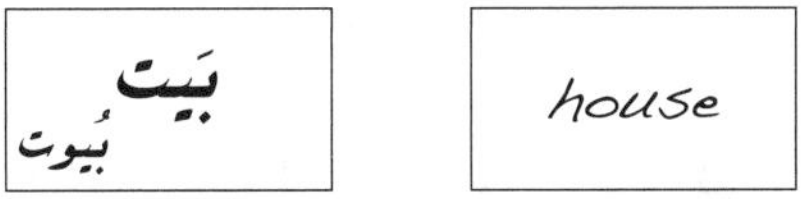

Tip: Just writing the plural will help you to remember it. Make sure that you can remember both the singular and the plural before the card passes into the next envelope.

What are these?

Look at the pictures and listen to the recording:

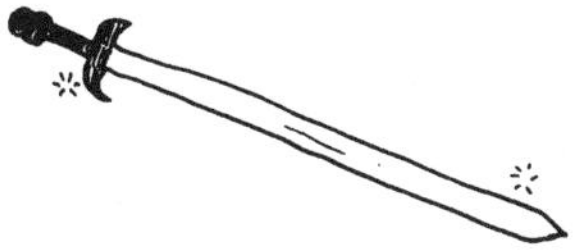

هذا سيف . هو سيف .

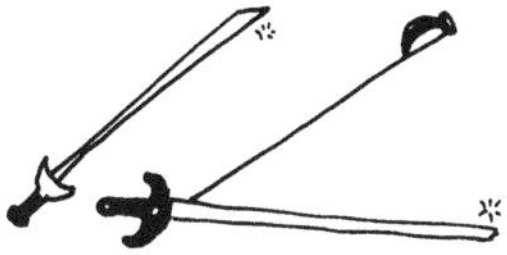

هذه سيوف . هي سيوف .

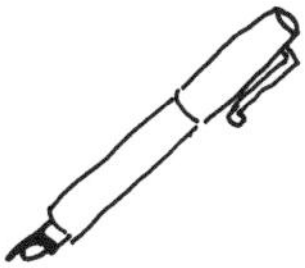

هذا قلم . هو قلم .

هذه أقلام . هي أقلام .

هذا ملك . هو ملك .

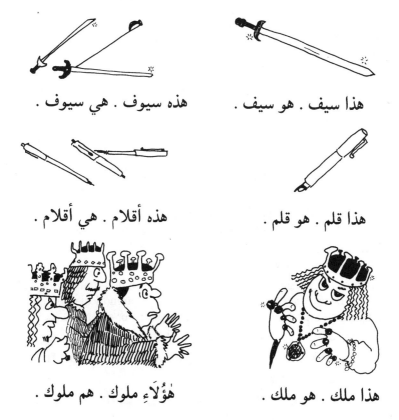

هٰؤُلاَءِ ملوك . هم ملوك .

Notice that there are two different ways of saying 'these' in Arabic: hādhihi suyūf (these are swords), or hā'ulā'i mulūk (these are kings).

هٰذا سيف .

هٰذَا + masculine singular

هٰذه سُيُوف .

هٰذِهِ + feminine singular *or* non-human plurals

هٰؤُلَاءِ ملوك .

هٰؤُلَاءِ + human plurals (masculine and feminine)

Although هؤلاء (hā'ulā'i) is the plural of هذا (hādhā) and هذه (hādhihi), it is only used when talking about *people*. Arabic divides plurals into:

1 Humans (people)
2 Non-humans (objects, ideas, animals, etc.)

In other words, you should use the same words with non-human plurals as you do with a *feminine singular* word. The same grammatical rules apply to non-human plurals as to the feminine singular. For example:

- Use هذه: هذه سيوف (These are swords.)
- Use هي: أين أقلامي؟ هي على المائدة (Where are my pens? They're on the table.)
- Use an adjective with a tā' marbūṭa: البيوت جميلة (The houses are beautiful.)

Modern Standard Arabic grammar treats all non-human plurals as feminine singular. There is no exception to this.

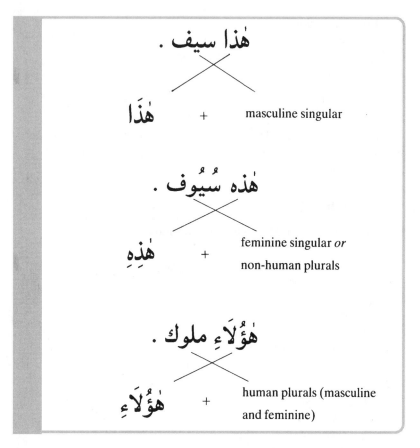

Exercise 4

Write sentences, as in the example:

١

هذه قلوب. هي قلوب.

٢

٣

٤

٥

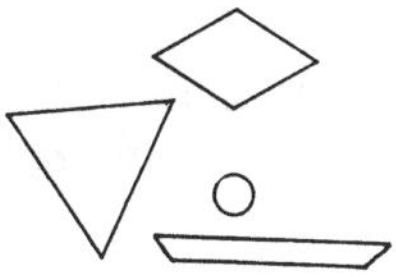

٦

Exercise 5

Make these sentences plural, as in the example:

١ هذا بَيت. هذه بيوت.

٢ هذا وَلَد.

٣ السَيف جَميل.

٤ هذا الكوب مَكسور.

٥ أين البَنك؟ هو هُناك.

٦ الدَرّاجة خفيفة.

٧ هَل هذا مُدَرِّس؟

٨ لا، هو مُحاسِب.

The party الحَفلة

Salwa is arranging a party for her son's fifth birthday. Listen to the items she needs for the party:

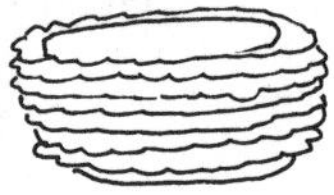
أطباق وَرَق

قُبّعات وَرَق

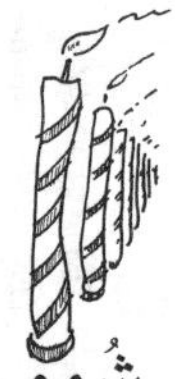
شُموع

أكواب بلاستيك

زجاجات كولا

أكياس بلاستيك

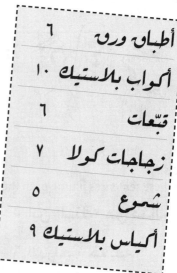

Exercise 6

Salwa has made a list of how many of each item she needs.

Ask the shopkeeper for each item, as in the example.

أطباق ورق	٦
أكواب بلاستيك	١٠
قبّعات	٦
زجاجات كولا	٧
شموع	٥
أكياس بلاستيك	٩

أريد ستّة أطباق ورق، من فضلك.

(urīd sittat aṭbāq waraq, min faḍlak)

I'd like six paper plates, please.

Now listen to Salwa buying some of these items in a party shop:

– صباح الخير. أريد أطباق وقبّعات ورق وأكواب بلاستيك من فضلك.

– حاضِر يا مَدام. أيّ لون؟ عِندَنا كُلّ الألوان: أبيَض، أحمَر، أخضَر، أزرَق...

– أُفَضِّل القبّعة الزَرقاء والطبَق الأحمَر.

– كَم يا مدام؟

– ٦ من فضلك، و١٠ أكواب بيضاء.

– طيّب... ٦ قُبّعات زَرقاء و٦ أطباق حَمراء و١٠ أكواب بيضاء... خمسة جنيهات من فضلك.

– تَفَضَّل.

– شُكراً. مَعَ السلامة يا مدام.

حاضِر (ḥāḍir)	certainly
أيّ (لون)؟ (ayy [lawn])	which [colour]?
كُلّ (الألوان) (kull [al-alwān])	all [the colours]
أُفَضّل (ufaḍḍil)	I prefer

Colours الألوان

You can usually make an adjective feminine by adding tā' marbūṭa, e.g. السرير جديد (as-sarīr jadīd), the bed is new, الحقيبة جديدة (al-ḥaqība jadīda̲), the bag is new. Adjectives describing basic colours are the main exception to this and have their own feminine forms.

Look at the masculine and feminine adjectives below and the three root letters that occur in both. (Remember to ignore long and short vowels.)

Root letters	*Feminine adj.*	*Masculine adj.*	
ب / ي / ض	بيضاء (bayḍā')	أبيض (abyaḍ)	white
ح / م / ر	حمراء (ḥamrā')	أحمر (aḥmar)	red

We can now see the pattern for the colour adjectives:

Masculine colour adjective:

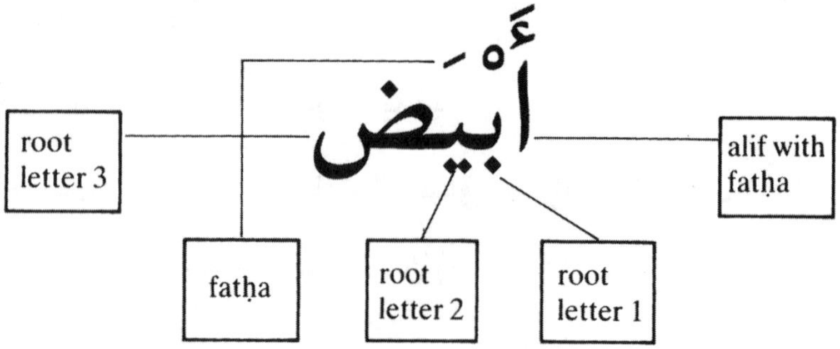

Feminine colour adjective:

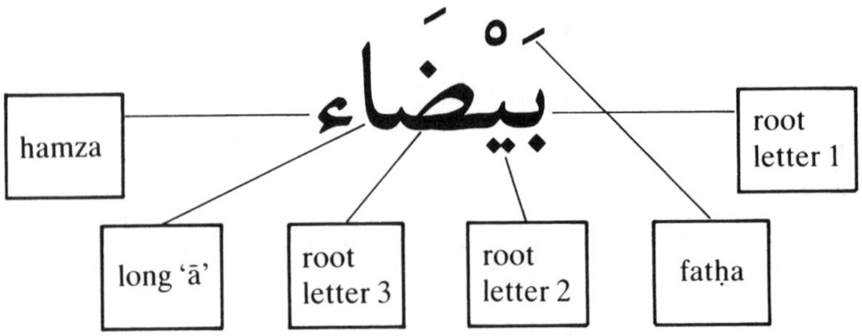

Remember that feminine adjectives will also be used with non-human plurals:

طبق أحمر (ṭabaq aḥmar)	a red plate
أطباق حمراء (aṭbāq ḥamrā')	red plates

Exercise 7

Here is a table for some other colours, showing the masculine adjectives. Fill in the column for the feminine adjectives:

Meaning	*Feminine (& non-human plurals)*	*Masculine*
green		أخضَر
blue		أزرَق
black		أسوَد
yellow		أصفَر

Now check your answers with the recording or in the answer section.

Exercise 8

Say and write these in Arabic, as in the example.

1 a red shirt قَميص أحمر

2 a red car

3 white plates

4 green bottles

5 yellow bags

6 the black dog

7 the blue bicycle

8 the yellow candles

Structure notes

The accusative case

The third, and final, case in Arabic is the *accusative* (النَّصب, an-naṣb). This is made by adding two fatḥas (ـً) on the end of the word for the *indefinite* (pronounced 'an') and one fatḥa for the *definite* (pronounced 'a').

The table below is a summary of all the case endings:

	Indefinite	*Definite*
Nominative	بنتٌ (bintun)	البنتُ (al-bintu)
Accusative	بنتاً (bintan)	البنتَ (al-binta)
Genitive	بنتٍ (bintin)	البنتِ (al-binti)

Note that the accusative indefinite has an extra alif written on the end of the word, called 'alif tanwīn'. The alif tanwīn is not written if the word ends in a tā' marbūṭa:

مدينةً (madīnatan) سيّارةً (sayyāratan)

The alif tanwin is one of the relatively few instances when a case ending can affect the basic script, so it helps if you understand why it is used.

The accusative case is used for the *object of a verb*:

أريد شموعاً. (urīd shumūɛan) I'd like some candles.

أُفَضِّل القبّعةَ الكبيرة. (ufaḍḍil al-qubbaɛata l-kabīra) I prefer the big hat.

and for *adverbial phrases* where the meaning is 'with', 'by', 'in the', etc.:

شُكراً (shukran) with thanks (i.e. 'thank you')

صباحاً (ṣabāḥan) in the morning

The accusative is also used after the *question word* كم؟ (kam, how many?). This explains the extra alif which appears when a noun not ending in tā' marbūṭa follows kam:

كم ولداً؟ (kam waladan) how many boys?

كم مدينةً؟ (kam madīnatan) how many towns?

Almost all nouns and adjectives, whether they are singular, dual, plural, masculine or feminine, have case endings in formal Arabic. The main exception to this is words of foreign origin (e.g.: راديو rādyū) when, although theoretically possible, case endings would be very clumsy.

Conversation

Going shopping
Look back at Salwa's party shopping list and the conversation on pages 140–1. Make up a similar conversation but ask for the other three items on the list (plastic bags, cola bottles and candles). Decide which colours you want the items to be. You could start like this:

أريد أكياس بلاستيك وزجاجات كولا وشموع من فضلك.
(urīd akyās bilastīk wa-zujājāt kūlā wa shumūع, min faḍlak)
I'd like some plastic bags, cola bottles and candles, please.

Once you've decided what to say, try taking the role of the customer on the recording.

Vocabulary in Unit 11

صَاحِب (أَصْحَاب) (ṣāḥib, aṣḥāb) friend/owner
سوق (أسواق) (sūq, awsāq) market
وَقْت (أَوْقات) (waqt, awqāt) time
شَكل (أَشْكال) (shakl, ashkāl) shape
سَيْف (سيوف) (sayf, suyūf) sword
قَلْب (قُلُوب) (qalb, qulūb) heart
ملِك (مُلوك) (malik, mulūk) king
شَيْخ (شُيوخ) (shaykh, shuyūkh) sheikh
شَمعة (شُموع) (shamعa, shumūع) candle
كوب (أَكْواب) (kūb, akwāb) cup, beaker
طَبَق (أَطْباق) (ṭabaq, aṭbāq) plate
كيس (أَكْياس) (kīs, akyās) bag (plastic, etc.), sack
قُبَعَّة (قُبَعَّات) (qubaععa, qubaععāt) hat
حَفْلة (حفلات) (ḥafla, ḥaflāt) party

بَلاَسْتيك	(bilāstīk) plastic
وَرَق	(waraq) paper
كولا	(kūlā) cola
أَيّ	(ayy) which?
كُلّ	(kull) all/every
لَوْن (أَلْوان)	(lawn, alwān) colour
أَبْيَض (بَيْضَاء)	(abyaḍ) white (*fem.* bayḍā')
أَسْوَد (سَوْدَاء)	(aswad) black (*fem.* sawdā')
أَخْضَر (خَضْرَاء)	(akhḍar) green (*fem.* khaḍrā')
أَحْمَر (حَمْرَاء)	(aḥmar) red (*fem.* ḥamrā')
أَزْرَق (زَرْقَاء)	(azraq) blue (*fem.* zarqā')
أَصْفَر (صَفْرَاء)	(aṣfar) yellow (*fem.* ṣafrā')
هؤلاءِ	(hā'ulā'i) these (for people only)
حاضِر	(ḥāḍir) certainly
أُفَضِّل	(ufaḍḍil) I prefer

unit 12

What happened yesterday?

What happened yesterday? ماذا حَدَثَ أَمْس؟

Look at the newspaper headline and the pictures:

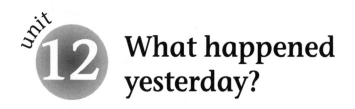

Exercise 1

See if you can match these Arabic words from the headline to the English:

thief/robber	أَمْس
investigation	سَرِقة
yesterday	مَعَ
theft/robbery	تَحْقيق
with	لِصّ

Now answer these questions in English:

1 Where is the bank?
2 How much money was stolen?
3 When did the robbery take place?
4 What is the name of the bank?
5 How many thieves are under investigation?

The two suspects both deny carrying out the robbery. Listen to the Ahmed Hamdi's alibi. (Follow the story from the top right, starting on page 149 and using the numbers on the pictures.)

«ذَهَبْتُ إلى مَطْعَم عربيّ ...»

«وأَكَلْتُ سَمَكًا .»

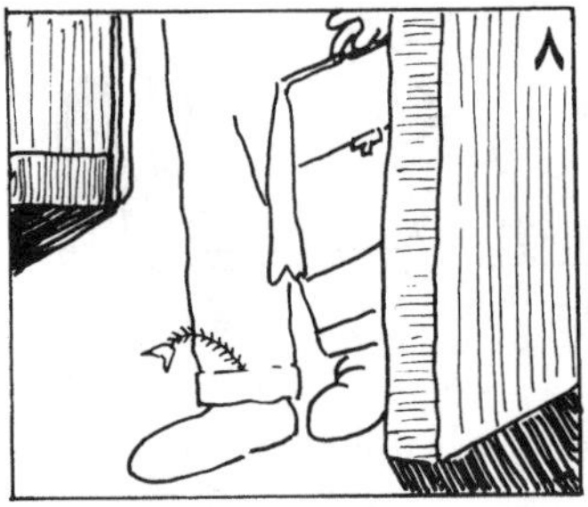

رَجَعْتُ من المكتب إلى بيتي مَسَاءً ...»

«وسَمِعْتُ عن السرقة في التليفزيون ...»

١

« أنا أحمد حمدي وبيتي في جنوب مدينة عمّان ... »

٢

«أمس خَرَجْتُ من بيتي صَبَاحًا ... »

٣

وذَهَبْتُ إلى مَكْتَبِي في وسط المدينة ... »

٤

« كَتَبْتُ خِطَابَات ... »

٥

« وشَرِبْتُ فِنْجان قَهْوَة . »

Look at these sentence tables. See how many different sentences you can make by choosing one word from each column, reading from *right to left*.

←

صباحًا. (ṣabāḥan) in the morning	البيت (al-bayt) the house	إلى (ilā) to	البيت (al-bayt) the house	من (min) from	ذهبتُ (dhahabtu) I went
مساءً. (masā'an) in the evening	المكتب (al-maktab) the office	من (min) from	المكتب (al-maktab) the office	إلى (ilā) to	رجعتُ (rajaعtu) I returned
	البنك (al-bank) the bank		البنك (al-bank) the bank		

بيتي. (baytī) my house	في (fī) in	شاي (shāy) tea	فنجان (finjān) a cup of	شربتُ (sharibtu) I drank
مكتبي. (maktabī) my office		قهوة (qahwa) coffee	زجاجة (zujājat) a bottle of	
		كولا (kolā) cola		
		ماء (mā') water		

Now look back at pages 148–9 and listen again to the story, following the words carefully.

Asking questions about the past

A policeman is checking Ahmed's alibi at the police station:

Exercise 2

Make more questions and answers about Ahmed's alibi, as in the example:

١ كتبت خِطابات / مكتب

هل كتبتَ خِطابات في مكتبك؟ نعم، كتبتُ خِطابات في مكتبي.

٢ ذهبت / مطعم أمريكيّ؟

٣ أكلت سمكًا / مطعم؟

٤ رجعت / بيت مساءً؟

٥ سمعت /سرقة /راديو؟

Exercise 3

The female suspect, Zaynab Shawqi, is a clerk in the Kuwaiti bank. Read her alibi once *without* writing. Then read it again filling in the missing words. (Start at picture 1, top right on page 153.)

« ـــــ إلى مطعم ـــــ ... »

« وفي المطعم سَمِعْتُ ـــــ السرقة في ـــــ . »

رجعت ـــــ المطعم ـــــ البنك ...

« وَجَدْتُ ـــــ المكسور ... ! »

« أنا زينب شَوْقِيّ و ______
في وسط مدينة عمّان . »

« أمس ... ذَهَبْتُ إلى ______
صباحًا ... »

« و ______ فِنْجان شَاي . »

« فَتَحْتُ الخَزانَة ... »

« وَجَلَسْتُ على مَكْتَبي . »*

(* على مكتبي = *at* my desk)

The policeman is now checking Zaynab's story:

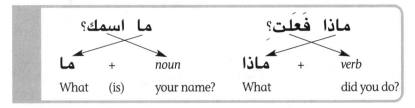

Questions with 'what?'

Arabic has two question words meaning 'what': ما (mā) is used in front of a *noun* and ماذا (mādhā) in front of a *verb*.

ما اسمك؟			ماذا فَعَلت؟		
ما	+	*noun*	ماذا	+	*verb*
What	(is)	your name?	What		did you do?

Notice that Arabic verbs are the same whether they are in questions or in sentences. *There is no question form ('did you/he?' etc.) in Arabic.*

Exercise 4

Choose a question word from the box to complete each of the questions and answers below. The first one is an example:

أين	متى	ما	ماذا	هل

١ **ماذا** شَرِبْتَ؟

شربتُ فنجان قهوة.

٢ أَين شَرِبْتَ القهوة؟

شربتُ القهوة في مكتبي.

٣ هل ذهبتَ إلى مطعم عربي؟

نعم، ذهبتُ إلى مطعم عربي.

٤ ______ أكلتَ في المطعم؟

أكلتُ سمكًا.

٥ ______ فعَلتَ في مكتبك؟

كَتَبتُ خِطابات.

٦ ______ اسمَك؟

اسمي أحمد حمدي.

٧ ______ سَمَعتَ عن السرقة؟

سَمِعْتُ عن السرقة مساءً.

Verbs in the past

The verbs you have met in this unit describe things which have happened in the past. They are in the past tense (الماضي al-māḍī). You will have noticed that the end of the verb changes slightly, depending on who carried out the action (depending on the *subject* of the verb).

Look at how this verb changes depending on the subject:

وَجَدْتُ (wajadtu)	I found
وَجَدْتَ (wajadta)	you *(masc.)* found
وَجَدْتِ (wajadti)	you *(fem.)* found
وَجَدَ (wajada)	he found
وَجَدَتْ (wajadat)	she found

Notice how Arabic does not normally use the personal pronouns (هو/أنت/أنا, etc.) with the verb as the *ending* tells you if it is 'I', 'you', etc.

Look again at the list above. You can see that the verb always begins with وَجَد (wajad). This is the *stem* of the verb and contains the three root letters. (The root letters و/ج/د are connected with the meaning of 'finding'.) The endings added to the stem tell you the subject of the verb:

Subject	*Ending*		*Stem*	*Meaning*
أنا	(-tu) تُ	+	وَجَد (wajad)	found
أنتَ	(-ta) تَ	+	ذَهَب (dhahab)	went
أنتِ	(-ti) تِ	+	خَرَج (kharaj)	went out
هو	(-a) ـَ	+	كَتَب (katab)	wrote
هي	(-at) ـَتْ	+	أَكَل (akal)	ate
		+	رَجَع (rajaع)	returned
		+	فَتَح (fataḥ)	opened
		+	جَلَس (jalas)	sat
		+	فَعَل (faعal)	did/made
		+	سَمِع (samiع)	heard
		+	شَرِب (sharib)	drank

In spoken dialects the final vowel is often dropped after anā and anta, so both become wajadt, and for huwa, which becomes wajad.

You may have noticed that without the vowels the word:

وجدت

could have at least four different meanings:

وَجَدْتُ I found

وَجَدْتَ you *(masc.)* found

وَجَدْتِ you *(fem.)* found

وَجَدَتْ she found

There is no automatic way of telling which meaning is intended. However, the context will usually give you a good indication.

Tip: The stems of the verbs are vowelled mainly with two fatḥas (wajad). Sometimes, however, the second vowel can be a kasra (see the last two verbs in the table). Do not spend too much time trying to remember these. The most important thing is to listen for the root letters.

Exercise 5

Write the correct form of the verb in the gap. The first is an example:

١ أمس، **خَرَجْتُ** (خرج) من البيت صباحًا. (أنا)

٢ ______ (ذهب) إلى البنك. (هي)

٣ هل ______ (أكل) التُّفّاحة؟ (أنتَ)

٤ أوّلاً، ______ (كتب) خطابات. (هو)

٥ أين ______ (سمع) عن السرقة؟ (أنتِ)

٦ ______ (ذهب) إلى البيت و ______ (جلس) على كرسيّ. (أنا)

٧ ______ (شرب) فنجان قهوة مع صاحبتها. (هي)

٨ ماذا ______ (فعل) أمس؟ (أنتَ)

Joining sentences together

Listen to these words and expressions you can use to link sentences together:

أَوَّلاً	(awwalan)	firstly
أَخيرًا	(akhīran)	finally
بَعْدَ ذَلِكَ	(baɛda thālika)	after that
قَبْلَ ذَلِكَ	(qabla thālika)	before that
ثُمَّ	(thumma)	then
فَـ...	(fa)	and/and so

The policeman has written Ahmed's alibi in his notebook. Read what he has written, paying special attention to the linking words and expressions.

التحقيق في سرقة البنك الكويتي

اسمه أحمد حمدي وبيته في جنوب
مدينة عمّان. خرج أمس من بيته
صباحًا وذهب إلى مكتبه في وسط
المدينة. أوّلاً كتب خطابًا وبعد ذلك
شرب فنجان قهوة. ثمّ ذهب إلى مطعم
عربي فأكل سمكًا. رجع إلى بيته مساءً
وأخيراً سمع عن السرقة في التليفزيون.

Exercise 6

Unfortunately, the policeman's notes about Zaynab were shredded by mistake. Can you write them out again in the right order?

فرجعَت إلى البنك.

وفتحت الخزانة.

أوّلاً شربَت فنجان شاي...

وبعد ذلك ذهبَت إلى المطعم

اسمها زينب شوقي

وبيتها في وسط مدينة عمّان.

ثمّ جلسَت على مكتبها

أخيرًا وجدَت الشبّاك المكسور.

أمس ذهبَت إلى البنك الكويتي صباحًا.

وسمعَت عن السرقة في الراديو.

Exercise 7

Join the two halves of the sentences, as in the example.

أكلتُ	ولدًا صغيرًا بجانب باب المدرسة.
شَرِبَت دينا	إلى بيتي مساءً.
وَجَدْتُ	على كرسيّ خشبيّ.
أولاً، فتحت زينب	سمكًا في المطعم أمس.
جلَسَت	خزانة البنك الكويتي صباحًا.
أخيرًا، رَجَعتُ	زجاجة كولا.

Exercise 8 ماذا فعل الملك أَمْس؟

Below you will find six things that the king did yesterday.

First, read the sentences and think about the order in which he might have done these things. (Note: قصر (qaṣr) = palace.)

- ❑ ذهب إلى مصنع السيّارات في جنوب المدينة.
- ❑ ذهب إلى مدرسة كبيرة في وسط المدينة.
- ❑ شرب فنجان قهوة مع المهندسين في المصنع.
- ❑ خرج من القصر الملكي.
- ❑ رجع إلى القصر الملكي.
- ❑ جلس مع الأولاد والبنات والمدرّسين.
- ❑ سمِعَ من المهندسين عن السيّارة الجديدة.

Listen to the news broadcast and put the sentences in the correct order. Write the numbers in the boxes.

Using as many of the linking phrases on page 158 as possible, write a newspaper article about what the king did yesterday. Start like this:

أوّلا خرج الملك من القصر صباحًا و...

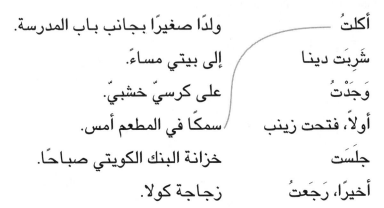

Using a dictionary

You have now reached the point where you should buy one or more dictionaries to help you expand your vocabulary by yourself and to look up words that you come across in magazines, newspapers, etc.

It is possible to put Arabic in alphabetical order in two ways:

1 According to the order of the letters in a word – as we do in English.
2 According to the order of the *root letters* in a word.

For example, imagine you want to look up this word: مكتب (maktab).
– with method 1 you would look under م/ك/ت/ب (reading right to left).
– with method 2 you would look under ك/ت/ب, the root letters.

Although the first method is becoming more common, especially as it means that alphabetisation can be carried out by a computer, the second method is still used in many standard reference works.

> So far, we have written the root letters separately: ك/ت/ب. For the sake of convenience, most linguists and dictionaries use the stem of the past tense to express the root. So we can say that كتب is the root of كتاب (kitāb) and مكتب (maktab); or that درس is the root of مدرسة (madrasa).

There are a number of Arabic–English dictionaries on the market, some designed for native speakers and some for learners of Arabic. We suggest that you buy one designed for learners, as the others do not always show you the vowels or the plurals (as a native speaker you are expected to know them).

The most popular dictionary designed for learners is *A Dictionary of Modern Arabic* by Hans Wehr (Otto Harrassowitz, 1993). Although originally compiled in the 1960s, it has been updated several times and is still the most respected Arabic–English dictionary for learners of Arabic. Words are listed under the root letters.

Appendix 1, which lists the Arabic letters in alphabetical order, will be a useful reference when you are using a dictionary.

Page 162 shows an example page from the Hans Wehr dictionary, showing the entries under the root درس.

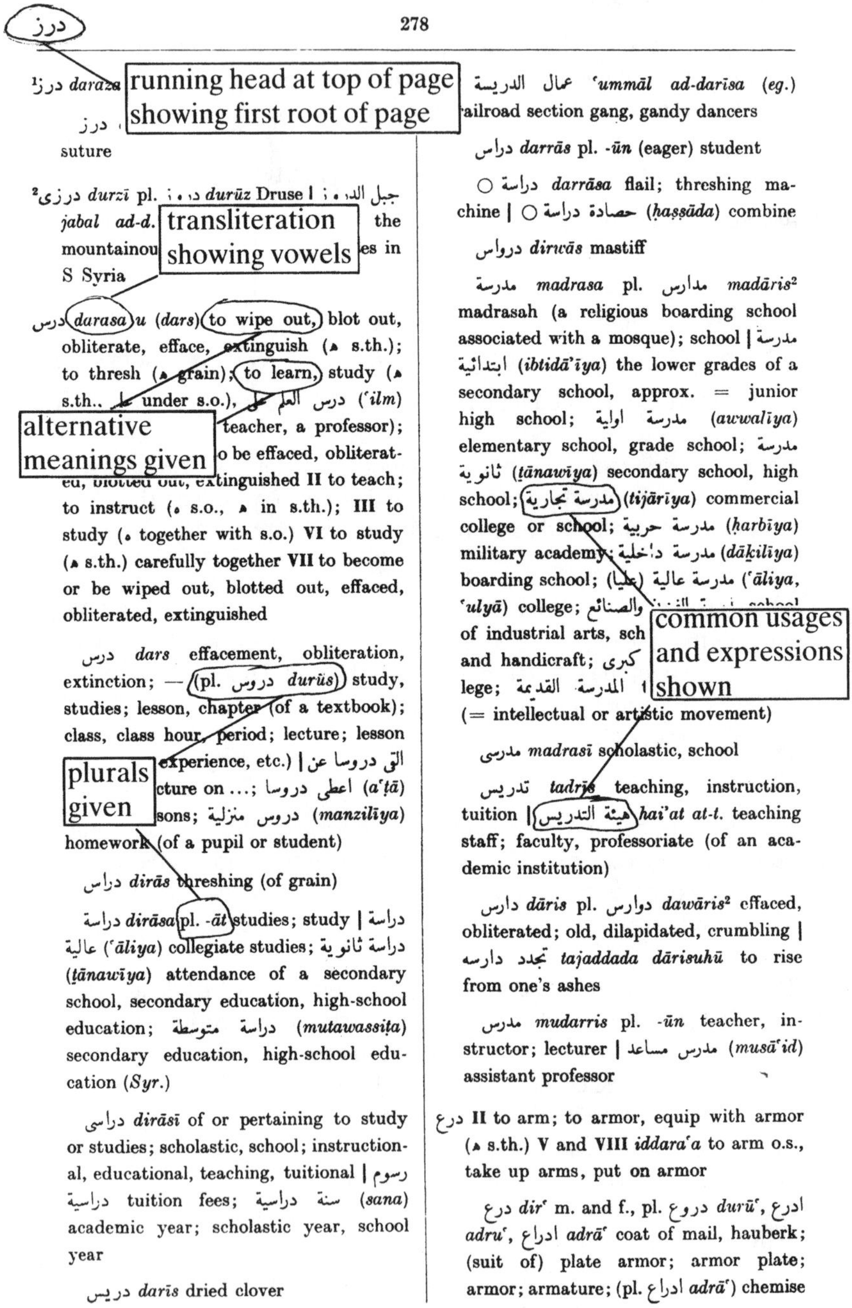

درز 278

running head at top of page showing first root of page

درز[1] *daraza* ... درز ... suture

درزى[2] *durzī* pl. دروز *durūz* Druse | جبل الدروز *jabal ad-d.* ... the mountainou... ...es in S Syria

transliteration showing vowels

درس *darasa* u (*dars*) to wipe out, blot out, obliterate, efface, extinguish (ه s.th.); to thresh (ه grain); to learn, study (ه s.th., على under s.o.), درس العلم على (*ʿilm*) ... teacher, a professor); ...o be effaced, obliterated, blotted out, extinguished **II** to teach; to instruct (ه s.o., ه in s.th.); **III** to study (ه together with s.o.) **VI** to study (ه s.th.) carefully together **VII** to become or be wiped out, blotted out, effaced, obliterated, extinguished

alternative meanings given

درس *dars* effacement, obliteration, extinction; — (pl. دروس *durūs*) study, studies; lesson, chapter (of a textbook); class, class hour, period; lecture; lesson ...experience, etc.) | القى دروسا عن ...cture on ...; اعطى دروسا (*aʿṭā*) ...sons; دروس منزلية (*manzilīya*) homework (of a pupil or student)

plurals given

دراس *dirās* threshing (of grain)

دراسة *dirāsa* pl. *-āt* studies; study | دراسة عالية (*ʿāliya*) collegiate studies; دراسة ثانوية (*ṯānawīya*) attendance of a secondary school, secondary education, high-school education; دراسة متوسطة (*mutawassiṭa*) secondary education, high-school education (*Syr.*)

دراسى *dirāsī* of or pertaining to study or studies; scholastic, school; instructional, educational, teaching, tuitional | رسوم دراسية tuition fees; سنة دراسية (*sana*) academic year; scholastic year, school year

دريس *darīs* dried clover

عمال الدريسة *ʿummāl ad-darīsa* (*eg.*) railroad section gang, gandy dancers

دراس *darrās* pl. *-ūn* (eager) student

○ دراسة *darrāsa* flail; threshing machine | ○ حصادة دراسة (*ḥaṣṣāda*) combine

درواس *dirwās* mastiff

مدرسة *madrasa* pl. مدارس *madāris*[2] madrasah (a religious boarding school associated with a mosque); school | مدرسة ابتدائية (*ibtidāʾīya*) the lower grades of a secondary school, approx. = junior high school; مدرسة اولية (*awwalīya*) elementary school, grade school; مدرسة ثانوية (*ṯānawīya*) secondary school, high school; مدرسة تجارية (*tijārīya*) commercial college or school; مدرسة حربية (*ḥarbīya*) military academy; مدرسة داخلية (*dāḵilīya*) boarding school; مدرسة عالية (علیا) (*ʿāliya*, *ʿulyā*) college; ... والصنائع ... school of industrial arts, sch... and handicraft; كبرى ... lege; المدرسة القديمة ... (= intellectual or artistic movement)

common usages and expressions shown

مدرسى *madrasī* scholastic, school

تدريس *tadrīs* teaching, instruction, tuition | هيئة التدريس *haiʾat at-t.* teaching staff; faculty, professoriate (of an academic institution)

دارس *dāris* pl. دوارس *dawāris*[2] effaced, obliterated; old, dilapidated, crumbling | تجدد دارسه *tajaddada dārisuhū* to rise from one's ashes

مدرس *mudarris* pl. *-ūn* teacher, instructor; lecturer | مدرس مساعد (*musāʿid*) assistant professor

درع **II** to arm; to armor, equip with armor (ه s.th.) **V** and **VIII** *iddaraʿa* to arm o.s., take up arms, put on armor

درع *dirʿ* m. and f., pl. دروع *durūʿ*, ادرع *adruʿ*, ادراع *adrāʿ* coat of mail, hauberk; (suit of) plate armor; armor plate; armor; armature; (pl. ادراع *adrāʿ*) chemise

Hans Wehr *A Dictionary of Modern Arabic* (Otto Harrassowitz, 1993)

Exercise 9 Dictionary work

(You will need a dictionary to do this exercise.)

Decide which are the root letters of these words (see Unit 11), and then find the words in your dictionary and write down the meaning. The first is an example:

Meaning المَعنى	Root المَصدَر	Word الكَلمة
minister	و ز ر	وَزير
______	______	سَفير
______	______	وِزارة
______	______	مَعْرَض
______	______	رِسالَة
______	______	عِلاقة

Structure notes

Sound masculine plural and dual case endings

The *sound masculine plural* (SMP) and *dual case* endings vary from the regular case endings. They affect the basic script and the pronounced part of the word. The SMP and dual endings are the same for both the definite and indefinite, so there are only two possible variations for each:

	SMP	*Dual*
Nominative	نجّارون (najjār<u>ūn</u>)	نجّاران (najjār<u>ān</u>)
Accusative + genitive	نجّارين (najjār<u>īn</u>)	نجّارين (najjār<u>ayn</u>)

The article on page 147 has the title التحقيق مع لصّين (at-taḥqīq maع liṣṣayn, The investigation is with two thieves). The dual ending is genitive as لصّين (liṣṣayn) follows the preposition مع (maعa).

Sound feminine plural

The *sound feminine plural* (SFP) has regular case endings, except for the accusative indefinite, which is the same as the genitive indefinite:

	Indefinite	*Definite*
Nominative	خطاباتٌ (khiṭābātun)	الخطاباتُ (al-khiṭābātu)
Accusative	خطاباتٍ (khiṭābātin)	الخطاباتَ (al-khiṭābāta)
Genitive	خطاباتٍ (khiṭābātin)	الخطاباتِ (al-khiṭābāti)

Notice that the SFP accusative indefinite, like tā' marbūṭa, does *not* have the extra alif tanwīn:

كتبْتُ خطاباً (katabtu khiṭāban)	I wrote a letter.
كتبْتُ خطاباتٍ. (katabtu khiṭābātin)	I wrote letters.

Vocabulary in Unit 12

لِصّ (لُصوص) (liṣṣ, luṣūṣ) thief/robber

سَرِقة (سَرِقات) (sariqa, sariqāt) theft/robbery

تَحْقيق (تَحْقيقات) (taḥqīq, taḥqīqāt) investigation

خِطاب (خِطابات) (khiṭāb, khiṭābāt) letter

قَصْر (قُصور) (qaṣr, quṣūr) palace

مَطْعَم (maṭɛam*) restaurant

مَكْتَب (maktab*) office/desk

فِنْجان (finjān*) cup

شاي (shāy) tea

قَهْوة (qahwa) coffee

سَمَك (samak) fish

كُولا (kūlā) cola

مَاء (mā') water

عَنْ (ɛan) about/concerning

* *Plurals of these words will be covered in later units.*

مَعَ (maعa) with

إلى (ilā) to/towards

مَلَكِيّ (malakī) royal

أَمْس (ams) yesterday

صَبَاح (ṣabāḥ) morning

مَسَاء (masā') afternoon/evening

مَتى؟ (mattā) when?

مَاذا؟ (mādhā) what? (+ *verb*)

خَرَج (kharaj) went out/exited

ذَهَب (dhahab) went

كَتَب (katab) wrote

شَرِب (sharib) drank

أَكل (akal) ate

رَجَع (rajaع) returned/went back

فَتَح (fataḥ) opened

جَلَس (jalas) sat down

سَمِع (samiع) heard

فَعَل (faعal) did/made

وَجَد (wajad) found

أَوّلاً (awwalan) firstly

أَخيرًا (akhīran) finally

بَعْدَ ذلِك (baعda dhālik) after that

قَبْلَ ذلِك (qabla dhālik) before that

ثُمَّ (thumma) then

فَـ... (fa) and/and so

unit 13

Wish you were here

Plural patterns 3 and 4

Look at the pictures and listen to the recording:

رِجَال

رَجُل

كِلَاب

كَلْب

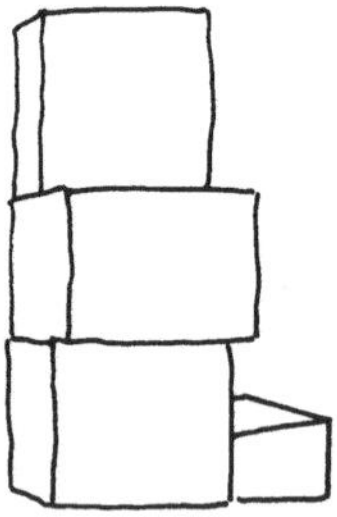

عُلَب

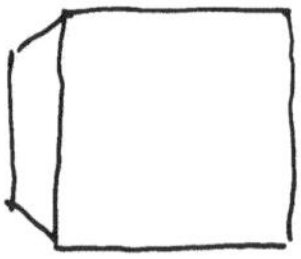

عُلْبَة

صُوَر

صُورَة

Pattern 3

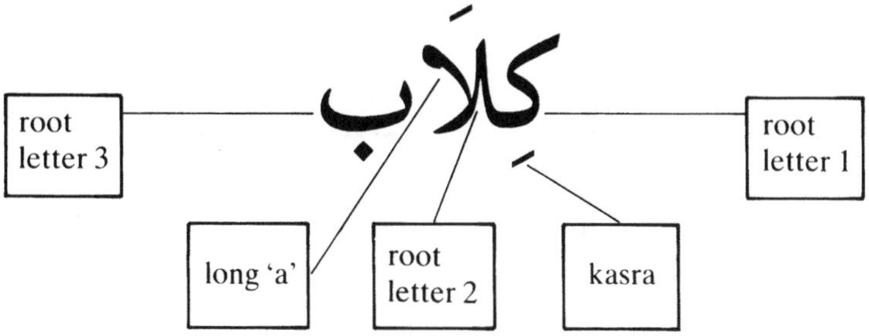

Pattern 4

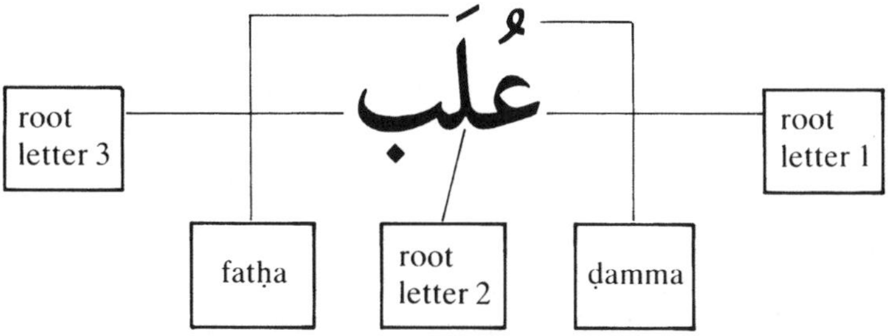

To express plural and other patterns in Arabic, the three root letters ف/ع/ل are used as a standard template (فعل = 'to do/to make'). We can therefore say that the plural pattern 3 is the فِعال (fiعāl) pattern, and pattern 4 is the فُعَل (fuعal) pattern. Here are the four broken plural patterns you have met so far:

Example	*Pattern*
أَقْلام ← pen قَلَم	(afعāl) أَفْعَال *Pattern 1*
بُيُوت ← house بَيت	(fuعūl) فُعُول *Pattern 2*
كِلاب ← dog كَلب	(fiعāl) فِعال *Pattern 3*
عُلَب ← box عُلبة	(fuعal) فُعَل *Pattern 4*

Exercise 1

Here are some more words that fit into the فِعال (fiʿāl) and فُعَل (fuʿal) plural patterns. Write the plurals, as in the example.

Plural	*Pattern*	*Singular*	
جِبال	فِعال	جَبَل	mountain
______	فِعال	جَمَل	camel
لعب	فُعَل	لُعْبَة	toy/game
______	فِعال	بَحْر	sea
______	فُعَل	تُحْفَة	masterpiece/artefact
______	فُعَل	دَوْلَة	nation/state
______	فِعال	ريح	wind

Now check your answers and repeat the patterns after the recording. Do this several times so that you begin to hear the rhythm of the patterns.

Exercise 2

Make questions and answers as in the example. (Remember that كم (kam) is followed by the singular – see page 121.)

١

كم كلبًا في الصورة؟

هناك أربعة كلاب.

٢

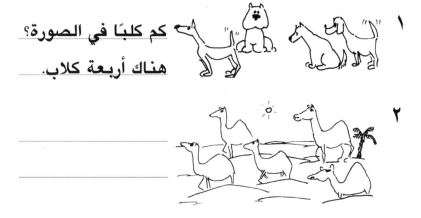

______

______

٣

٤

٥

٦

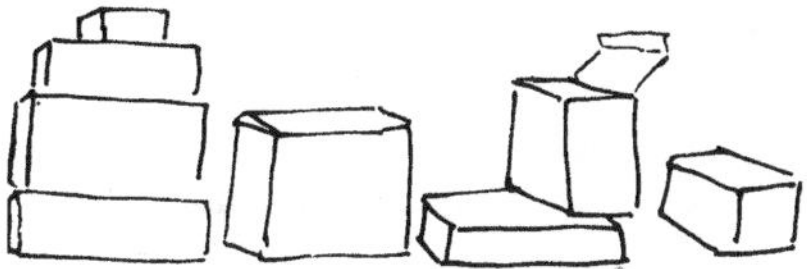

علبة

علب

Numbers 11–100

ثمانية

Numbers 11–19

Listen to the recording and repeat the numbers 11 to 19.

١١	أَحَد عَشَر	١٦	سِتَّة عَشَر
١٢	اِثْنا عَشَر	١٧	سَبعة عَشَر
١٣	ثَلاثَة عَشَر	١٨	ثَمانية عَشَر
١٤	أَربعة عَشَر	١٩	تِسعَة عَشَر
١٥	خَمسة عَشَر		

The pronunciation of Arabic numbers can vary depending on the accent of the speaker and the formality of the language. In this course you will learn an informal pronunciation that will be understood universally.

Exercise 3

Draw lines between the columns, as in the example.

١٤	ستّة عشر	11
١٧	ثلاثة عشر	14
١١	خمسة عشر	16
١٦	أحد عشر	19
١٩	ثمانية عشر	15
١٢	تسعة عشر	18
١٨	اثنا عشر	17
١٣	سبعة عشر	12
١٥	أربعة عشر	13

Exercise 4

Say and write these numbers:

١٤	١٥
٥	٤
١٨	١٢
١٦	٩

Numbers 20–100

Now listen to the numbers 20 upwards:

٢٠	عِشْرين	٢١	واحد وعِشْرين
٣٠	ثَلاثين	٢٢	اِثنان وعِشْرين
٤٠	أَرْبَعين	٢٣	ثَلاثة وعِشْرين
٥٠	خَمْسين	٥٦	سِتّة وخَمْسين
٦٠	ستِّين	٨٨	ثَمانية وثَمانين
٧٠	سَبْعين	٩٥	خَمْسة وتِسعين
٨٠	ثَمانين		
٩٠	تِسعين		
١٠٠	مِئَة		

Notice that to say 'twenty-one', 'fifty-six', etc. in Arabic, you say wāḥid wa-ع‍ishrīn ('one and twenty'), sitta wa-khamsīn ('six and fifty'), etc. The units come *before* the tens.

Tip: The tens from 20 to 90 have an alternative ending, ون (-ūn): ع‍ishrūn, thalāthūn, etc. However, most spoken dialects use the ين (-īn) ending consistently and so this is the more useful pronunciation to learn initially. See the 'Structure notes' at the end of the unit for more details.

Exercise 5

Write these numbers in figures, as in the example. (Remember: figures go from *left to right*, as they do in English.)

١ ستة وأربعين ← ٤٦

٢ واحد وثمانين

٣ خمسة وثلاثين

٤ مئة وأربعة وعشرين

٥ ثلاثة وتسعين

٦ اثنان وسبعين

٧ مئة وخمسة وثمانين

٨ مئة وسبعة وخمسين

Numbers 11 upwards with singular noun

The numbers 11 upwards are followed by a *singular* noun. In addition, the singular noun following a number above 11 will have the extra alif tanwīn (-an ending) if the noun *does not* end in tā' marbūṭa. This is similar to what happens after kam? (how many?).

١٢ جبلاً	(ithnāʿashar jabalan)	twelve mountains
٣٠ سيّارة	(thalāthīn sayyāra)	thirty cars

It is as if in English we were to say 'three cars' but 'thirty car'. This may seem bizarre to a learner, but it is important to remember as it is true even of spoken dialects.

In high-level Modern Standard Arabic, numbers used in a sentence can change slightly depending on whether they are referring to a masculine or a feminine noun, and what function they have in the sentence. However, these changes are complicated and not often seen or heard. Many native speakers do not remember them in detail, and as a beginner you can stick to the forms given here. Be prepared, however, to hear or see some variations.

Exercise 6

How many are there? Say and write, as in the example.

16 x

58 x

61 x

٦١ رجلاً
(wāḥid wa-sittīn rajulan)

18 x
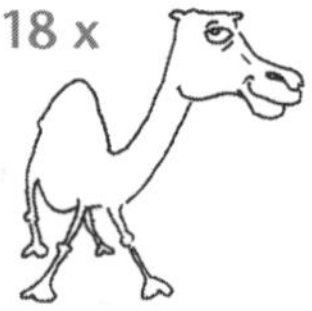

49 x

23 x

93 x

28 x

72 x

What's the weather like? كَيف حال الطَّقس؟

Temperature دَرَجة الحَرارة

Look at the thermometer and the descriptions of the temperatures.

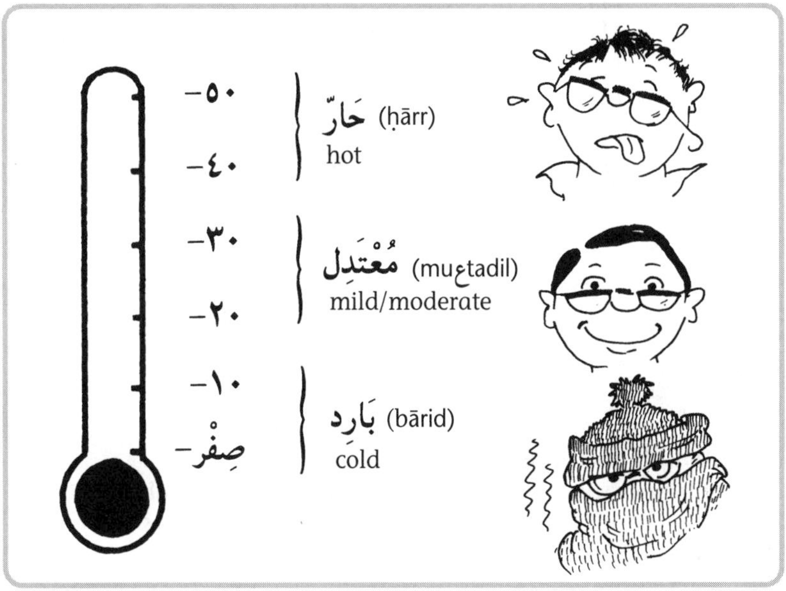

Now listen to the recording and look at the following descriptions:

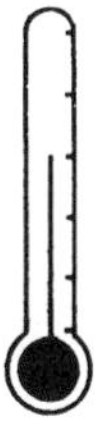

ما هي دَرَجَة الحرارة؟

دَرَجَة الحرارة ٣٠

الطَّقْس مُعْتَدِل.

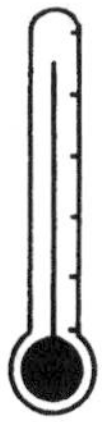

ما هي دَرَجَة الحرارة؟

دَرَجَة الحرارة ٤٥.

الطَّقس حارّ.

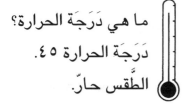

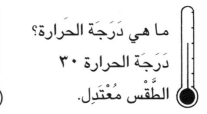

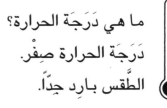

ما هي دَرَجَة الحرارة؟

دَرَجَة الحرارة صِفْر.

الطَّقس بارِد جِدّاً.

Exercise 7

Following the examples on page 173, make questions and answers for these thermometers.

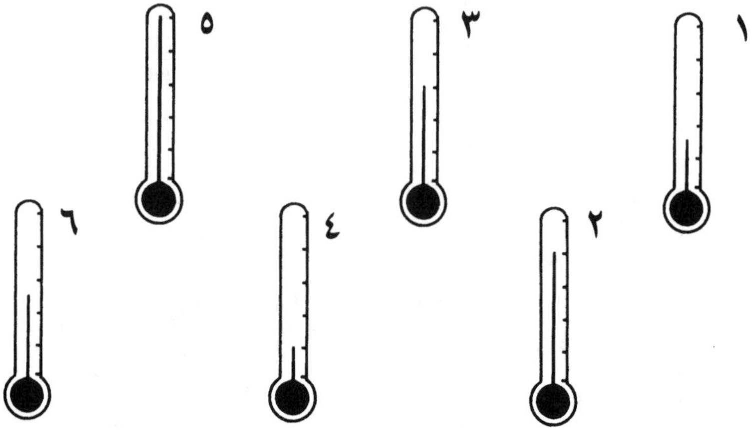

Describing the weather

Look at the newspaper weather chart on page 175. The right-hand column is a list of place names. Then there are two columns of figures. What do you think these represent?

- The first (right-hand) column of figures is the minimum ('smallest') temperature: الصُغرى (aṣ-ṣughrā)
- The second is the maximum ('biggest') temperature: الكُبرى (al-kubrā)

The final left-hand column is a general description of the weather.

Find الرياض (ar-riyāḍ, Riyadh) in the list of towns and look at its temperatures and the description of the weather. Now listen to the following:

ما هي دَرَجَة الحرارة الصُغرى في الرّياض؟

دَرَجَة الحرارة الصُغرى ٢٥.

وما هي دَرَجَة الحرارة الكُبْرى؟

دَرَجَة الحرارة الكُبْرى ٤٣.

كَيْفَ حَال الطَّقس في الرّياض؟

الطَّقّس حارّ وصَحْو.

حالة الطقس

	الصغرى	الكبرى	
مكة المكرمة	٢٩	٤٢	صحو
المدينة المنورة	٢٦	٤١	صحو
الرياض	٢٥	٤٣	صحو
جدة	٢٧	٣٨	صحو
الظهران	٣١	٤٤	صحو
ابها	١٦	٢٩	غائم
الطائف	٢٤	٣١	صحو
البحرين	٢٠	٣٧	صحو
القاهرة	٢٠	٣٤	صحو
بيروت	١٨	٣٢	صحو
الجزائر	١٩	٣٤	صحو
تونس	١٧	٢٥	صحو
الرباط	٢٠	٣١	صحو
امستردام	١٠	١٨	غائم
اثينا	١٥	٢٩	صحو
برلين	١٥	٢٢	غائم
بروكسل	٩	٢٣	غائم
كوبنهاجن	١٣	٢٢	صحو
دبلن	١١	١٨	غائم
فرانكفورت	٣	٣٠	صحو
جنيف	١٧	٢٣	صحو
هلسنكي	١٩	٢٥	غائم
هونج كونج	٢٦	٣١	صحو
جاكرتا	٢٣	٣٣	غائم
كوالالمبور	٢٣	٣٣	صحو
لشبونة	١٩	٣٠	صحو
لندن	١٢	٢٠	غائم
مدريد	١٧	٣٥	صحو
مانيلا	٢٣	٣٣	غائم
مونتريال	٢٢	٢٧	صحو
موسكو	١٨	٢٤	صحو
نيودلهي	٢٨	٣٥	غائم
نيويورك	٢٦	٣٧	غائم
نيقوسيا	٢٢	٣٧	صحو
باريس	١٣	٢	غائم
روما	١٨	٢٤	غائم
استوكهولم	٢٠	٢٥	غائم
سيدني	٩	١٧	صحو
طوكيو	٢٣	٣٠	صحو
فيينا	١٥	٢٣	غائم

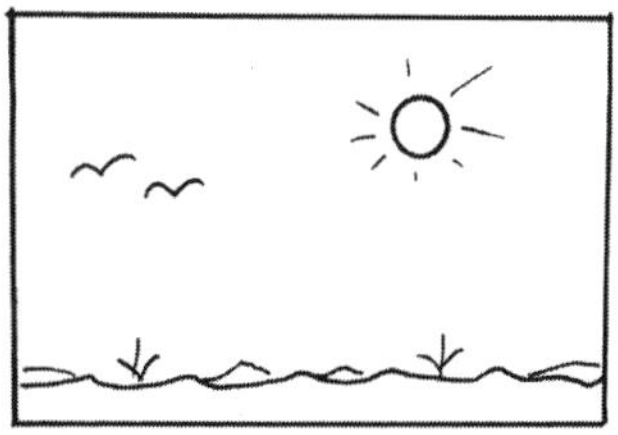

الطقس صَحْو. The weather's clear.

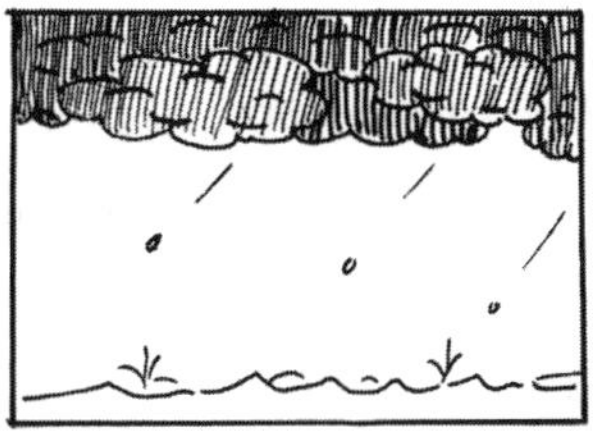

الطقس غَائِم. The weather's cloudy.

Exercise 8

Now answer these questions using the chart on page 175.

١   ما هي دَرَجَة الحَرارة الصُغْرى في بيروت؟

٢   ما هي دَرَجَة الحَرارة الكُبْرى في أثينا؟

٣   كَيْفَ حَال الطَّقس في دبلن؟

٤   كَيْفَ حَال الطَّقس في طوكيو؟

٥   هل الطقس غائم في مدريد؟

٦   هل الطقس بارد في القاهرة؟

٧   هل دَرَجَة الحَرارة الكُبْرى في هونج كونج ٣١؟

٨   هل دَرَجَة الحَرارة الصُغْرى في البحرين ٤٠؟

٩   هناك كم مدينة في القائمة؟

١٠ الطقس صحو في كم مدينة في القائمة؟

Writing notes and postcards

Look at these useful words and phrases for writing notes or postcards in Arabic.

عَزيزي (azīzī)	Dear ... (to a male)	
عَزيزتي (azīzatī)	Dear ... (to a female)	
كَيْفَ حالكَ؟ (kayf ḥālak)	How are you? (to a male)	
كَيْفَ حالكِ؟ (kayf ḥālik)	How are you? (to a female)	
أنا/نَحنُ بخَير. (anā/naḥnu bi-khayr)	I'm/we're fine.	
مَعَ تَحيّاتي (maɛa taḥiyyātī)	Best wishes ('with my greetings')	

Exercise 9

Zaynab is on holiday with her family and has written a postcard to her brother. Answer the questions below. Don't worry about every word; just try to get the gist. Note: متحف (matḥaf) = museum; فندق (funduq) = hotel.

1 What's Zaynab's brother called?
2 Where is Zaynab on holiday?
3 What's the weather like?
4 Where did Zaynab go yesterday morning?
5 What kind of food did they eat?
6 Where did Zaynab go after eating?
7 What did Nadir and the boys do?
8 What does Zaynab ask at the end of the postcard?

عزيزي أحمد،
كيف حالك؟ أنا بخير. أنا في لندن
مع نادر والأولاد. الطقس بارد
وغائم. ذهبنا أمس صباحًا إلى وسط
المدينة وأكلنا في مطعم ياباني.
بعد ذلك ذهبتُ إلى متحف ولكن
نادر والأولاد رجعوا إلى الفندق.
وأنتم؟ ماذا فعلتم؟ هل كتبتم
لي خطابًا؟
مع تحياتي زينب

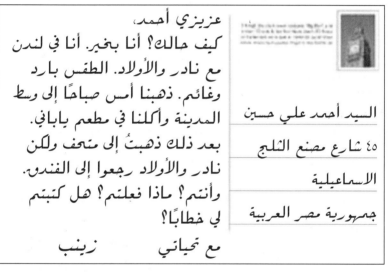

السيد أحمد علي حسين
٤٥ شارع مصنع الثلج
الاسماعيلية
جمهورية مصر العربية

Past verbs in the plural

The postcard above contains several examples of verbs in the plural:

ذهبنا إلى وسط المدينة. (dhahabnā ilā wasaṭ il-madīna.)	We went to the centre of town.
أكلنا في مطعم ياباني. (akalnā fī maṭɛam yabānī.)	We ate in a Japanese restaurant.
رجعوا إلى الفندق. (rajaɛū ilā l-funduq.)	They returned to the hotel.
هل كتبتم لي خطابًا؟ (hal katabtum lī khiṭāban?)	Did you *(pl.)* write me a letter?

Example	*Ending*	*Subject*
I studied دَرَسْتُ	(-tu) تُ	أنا I
you *(m.)* wrote كَتَبْتَ	(-ta) تَ	you *(m.)* أنتَ
you *(f.)* went ذَهَبْتِ	(-ti) تِ	you *(f.)* أنتِ
he returned رَجَعَ	(-a) ـَ	he هُوَ
she ate أَكَلَتْ	(-at) ـَتْ	she هِيَ
we opened فَتَحْنا	(-nā) نا	we نَحنُ
you *(pl.)* did فَعَلْتُمْ	(-tum) تُمْ	you *(pl.)* أنتُم
they went out خَرَجوا*	(-ū) وا*	they هُم

*The alif is a spelling convention and is not pronounced.

Exercise 10

Zaynab has now moved on to Paris and has sent this postcard to her friend, Sara. Fill in the gaps in her message.

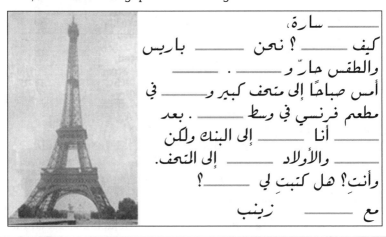

____ سارة،
كيف ____؟ نحن ____ باريس
والطقس حارّ و ____ . ____
أمس صباحًا إلى متحف كبير و____ في
مطعم فرنسي في وسط ____ . بعد
____ أنا ____ إلى البنك ولكن
____ والأولاد ____ إلى المتحف.
وأنتِ؟ هل كتبتِ لي ____؟
مع ____ زينب

Structure notes

Numbers

The numbers 20, 30, 40, etc. have the same endings as the sound masculine plural: they end in ون -ūn in the nominative, and ين -īn in the accusative and genitive. Only in more formal Standard Arabic are the nominative numbers generally used. The -īn pronunciation is more practical for a learner to use.

Conversation

Talking about a vacation
Imagine you are Zaynab and have just come back from your vacation in London and Paris. A friend has rung to ask you about your trip.

Review the information in the postcard from London on page 177, and then play the role of Zaynab in the telephone conversation on the recording.

Vocabulary in Unit 13

عُلبَة (عُلَب) (ɛulba, ɛulab) box/tin/packet

لُعبَة (لُعَب) (luɛba, luɛab) toy/game

تُحْفَة (تُحَف) (tuḥfa, tuḥaf) masterpiece/artefact

دَوْلَة (دُوَل) (dawla, duwal) nation/state

رَجُل (رِجَال) (rajul, rijāl) man

جَبَل (جِبَال) (jabal, jibāl) mountain

جَمَل (جِمَال) (jamal, jimāl) camel

بَحْر (بِحَار) (baḥr, biḥār) sea

ريح (رِياح) (rīḥ, riyāḥ) wind

حَال (أحوال) (ḥāl, aḥwāl) state/condition

الطَّقْس (aṭ-ṭaqs) the weather

دَرَجة الحَرارة (darajat al-ḥarāra) temperature ('degree of heat')

حَارّ (ḥārr) hot

مُعْتَدِل (muɛtadil) mild/moderate

بارِد (bārid) cold

صَحْو (ṣaḥw) clear/fine

غائِم (ghā'im) cloudy/overcast

عَزيزي/عَزيزَتي (ɛazīzī/ɛazīzatī) Dear ... *(starting a letter)*

مَع تَحِيَّاتي (maɛa taḥiyyātī) Best wishes *(finishing a letter)*

كَيْفَ (kayfa) how

كَيْف حَالك/حَالِك؟ (kayf ḥālak/ḥālik) How are you? *(masc./fem.)*

مَتحَف (matḥaf) museum

فُنْدُق (funduq) hotel

أحَد عَشَر (aḥad ɛashar) eleven

اثنا عَشَر (ithnā ɛashar) twelve

ثلاثة عَشَر (thalāthat ɛashar) thirteen

أربعة عَشَر (arbaɛat ɛashar) fourteen

خَمْسة عَشَر (khamsat ɛashar) fifteen

سِتَّة عَشَر (sittat ɛashar) sixteen

سَبْعة عَشَر (sabɛat ɛashar) seventeen

ثَمانية عَشَر (thamānyat ɛashar) eighteen

تِسعَة عَشَر (tisɛat ɛashar) nineteen

عِشْرين (ɛishrīn) twenty

ثلاثين (thalāthīn) thirty

أربعين (arbaɛīn) forty

خَمسين (khamsīn) fifty

ستِّين (sittīn) sixty

سَبْعين (sabɛīn) seventy

ثَمانين (thamānīn) eighty

تِسعين (tisɛīn) ninety

مائة (mi'a) a hundred

صِفر (ṣifr) zero

unit

14 All the President's men

Days of the week أيّام الأُسبوع

Listen to the recording and look at the days of the week:

يَوْم السَّبْت	Saturday
يَوْم الأَحَد	Sunday
يَوْم الاِثْنَيْن	Monday
يَوْم الثُّلاثاء	Tuesday
يَوْم الأَرْبَعاء	Wednesday
يَوْم الخَمِيس	Thursday
يَوْم الجُمْعَة	Friday

Tip: It is possible to shorten the days of the week, omitting the word يَوم (yawm, day) to make السبت (as-sabt, Saturday), etc.

Listen to these sentences:

يَوْم الأَرْبعاء بعدَ يَوْم الثُّلاثاء. Wednesday is after Tuesday.
(yawm il-arbaؕāʼ baؕda yawm ath-thulāthāʼ)

يَوْم الأِثْنَيْن قبل يَوْم الثُّلاثاء. Monday is before Tuesday.
(yawm il-ithnayn qabla yawm ath-thulāthāʼ)

(qabla) قَبل	before
(baؕda) بَعد	after

Exercise 1

Fill in the gaps and draw the lines, as in the example:

Friday	الأربعاء	يوم
Tuesday	السبت	____
Thursday	الاثنين	____
Sunday	____	يوم
Wednesday	____	____
Saturday	____	____
Monday	____	____

Exercise 2

Now complete these sentences, as in the example:

يَوْم الجُمعَة قبل يَوْم السَّبْت.

يَوْم الخَميس ____ يَوْم الأَربِعَاء.

يَوْم الأحَد ____ يَوْم الاِثْنَيْن.

يَوْم الثُلاثَاء ____ يَوْم الأَربِعَاء.

____ السَّبْت بعد ____ .

Make four more similar sentences of your own.

Arabic words in English

In Unit 10 you met some English words that have been adopted into Arabic. There are also a number of words that have come the other way, usually making their way into English via Arabic literature and science or from contact, through trade for example, between Arabic speakers and Europeans.

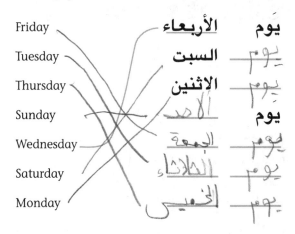

You have already met the word قطن (quṭn), from which we get our word 'cotton', and the word جمل (jamal), from which we get our word 'camel'.

Exercise 3

Here are some more English words derived from Arabic. See whether you can match them to the Arabic words on the right.

algebra	زَعْفَران
emir, prince	الكُحول
saffron	وَزير
alkali	الجَبْر
vizier, minister	تَمْر هِنْدي*
tamarind	أَمير
alcohol	القِلي

**Literally, 'Indian dates'.*

Plural pattern 5

Here are two of the words from Exercise 3. Listen and repeat them with their plurals several times until you can recognise and repeat the pattern.

Plural	*Singular*	
(wuzarā') وُزَراء	(wazīr) وَزير	minister
(umarā') أُمَراء	(amīr) أَمير	prince

Pattern 5

فُعَلاء (fuعalā')

This plural pattern is used for most words referring to male humans which have the pattern فعيل (faعīl) in the singular. It cannot be used for words that are not male humans.

Exercise 4

Listen to these words, pausing after each one. (They can all be made plural by using pattern 5.) Say the plural, following the same pattern, and then release the pause button to check your answer.

سَفير	ambassador
رَئيس	president/head (of)
زَعيم	leader
وَكيل	agent

Repeat this exercise until you are confident of the pattern. Then read the box below and then write down the plurals.

Hamza as a root letter

Notice that أَمير and رَئيس both have hamza as one of their root letters.

In the case of أَمير, hamza is the first root letter; and in the case of رَئيس, the second root letter.

The fact that hamza is one of the root letters makes no difference to the patterns except that how the hamza is written may change. At the beginning of a word, hamza is written on an alif, but in the middle or at the end of a word you may also find it sitting on a yā' (with no dots), on a wāw, or by itself on the line:

رئيس	(ra'īs)
رؤساء	(ru'asā')

Hamza is listed in the dictionary under alif. So for رئيس (ra'īs) you would look under راس, and for أمير under امر.

The feminine

Note that a female minister, ambassador, etc. will have a tā' marbūṭa in the singular, with the plural made by using the sound feminine plural (-āt):

Plural	Singular	
أَميرات (amīrāt)	أَميرة (amīra)	princess
وزيرات (wazīrāt)	وزيرة (wazīra)	*(female)* minister

Exercise 5
Write out the feminine singulars and plurals for the words in Exercise 4.

fiɛāla nouns
Words with the فعيل (faɛīl) pattern referring to male people can usually be made into general nouns from the same root letters using the pattern فعالة (fiɛāla), for example فعيل (wazīr, minister) is changed to وِزارة (wizāra, ministry).

Exercise 6
Complete the table below, as in the example:

Meaning	General noun	Root letters
ministry	وِزارة	و ز ر
embassy	سِفارة	س ف ر
emirate	إمارة	ا م ر
agency		و ك ل
leadership	زِيادة	ز ى م
presidency/chair	رِئاسة	ر أ س

What did the President do last week?
ماذا فعل الرئيس في الأسبوع الماضي؟

This is the President's schedule showing what he did last week. Initially, have a quick look at the schedule and the word list opposite and see whether you can identify some of the things the President did each day.

الظهر	الصباح	
معرض البنوك العربية	اجتماع مع السفير الفرنسي	السبت
مؤتمر المدرّسين العرب	الرئيسة البريطانية في مكتبي	الأحد
اجتماع مع السفيرة الايطالية	افتتاح المصنع الجديد	الاثنين
جلسة مع زعماء الأحزاب	الأمير محمود في مكتبي	الثلاثاء
اجتماع مع سفراء السودان واليمن والبحرين	الأمير حسين في القصر	الأربعاء
افتتاح المتحف الملكي	جلسة عمل مع الوزراء	الخميس

(ijtimāع (maعa)) **اجتماع (مع)**	meeting (with)
(iftitāḥ) **افتتاح**	opening (ceremony)
(maعraḍ) **مَعرَض**	exhibition
(mu'tamar) **مُؤتَمَر**	conference
(jalsa) **جَلسة**	session
(jalsat عamal) **جَلسة عَمَل**	working session, workshop
(ḥizb/aḥzāb) **حِزب/أحزاب**	party/parties *(political)*

Now find Saturday (السبت) and Sunday (الأحد) in the schedule.

Listen to a reporter asking the President's press agent about what he did on these days.

Look at these sentence tables. You can use these to make different sentences about what the President did last week by choosing one word from each column (reading from *right to left*).

مع ... with ...	اجتماعًا	الرئيس the President	عقد convened
	جلسة		
لـ ... for ...	جلسة عمل		حضر attended
	مؤتمرًا		
في ... in ...	معرضًا		
	افتتاحًا		

في مكتبه in his office	الرئيسة	الرئيس the President	استقبل * received
	الوزير		
في القصر in the palace	السفير		

**This type of verb will be covered in more detail in Unit 19.*

Word order

You may have noticed that the verb usually comes first in Arabic sentences, *before* the subject or the rest of the sentence: عقد الوزير اجتماعًا (ɛaqada al-wazīr ijtimāɛan, literally 'convened the minister a meeting'); فتحت زينب الخزانة (fataḥat zaynab al-khizāna, 'opened Zaynab the safe'). This is in contrast to English where we always put the verb *after* the subject: The minister convened a meeting; Zaynab opened the safe.

Arabic order:

عقد الوزير اجتماعًا مع ...

3 rest of sentence	2 subject	1 verb

English order:

The minister convened a meeting with…

1 subject	2 verb	3 rest of sentence

However, Arabic word order is more flexible than English and you sometimes find the verb and the subject the other way around. This is especially true of less formal Arabic as it reflects what happens in spoken dialects where the verb usually comes after the subject. For the moment, it is easier to stick to the more standard order above.

Exercise 7

Looking at the President's schedule on page 186, complete the questions and answers for Monday and Tuesday.

ماذا ______ الرئيس ______ الاثنين؟

حضر افتتاح ______ ______ صباحًا،

وعقد ______ مع ______ ______ ظهرًا.

______ ______ الرئيس ______ الثلاثاء؟

استقبل الرئيس ______ في ______ صباحًا، وبعد

ذلك ______ ______ مع ______ الأحزاب ______ .

Now make similar questions and answers for Wednesday and Thursday.

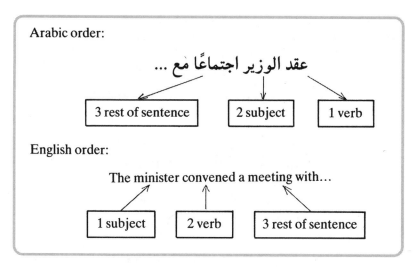

The cabinet مَجلِس الوُزَراء

رئيس الوزراء Prime Minister

نائِب رئيس الوزراء Deputy Prime Minister

وزير... Minister of ...

الدِّفاع
Defence

الاقتِصاد
the Economy

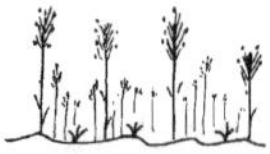

الزِّراعة
Agriculture

الصِّناعة
Industry

التَّعليم
Education

العَدل
Justice

الخارِجيّة
the Exterior

الدّاخليّة
the Interior

الثَّقافة
Culture

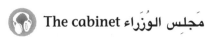

الصِّحة
Health

Tip: Notice how Arabic puts al- ('the') before *every* department, whereas English only sometimes does.

Listen a few times to the recording of the cabinet ministers, looking at page 190. Then listen again without looking at the text. Pause the recording after each minister and check whether you can remember the meaning.

Exercise 8

Look at the newspaper headlines below. Decide which *two* people, or groups of people, are the subject of each headline.

١ استقبل الأمير عبد الله سفير باكستان

٢ الرئيس المصري استقبل أميرة سعودية

٣ اجتماع بين وزيرة التعليم وزعماء المدرّسين

٤ رسالة لوزير الزراعة من الرئيس الألماني

٥ اجتماع بين الأمير سلمان والسفير البريطاني

٦ الرئيس السوري استقبل نائب وزير الخارجية

٧ رسالة من وزير العدل إلى الرئيس العراقي

٨ رسالة من أمير الكويت إلى سفراء أوروبا

Now describe the headlines, using one of the three model sentences below:

استقبل الأمير عبد الله سفير باكستان.

Prince Abdullah received the Ambassador of Pakistan.

حضرت وزيرة التعليم اجتماعًا مع زعماء المدرّسين.

The *(female)* Minister of Education attended a meeting with teachers' leaders.

كتب وزير العدل رسالة إلى الرئيس العراقيّ.

The Minister of Justice wrote a message to the Iraqi President.

Exercise 9

The following article gives details about the visit of the British Minister of Defence to Saudi Arabia. It is typical of the kind of account that appears regularly in the Arabic newspapers.

من جانب (min jānib)
on the part of

مساعد (musāɛid)
aide/assistant

شؤون عسكرية
(shu'ūn ɛaskariyya)
military affairs

السيّد (as-sayyid)
Mr

الأمير حسن عقد جلسة عمل
مع وزير الدفاع البريطاني

الرياض : استقبل الأمير حسن نائب رئيس مجلس الوزراء في مكتبه بالرياض صباح أمس وزير الدفاع البريطاني وبعد ذلك عقد الأمير حسن والوزير البريطاني جلسة عمل.
وحضر الجلسة من جانب السعودي الأمير أشرف نائب وزير الدفاع والأمير محمد مساعد وزير الدفاع ومساعد وزير الدفاع للشؤون العسكرية السيد عثمان حمدي.

First try to work out where and when the meeting took place. Then decide whether the following are true (✔) or false (✘), as in the example.

١ ذهب وزير الدفاع البريطانيّ إلى الرياض. ☑
٢ استقبل الأمير حسن الوزير البريطاني. ☐
٣ استقبل الأمير الوزير في مكتبه ظهر أمس. ☐
٤ الأمير حسن هو رئيس الوزراء. ☐
٥ بعد الاستقبال رجع الوزير البريطاني إلى لندن. ☐
٦ الأمير حسن هو وزير الدفاع السعودي. ☐
٧ الأمير أشرف هو نائب وزير الدفاع. ☐
٨ حضر الجلسة من جانب السعودي أميران ومساعد. ☐

Singular and plural verbs

Look at these three sentences from the article in Exercise 9:

استقبل الأمير حسن... وزير الدفاع البريطانيّ...

عقد الأمير حسن والوزير البريطاني جلسة عمل.

حضر الجلسة... الأمير أشرف... والأمير محمّد... والسيّد عثمان حمدي.

How many people are the subject of each sentence?

- The first sentence has only one subject: الأمير حسن (Prince Hassan).
- The second sentence has two subjects: الأمير حسن والوزير البريطاني (Prince Hassan and the British minister).
- The third sentence has three subjects: الأمير أشرف... والأمير محمّد... والسيّد عثمان حمدي (Prince Ashraf, Prince Mohammed and Mr Uthman Hamdi).

All the verbs, however, are in the masculine *singular*. If a verb comes *before* its subject it will always be singular, even if the subject is plural. The verb will change according to whether the subject is masculine or feminine, but not according to whether it is singular or plural.

Verbs that come *after* the subject will be singular for a singular subject and plural for a plural subject:

استقبل الوزراء السفير الفرنسي وعقدوا اجتماعًا.

plural verb after subject — *subject (masc. plural)* — *singular verb before subject*

The ministers received the French Ambassador and held a meeting.

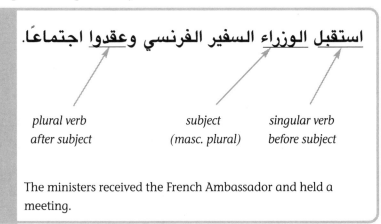

Exercise 10

Choose a verb from the box to fill each gap in the sentences, using the masculine, feminine, singular or plural as appropriate. You can use a verb more than once. The first sentence is an example.

عقد	كتب	ذهب	سمع
أكل	جلس	فعل	رجع
شرب	خرج	وجد	حضر

١ خرج السفراء من السفارة وذهبوا إلى القصر الملكيّ.

٢ ______ الوزير جلسة عمل مع السفير اليمنيّ.

٣ ______ الزعماء إلى المصنع و______ عن السيارة الجديدة.

٤ ______ الرئيسة على مكتبها و______ رسالة إلى وزير الدفاع.

٥ ______ الرجال سمكًا في المطعم، وبعد ذلك ______ زجاجات كولا.

٦ ______ وزيرة الاقتصاد افتتاح بنك جديد.

٧ ______ زينب إلى البنك و______ الشبّاك المكسور.

٨ ماذا ______ الرئيسة يوم الثلاثاء؟

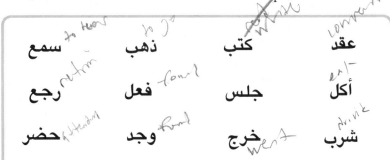

Structure notes

More about iḍāfa

Look at these two phrases:

السفير الألمانيّ the German Ambassador

سفير ألمانيا the Ambassador of Germany

These are two different phrases expressing the same meaning. (The English translations are also different ways of expressing the same meaning.)

The first phrase uses an adjective to describe the nationality of the ambassador. The adjective 'al-almānī' comes after the noun 'as-safīr' in Arabic, and both have the article 'al-' as the adjective describes a definite noun.

The second phrase is an iḍāfa construction (two or more nouns together). Remember that only the last noun in an iḍāfa can have 'al-' (although it does not have to). So, in the second phrase above, the word 'safīr' does not have 'al-', even though it means '<u>the</u> ambassador'.

If you want to use an adjective to describe an iḍāfa, the adjective must come after the *whole* iḍāfa. You cannot put an adjective in the middle of the nouns in an iḍāfa:

وزير الخارجية الإيراني the Iranian Minister of the Exterior

You could also use an iḍāfa with three nouns that would have the same meaning as the above:

وزير خارجية إيران the Minister of the Exterior of Iran

Notice that the word khārijiyya doesn't have 'al-' as it is no longer the *last* word in the iḍāfa.

Optional exercise

Look back at the headlines in Exercise 8. List all the examples of phrases using an adjective for nationalities and those using just an iḍāfa. For example:

سفير باكستان the Ambassador of Pakistan (iḍāfa)

الرئيس المصريّ the Egyptian President *(noun + adjective)*

Now reverse the form of the phrases, for example:

السفير الباكستانيّ the Pakistani Ambassador

رئيس مصر the President of Egypt

Vocabulary in Unit 14

أُسْبُوع (usbūع) week

يَوْم (أيَّام) (yawm, ayyām) day

(يَوْم) السَّبْت (yawm as-sabt) Saturday

(يَوْم) الأحَد (yawm al-aḥad) Sunday

(يَوْم) الاِثْنَيْن (yawm al-ithnayn) Monday

(يَوْم) الثُلاثـاء (yawm ath-thulāthā') Tuesday

(يَوْم) الأربِعـاء (yawm al-arbiعā') Wednesday

(يَوْم) الخَمِيس (yawm al-khamīs) Thursday

(يَوْم) الجُمعَة (yawm al-jumعa) Friday

بَعْدَ (baعda) after

قَبْلَ (qabla) before

وَزِير (وُزَرَاء) (wazīr, wuzarā') minister

وِزارة (وِزارات) (wizāra, wizārāt) ministry

أَمير (أُمَراء) (amīr, umarā') emir, prince

إمـارَة (إمـارات) (imāra, imārāt) emirate

سَفِير (سُفَرَاء) (safīr, sufarā') ambassador

سِفَـارَة (سِفَـارات) (sifāra, sifārāt) embassy

رَئِيس (رُؤَسَـاء) (ra'īs, ru'asā') president, head (of)

رِئـاسَة (رِئـاسات) (ri'āsa, ri'āsāt) presidency, chair

زَعِيم (زُعَمـاء) (zaعīm, zuعamā') leader

زِعـامة (زعـامـات) (ziعāma, ziعāmāt) leadership

وَكِيل (وُكَلاء) (wakīl, wukalā') agent

وِكـالة (وِكـالات) (wikāla, wikālāt) agency

مُسـاعِـد (مُسـاعِدون) (musāعid, musāعidūn) aide, assistant

نَائِب (nā'ib) deputy

مَجْلِس الوُزَراء (majlis al-wuzarā') the Cabinet (council of ministers)

ظُهْر (ẓuhr) noon

ظُهْرًا / بَعْد الظُهْر (ẓuhran/baɛda l-ẓuhr) in the afternoon

عَقَد (ɛaqad) held/convened (meeting, wedding, etc.)

حَضَر (ḥaḍar) attended (meeting, etc.)

اِسْتَقْبَل (istaqbal) received, welcomed

اِجْتِمَاع (اِجْتِمَاعات) (ijtimāɛ, ijtimāɛāt) meeting

جَلْسَة (عَمَل) (jalsat (ɛamal)) (working) session

مُؤْتَمَر (مُؤْتَمَرات) (mu'tamar, mu'tamarāt) conference

مَعْرَض (مَعَارِض) (maɛraḍ, maɛāriḍ) exhibition

اِفْتِتَاح (اِفْتِتَاحات) (iftitāḥ, iftitāḥāt) opening (ceremony)

الدِفَاع (ad-difāɛ) defence

الاِقْتِصَاد (al-iqtiṣād) the economy

الزِراعة (az-zirāɛa) agriculture

الصِناعة (aṣ-ṣināɛa) industry

التَعْليم (at-taɛlīm) education

العَدْل (al-ɛadl) justice

الخَارجيّة (al-khārijiyya) the exterior

الداخليّة (ad-dākhiliyya) the interior

الثَقَافة (ath-thaqāfa) culture

الصِحَّة (aṣ-ṣiḥḥa) health

حِزْب (أَحْزاب) (ḥizb, aḥzāb) (political) party

شَأْن (شُؤُون) (sha'n, shu'ūn) affair, matter

عَسْكَريّ (ɛaskarī) military

unit 15 Review

Exercise 1

Fill in the missing figures and words in the table below. Remember to start with the *right-hand* column.

٣٠	ثلاثين	١١	أحد عشر	١	وَاحِد
٤٠	أربعين	١٢	اثنا عشر	٢	اِثْنَان
٥٠	خمسين	١٣	ثَلاثَة –	٣	ثَلاثَة
٦٠	ستين	١٤	أربعة عشر	٤	أربعة
٧٠	سبعين	١٥	خَمْسَة عشر	٥	خَمْسَة
٨٠	ثمانين	١٦	ستة عشر	٦	ستة
٩٠	تسعين	١٧	سبعة عشر	٧	سبعة
٩٥	خمسة وتسعين	١٨	ثمانية عشر	٨	ثَمانية
٤٣	ثلاثة وأربعين	١٩	تسعة عشر	٩	تسعة
٣٤	أربعة وثلاثين	٢٠	عشرين	١٠	عَشرَة

Exercise 2

Now write down the numbers you hear on the recording. The first is an example.

١ ٩٤

Exercise 3

Can you finish these sequences of numbers?

٢ ٤ ٦ ٨ ١٠ ١٢ ١٤ ١٦ ١٨ ٢٠ ٢٢

٣ ٦ ٩ ١٢ ١٥ ١٨ ٢١ ٢٤ ٢٧ ٣٠ ٣٣

١١ ٢٢ ٣٣ ٤٤ ٥٥ ٦٦ ٧٧ ٨٨ ٩٩ ١١٠ ١٢١

٧ ١٤ ٢١ ٢٨ ٣٥ ٤٢ ٤٩ ٥٦ ٦٣ ٧٠ ٧٧

١ ١ ٢ ٣ ٥ ٨ ١٣ ٢١ ٣٤ ٥٥ ٨٩

Exercise 4

The following is a newspaper extract about international aid. Firstly, look at the article and additional vocabulary and try to answer the questions on page 200 in English.

طائِرة (طائِرات) (ṭā'ira (ṭā'irāt)) plane

بلغ (balagh) reached

وصل (waṣal) arrived

معونات (maɛūnāt) aid

نقل (naqal) carried

وزن (wazn) weight

الولايات المتّحدة (al-walāyāt al-muttaḥida) the United States

١١٣ طائرة معونة إلى السودان

الخرطوم –
مكتب « الشرق الأوسط »
بلغ عدد طائرات المعونات العربية والغربية التي وصلت إلى الخرطوم حتى أمس ١١٣ طائرة نقلت معونات بلغ وزنها ٢٢٩١ طنا كالتالي :

الدولة	عدد الطائرات
السعودية	٥١
مصر	١٣
الكويت	١١
اليمن	١٠
ليبيا	٥
الجزائر	٣
تونس	١
بلجيكا	٤
بريطانيا	٣
ابطاليا	٣
تركيا	٢
نيجيريا	٢
الولايات المتحدة	١
اليونان	١

1 Where are the aid planes going?   *Kartom*
2 How many aid planes have been sent altogether?   *113*
3 How many tonnes of aid have so far been sent?   *2291*
4 Which country has sent the most planes?   *Saudi Arabia*
5 Which western country has sent the most planes?   *Belgium*
6 Which newspaper reported this news item?   *Athary Arwort*

Now look at the list of countries and answer these questions in Arabic.
(Give short answers.)

> Remember:
>
> كَم   +   singular noun
>
> 3–10   +   plural noun
>
> 11 upwards +   singular noun
>
> For 2 things, use the *dual ending*: طائِرتان (2 planes)
>
> For 1 thing, use the *singular* with no number: طائِرة (a/one plane)

١   هناك كم دولة في القائمة؟   *١٥ دولة*

٢   هل فرنسا في القائمة؟   *لا*

٣   هل مصر بين السعودية واليمن في القائمة؟   *لا*

٤   كم طائرة للسعودية؟   *٦١ طائرة*

٥   كم طائرة لليبيا؟   *خمس طائرات*

٦   هل لليمن عشر طائرات؟   *نعم*

٧   كم طائرة لنيجيريا؟   *طائرتان*

٨   هل لمصر ١٤ طائرة؟   *لا*

٩   هل لأمريكا طائرة؟   *نعم*

١٠ هل لسوريا طائرة؟   *لا*

Exercise 5

So far you have met seven Arabic plural patterns:

(ūn/īn)	ون/ين	مُدَرِّس	←	مُدَرِّسون
(āt)	ات	مُدَرِّسة	←	مُدَرِّسات
(afعāl)	أَفعال	قَلَم	←	أقلام
(fuعūl)	فُعول	بيت	←	بيوت
(fiعāl)	فِعال	كلب	←	كلاب
(fuعal)	فُعَل	دولة	←	دُوَل
(fuعalā')	فُعَلاء	وزير	←	وزراء

Copy out the table below the box and then, in the correct columns, write the *plurals* of these words you know, as in the example:

وَلَد	شَمعة	زَعيم	أميرة	سوق
تُحفة	جُنَيه	شأن	لِصّ	سَيف
سيّارة	عُلبة	كُرة	سَفير	بَنك
مُساعِد	لُعبة	دَرّاجة	قَلب	رَجُل
وَكيل	جَبَل	صورة	جَمَل	تِليفون
بَحر	شَيخ	رَئيس	مَلِك	حِزب
فيلم	كيس	سِفارة	كوب	طَبَق

ون/ين	ات	فعال	فُعول	فِعال	فُعَل	فُعَلاء
مساعدون	أميرات	أولاد	شموع	رجال	تحف	زعماء

Exercise 6

Now make questions and answers for each picture, as in the example.

١

٢

كم كلبًا في الصورة؟

هناك ثلاثة كلاب في الصورة.

٣

٤

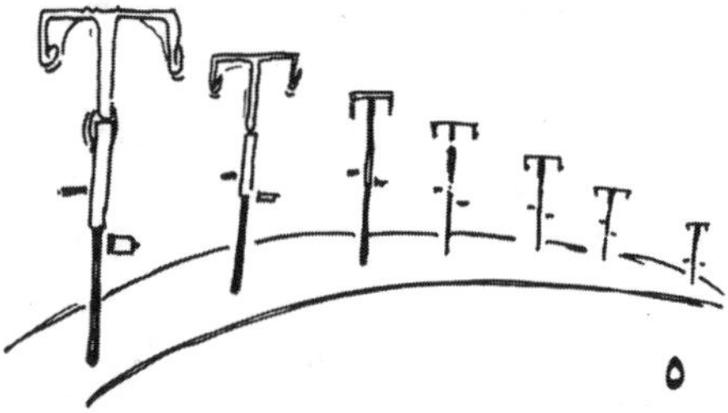

٥

٦

٧

٨

Exercise 7

Match the items to the material from which they are made, as in the example:

ذَهب	مائدة
قُطْن	قلادة
خَشَب	حقيبة
جلد	شُبّاك
زُجاج	قَميص

Now request the items, like this:

أريد مائدة خشب، من فضلك.

I'd like a wooden table, please.

Exercise 8

Complete this table:

Meaning	*Feminine*	*Masculine*
green	خَضْراء	أَخْضَر
blue	زرقا	أَزْرَق
white	بيضا	أبيض
black	سودا	أسود
yellow	صفرا	أَصْفَر
red	حمرا	احمر

Now choose a colour to fill each gap in the sentences on page 204.

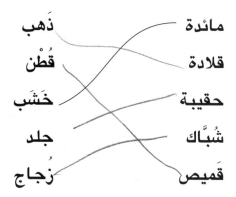

> *Remember:*
>
> Always use the *feminine singular* for non-human plurals.

١   باب بيتي *الازرق*.

٢   سيّارتي *سودا*.

٣   البحر *الأحمر* في شرق مصر.

٤   وجدتُ طماطم *حمرا* في السوق.

٥   راية (flag) مصر *بيضا* و *حمرا* و *سودا*.

Exercise 9

Remind yourself of the verb in the past by reviewing the table on
page 178. Then write the correct form of the verb in brackets to
complete the story (note: فِرعونيّ fir‌ɛūnī = pharaonic).

> *Remember:*
>
> 1 You do not need to write the pronoun, just the right form of
>   the verb.
>
> 2 The verb is singular when it is *before* the subject.

في الأسبوع الماضي، *ذهب* (ذهب) أحمد وفاطمة

وصاحبهما الألماني هَانْز إلى القاهرة و *وصلوا* (وصل)

هناك يوم السبت مساءً.

يوم الأحد *خرج* (خرج) الأصحاب صباحًا و *ذهبوا*

(ذهب) إلى المتحف المصري في وسط المدينة، و *وجدوا*

(وجد) هناك معرضًا لتُحَف فَرعونيّة. بعد ذلك *ذهبوا*

(ذهب) إلى مطعم بجانب المتحف و *أكل* (أكل) أحمد

وفاطمة سمكًا من البحر الأحمر، ولكن هـانز ـــ أكلَ (أكل)

بورجر.

يوم الاثنين ـــ حضرَ (حضر) أحمد وهـانز مؤتمرًا ثقافيًّا،

ولكن فاطمة ـــ جلستْ (جلس) في البلكون و(كتب) خطابًا

لأُمّها. أخيرًا، رجعَ (رجع) الأصحاب يوم الثلاثاء.

Exercise 10

Listen to the interview with the Minister of the Economy and fill in the gaps in his diary. Listen once without writing and then again, pausing if necessary.

الظهر	الصباح	
جلسة عمل مع المفتّش العام*	افتتاح البنك الياباني الجديد	الأحد
السفير دالي في مكتبي		الاثنين
اجتماع مع وزير العدل	مؤتمر وزراء الاقتصاد العرب	الثلاثاء
الأمير أحمد في القصر الملكي	البنوك الإسلامية	الأربعاء
	وزير الاقتصاد في الوزارة	الخميس

* المفتِّش العامّ (al-mufattish al-ᵉāmm) = the Inspector General

Now make eight questions using the diary on page 205 and as many of the question words below as you can. Two examples have been given for you.

هَل؟ *(question marker)*	أَين؟ where?	مَتى؟ when?
لِماذا؟ why? ('for what?')	ماذا؟ what?	

متى حَضَر الوزير مؤتمر وزراء الاقتصاد العَرَب؟

لماذا ذهب إلى وزارة الزراعة يوم الثلاثاء ظهراً؟

Conversation

Review

You're going to take part in two conversations which review some of the conversational language connected to shopping.

Below you will find some indicators as to what you want to buy. Prepare what you think you'll need to say.

Conversation 1

- you'd like a bag (حَقيبة)
- you'd prefer a leather bag
- you like black, but you don't like blue
- your budget is 40 pounds

Conversation 2

- you'd like half a kilo of apples
- you'd prefer the red apples
- you also want a box of figs
- you want a plastic bag

Now join in the conversations on the recording, speaking when prompted. You could also practise with a native speaker, another learner or a teacher, with one of you playing the part of the storekeeper.

Vocabulary in Unit 15

طـائِرة (طـائِرات) (ṭā'ira, ṭā'irāt) plane

بَلَغ (balagh) reached

وَصَل (waṣal) arrived

مَعونـة (مَعونـات) (maعūna, maعūnāt) aid/relief/help

نَقَل (naqal) carried

وَزن (أوزان) (wazn, awzān) weight

الـولايـات المتَّحِدة (al-walāyāt al-muttaḥida) the United States

رايـة (رايـات) (rāya, rāyāt) flag/banner

لمـاذا؟ (limādhā) why?

فِرعونيّ (firعūnī) pharaonic

مُفَتِّش (ون/ين) (mufattish) inspector

عـامّ (عāmm) general

unit 16

Every day

What's the time? كم الساعة؟

Look at the clocks and listen to the times on the recording:

كم الساعة ؟

الساعة السابعة .

كم الساعة ؟

الساعة الواحدة .

كم الساعة ؟

الساعة الثالثة .

كم الساعة ؟

الساعة العاشرة .

(as-sāɛa al-wāḥida)	الساعة الواحدة	one o'clock
(as-sāɛa ath-thānya)	الساعة الثانية	two o'clock
(as-sāɛa ath-thālitha)	الساعة الثالثة	three o'clock
(as-sāɛa ar-rābiɛa)	الساعة الرابعة	four o'clock
(as-sāɛa al-khāmisa)	الساعة الخامسة	five o'clock
(as-sāɛa as-sādisa)	الساعة السادسة	six o'clock
(as-sāɛa as-sābiɛa)	الساعة السابعة	seven o'clock
(as-sāɛa ath-thāmina)	الساعة الثامنة	eight o'clock
(as-sāɛa at-tāsiɛa)	الساعة التاسعة	nine o'clock
(as-sāɛa al-ɛāshira)	الساعة العاشرة	ten o'clock
(as-sāɛa al-ḥādya ɛashara)	الساعة الحادية عشرة	eleven o'clock
(as-sāɛa ath-thānya ɛashara)	الساعة الثانية عشرة	twelve o'clock

as-sāɛa athānya/ath-thālitha, etc. literally means 'the second/third hour'. In spoken Arabic you will often hear the regular (cardinal) numbers used with time, for example as-sāɛa ithnayn/thalātha, two/three o'clock.

Tip: ساعة (sāɛa) can also mean 'clock' or 'watch' as well as 'hour'.

Exercise 1

Say and write questions and answers for these times:

١
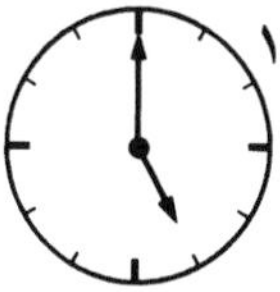

٢

٣

٤

٥

More about time

(as-sāɛa ... wan-niṣf)	**الساعة ... والنِصف**	half past ...
(as-sāɛa ... wath-thulth)	**الساعة ... والثُلث**	twenty past ...
(as-sāɛa ... war-rubɛ)	**الساعة ... والرُبع**	quarter past ...
(as-sāɛa ... illā thulthan)	**الساعة ... إلا ثُلثًا**	twenty to ...
(as-sāɛa ... illā rubɛan)	**الساعة ... إلا رُبعًا**	quarter to ...

Arabic uses the words niṣf, half, and rubɛ, quarter, to describe 30 and 15 minutes as English does. In addition, the word thulth, third, is used to describe 20 minutes (a third of an hour).

Look at the following clocks and listen to the times on the recording:

الساعة الثالثة والنصف .

الساعة السادسة والثلث .

الساعة الخامسة والربع .

الساعة الخامسة إلَّا رُبْعًا .

الساعة الثانية عشرة إلَّا ثُلْثًا .

الساعة العاشرة وخمس دَقَائِق .

الساعة الواحدة وعشر دَقَائِق .

الساعة السادسة إلَّا خمسة وعشرين دَقِيقَة .

Exercise 2

Now say and write questions and answers for these times:

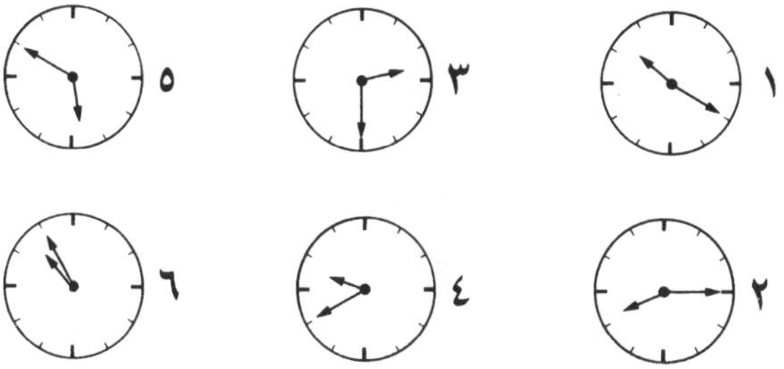

'At' and 'on'

Arabic doesn't have the equivalent of the English words 'at' or 'on' when talking about time. Days of the week and times are simply put directly after the event they describe:

متى الحفلة؟ (matā l-ḥafla?)	When's the party?
الحفلة يوم الخميس الساعة الثالثة. (al-ḥafla yawm al-khamīs as-sāعa ath-thālitha)	The party's on Thursday at three o'clock.

Exercise 3

Salwa and her friend Nabil want to go to the cinema and they're discussing what films are showing. Listen and fill in the days and times below.

	Arabic film	*American film*	*French film*
Thursday showing times			3 6
Friday showing times	4		
Saturday showing times			

Every day كُلّ يوم

Listen to what Mahmoud does every day (starting top right, page 213).

وَيكْتُب دُرُوسـهُ .

وبعد ذلك يأكل العَشاء .

وَيَشْرَب زجاجة كولا ولكن أخته فاطمة تَشْرَب فنجان شاي .

أخيرًا يَلْبَس البيجاما
الساعة التاسعة إلّا ربعًا .

كُلّ يوم
يَغْسِل محمود وَجْهَهُ الساعة السابعة .

وَيأْكُل الإِفْطار الساعة
السابعة والنصف .

ثمَ يَخْرُج من
البيت الساعة الثامنة .

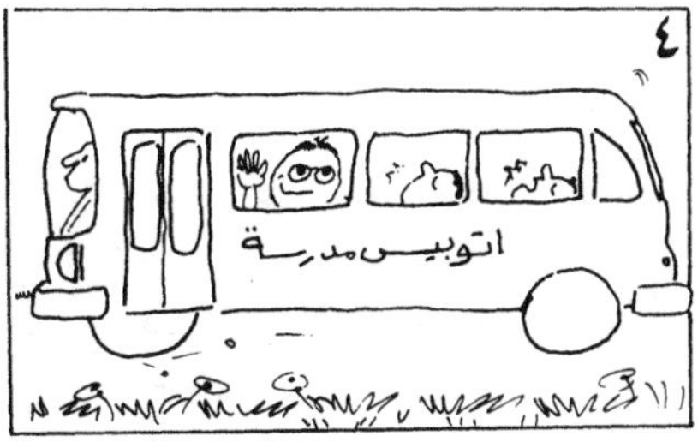

وَيذْهَب إلى المدرسة
بالأوتوبيس .

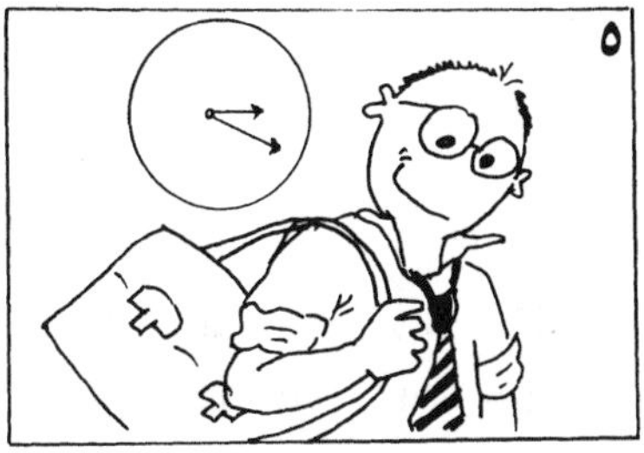

يرْجَع الساعة
الثالثة والثلث .

الإفْطَار
breakfast

الغَدَاء
lunch

العَشَاء
dinner

Means of transportation are preceded by بالـ (bil-, by [the]):

يَذْهَب
he goes

بالأُوتُوبِيس
by bus

بالطائرة
by plane

بالسيّارة
by car

بالقِطَار
by train

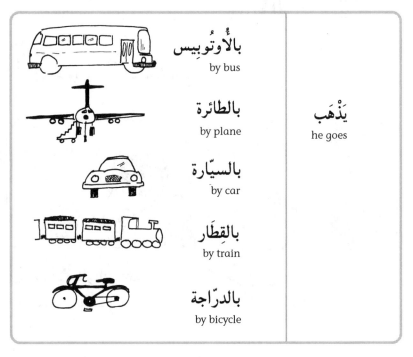

بالدرّاجة
by bicycle

He and she

Look at these sentences, taken from the picture story.

كلّ يوم يَشْرَب محمود زجاجة كولا. (kull yawm yashrab maḥmūd zujājat kūlā)	Every day Mahmoud drinks a bottle of cola.
كلّ يوم تَشْرَب فاطمة فنجان شاي. (kull yawm tashrab fāṭima finjān shāy)	Every day Fatima drinks a cup of tea.

Notice that the verb 'drinks' changes from <u>ya</u>shrab for Mahmoud ('he', huwa) to <u>ta</u>shrab for Fatima ('she', hiya):

(هُوَ) يَشْرَب

(هِيَ) تَشْرَب

Similarly the verb 'goes' would change from يذهب (<u>ya</u>dhhab) to تذهب (<u>ta</u>dhhab):

يذهب محمود إلى المدرسة بالأوتوبيس. (yadhhab maḥmūd ilā l-madrasa bil-ūtūbīs)	Mahmoud goes to school by bus.
تذهب فاطمة إلى المدرسة بالدراجة. (tadhhab fāṭima ilā l-madrasa bid-darrāja)	Fatima goes to school by bicycle.

Exercise 4

Listen to what Mahmoud's sister, Fatima, does every day, and match the sentences to the times, as in the example.

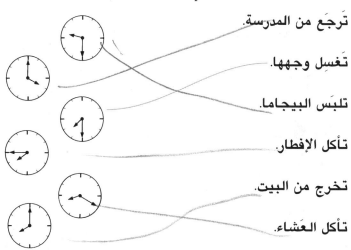

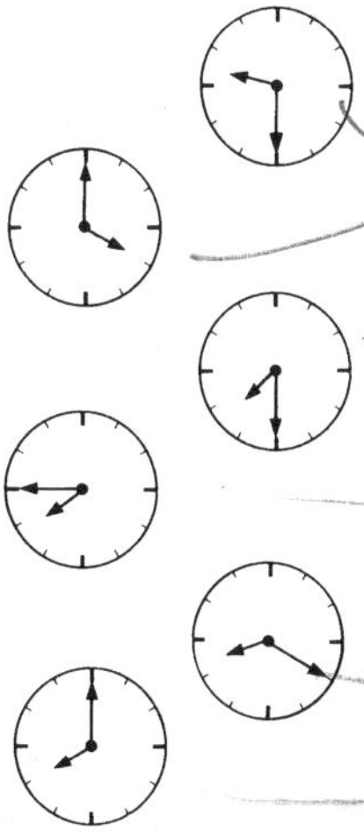

تَرجَع من المدرسة.

تَغسِل وجهها.

تلبَس البيجاما.

تأكل الإفطار.

تخرج من البيت.

تأكل العَشاء.

Now write a paragraph about what Fatima does every day. Use some of the words and phrases you know to join the sentences. Begin like this:

كلّ يوم تغسل فاطمة وجهها الساعة السابعة والنصف ثمّ...

Negative statements

Listen to the recording and look at the pictures and sentences below:

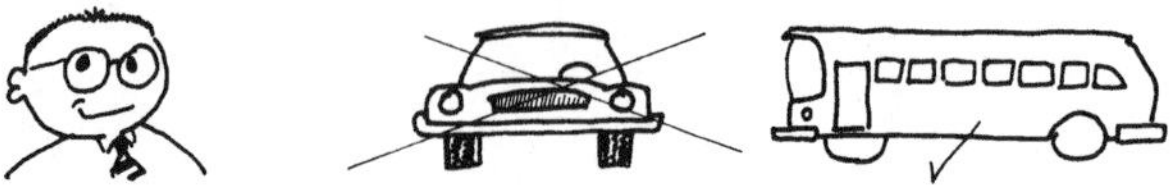

لاَ يذهب محمود إلى المدرسة بالسيّارة ، يذهب بالأوتوبيس.

لاَ تشرب فاطمة زجاجة كولا ، تشرب فنجان شاي.

| لا | يذهب |

لاَ + *present verb* = *present negative*

Exercise 5

Make sentences for these pictures, following the models above.

٣

١

٤

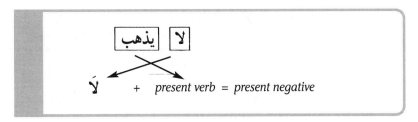

٢

Asking questions about every day

Listen to Mahmoud's and Fatima's teachers asking them about their everyday routines.

Present tense

In this unit you have met some verbs in the present tense, used when talking about what happens routinely or what is happening now. In the past tense, endings are added *after* the root letters to show the subject. The present tense is mainly formed by adding prefixes *before* the root, although there are sometimes also endings.

Here is an example of a present verb, using the verb 'drink'. The prefixes and endings around the root are underlined.

I drink	(ashrab) أَشْرَب
you *(masc.)* drink	(tashrab) تَشْرَب
you *(fem.)* drink	(tashrabīna) تَشْرَبين
he drinks	(yashrab) يَشْرَب
she drinks	(tashrab) تَشْرَب
we drink	(nashrab) نَشْرَب
you *(pl.)* drink	(tashrabūna) تَشْرَبون
they drink	(yashrabūna) يَشْرَبون

'She' and the three words for 'you' all start with ta- in the present tense. The feminine 'you' ends in -īna and the plural 'you' and 'they' end in -ūna. (In spoken dialects these endings are often shortened to -ī and -ū.)

Note that when two alifs combine in Arabic, they are written as one with a wavy madda sign above, pronounced ā. For example:

I eat	(ākul) [أ + أكل] آكل

Exercise 6

Think of three more questions and answers each for Mahmoud and Fatima, following the examples on page 217.

Exercise 7

Now talk about what you do everyday. First, think about your daily routine. What time do you have a wash? Have your breakfast? Leave the house in the morning? How do you travel? Return from work, university (جامِعة jāmiʿa) or school? Have dinner? What do you drink in the evening?

Then write a paragraph about what you do every day. Start like this:

كلّ يوم أغسل وجهي الساعة...

Education التعليم

At school في المدرسة

Look at the different subjects and listen to the recording.

Take care to distinguish between the similar words used for sport and mathematics/arithmetic:

sport = الرياضة (ar-riyāḍa)
mathematics/arithmetic = الرياضيّات (ar-riyāḍiyyāt)

Look at the timetable and try to remember the names of the subjects.

الخميس	الأربعاء	الثلاثاء	الاثنين	الأحد	السبت	
⚗️	اب ت	٢+٢=٤	🧒	🧒	🧙	٨:٠٠ 〈 〉 ١٠:٣٠
٢+٢=٤	🧒	abc	اب ت	٢+٢=٤	اب ت	١٢:٠٠
←					غداء	١٣:٣٠
╱	🤾	🎵	🎨	🤾	🌍	١٥:٠٠

 What does the class study? Listen to the headteacher asking the class teacher what her class studies on Saturday morning:

نَدْرُس التاريخ من الساعة الثامنة والنصف حَتَّى الساعة العاشرة وندرس العربيّة بعد ذلك حَتَّى الساعة الثانية عشرة .

ماذا تَدْرُسُون يوم السبت صباحًا ؟

(min ... hattā ...) ... مِن ... حَتَّى ... from ... until ...

Exercise 8

Look at the school timetable and make up more questions and answers between the parent and the teacher for the following:

١ يوم الثلاثاء ظهرًا

٢ يوم الثلاثاء صباحًا

٣ يوم الاثنين ظهرًا

٤ يوم الخميس صباحًا

٥ يوم السبت ظهرًا

٦ يوم الأحد ظهرًا

٧ يوم الاثنين صباحًا

Exercise 9

Now complete this paragraph about the children's school day. (Remember: use a *singular* verb *before* a plural subject, a *plural* verb *after* a plural subject.)

كلّ يوم ______ الأولاد من بيوتهم الساعة الثامنة إلا ربعًا

و______ إلى المدرسة بالأوتوبيس. يدرسون حتّى الساعة

______ وبعد ذلك ______ الغداء.

بعد الغداء يدرسون من ______ الواحدة والنصف ______

الساعة الثالثة ثم ______ من المدرسة إلى بيوتهم.

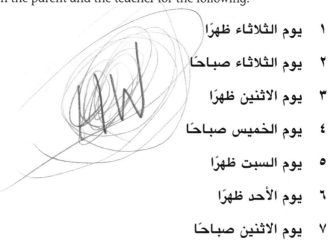

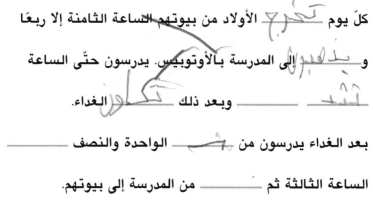

At university في الجامعة

Here is some more useful vocabulary for talking about university life:

(muḥāḍara) مُحاضرة	lecture
(kulliya) كُلّيّة	faculty/college
(maktaba) مكتَبة	library
(ustādh) أُستاذ	professor
(aṭ-ṭibb) الطِّبّ	medicine
(al-handasa) الهَندَسة	engineering
(al-ḥuqūq) الحُقوق	law

Exercise 10

Listen to Hisham talking about a typical day at university. Make notes in English about the following:

- the name of his university
- his degree subject
- his daily routine.

Vocabulary learning

The *middle vowel* of the present tense changes from one verb to the next:

يشرَب (yashrab) drinks
يخرُج (yakhruj) goes out
يغسِل (yaghsil) washes

There is no automatic way of knowing which is the middle vowel, but the dictionary will show the present tense vowel separately:

> غسل *ḡasala* (*i*) (*ḡasl*) to wash (ب ه, ه s.o., s.th. with), launder (ب ه s.th. with); to cleanse, clean (ه s.th., e.g., the teeth); to purge, cleanse, clear, wash (ه s.th., من of); to wash (ه against s.th.) II to

It is best to learn the past and present verbs together. If you are using the card system, write the middle vowel on the present verb:

غسل/يغسِل	*to wash*

Structure notes

Present tense

Those parts of the present tense that do not have a *suffix* (extra letters on the end) end with a ḍamma (u), but this is generally only pronounced in more formal Arabic. The present verb with its full endings would be:

I drink	(ashrabu) أَشْرَبُ
you *(masc.)* drink	(tashrabu) تَشْرَبُ
you *(fem.)* drink	(tashrabīna) يَشْرَبِين
he drinks	(yashrabu) يَشْرَبُ
she drinks	(tashrabu) تَشْرَبُ
we drink	(nashrabu) نَشْرَبُ
you *(pl.)* drink	(tashrabūna) تَشْرَبون
they drink	(yashrabūna) تَشْرَبون

Vocabulary in Unit 16

سَاعَة (سَاعَات) (sāɛa, sāɛāt) hour/watch/clock

دَقيقة (دَقائِق) (daqīqa, daqā'iq) minute

نِصْف (niṣf) half (*also* 30 minutes)

ثُلْث (thulth) third (*also* 20 minutes)

رُبْع (rubɛ) quarter (*also* 15 minutes)

كُلّ (kull) every/all

كُلّ يَوم (kull yawm) every day

إفْطار (ifṭār) breakfast

غَدَاء (ghadā') lunch

عَشَاء (ɛashā') dinner/supper

أُوتوُبيس (ـات) (ūtūbīs, ūtūbīsāt) bus

قِطار (قِطارات) (qiṭār, qiṭārāt) train

دَرَس/يَدْرُس (daras/yadrus) to study
غَسَل/يغسِل (ghasal/yaghsil) to wash
لبِس/يلبَس (labis/yalbas) to wear/put on
وَجْه (وجُوه) (wajh, wujūh) face
دَرْس (دُرُوس) (dars, durūs) lesson/class
تَعْليم (taعlīm) education
الرِّياضَة (ar-riyāḍa) sport
التَّاريخ (at-tārikh) history
التَرِبية الدينيَّة (at-tarbīyya ad-dīnīyya) religious education
الجُغرافيا (al-jughrāfiyā) geography
الكيمياء (al-kīmiyā') chemistry
الموسيقى (al-mūsīqā) music
الرَسْم (ar-rasm) drawing/art
العَرَبيّة (al-عarabīyya) Arabic (language)
الاِنجليزية (al-injilīzīyya) English (language)
الرياضيَّات (ar-riyāḍiyyāt) mathematics
مُحاضَرة (ات) (muḥāḍara, muḥāḍarāt) lecture
كُلِّية (كُلِّيات) (kulliya, kulliyāt) faculty/college
مكتَبة (مكتَبات) (maktaba, maktabāt) library
أُستاذ (ustādh) professor
الطِّبّ (aṭ-ṭibb) medicine
الهَندَسة (al-handasa) engineering
الحُقوق (al-ḥuqūq) law
حَتَّى (ḥattā) until

17 Eating and drinking

At the grocer's عِنْدَ البَقَّال

 Look at the pictures and listen to the recording:

١ جُبْنة

٢ بَيْض

٣ خُبْز

٤ مَعْجُون الأَسْنَان

٥ حَلِيب

٦ زَيْت

٧ عَصِير بِرتقال

٨ مَسْحُوق الغَسِيل

٩ صَابُون

Exercise 1

Here are some more things you might buy in a grocer's shop. The Arabic is very similar to the English. Can you match them?

biscuits	أَرُزّ
shampoo	سُكَّر
rice	مَكَرُونَة
cake	شَامْبُو
sugar	بَسْكَوِيت
macaroni	كَعْك

Describing packaging

Here are some useful words to describe food packaging.

زُجاجة	(zujāja)	bottle
أنبوبة	(anbūba)	tube
علُبة	(ɛulba)	box/packet/tin/carton
كيس	(kīs)	bag/sack
قطِعة	(qiṭɛa)	piece

Now listen to these examples:

زُجاجة زَيت

عُلبة بَسكَويت

أنبوبة مَعجون الأسنان

كيس سُكّر

قطعة جِبنة

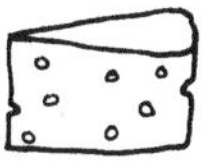

These are iḍāfa phrases, so the tā' marbūṭa will be pronounced if the first word is feminine: zujāj<u>at</u> zayt (a bottle of oil); ع‍ulb<u>at</u> baskawīt (a packet of biscuits), etc.

Exercise 2

Write the words in the box in one of the columns, as in the example. (There may be more than one correct answer.)

عصير برتقال	كولا	جبنة	حليب
مسحوق الغسيل	ماء	سكّر	شاي
معجون الطماطم	كعك	بُنّ	طماطم
مكرونة	تين	تفّاح	أرزّ

أنبوبة	قطعة	كيس	علبة	زجاجة
			حليب	

Listen to a customer buying some provisions.

صَباح الخَير	(ṣabāḥ al-khayr)	good morning
صَباح النور	(ṣabāḥ an-nūr)	good morning *(reply)*
مَساء الخَير	(masā' al-khayr)	good afternoon/evening
مَساء النور	(masā' an-nūr)	good afternoon/evening *(reply)*
مَعَ السلامة	(maɛa salāma)	goodbye
الله يُسَلِّمك	(āllah yusallimak(-ik))	goodbye *(reply to man/woman)*
أعطِني	(aɛṭinī)	give me
تَفَضَّل/تَفَضَّلي	(tafaḍḍal/tafaḍḍalī)	here you are *(to man/woman)*
تَحت أَمرك	(taḥt amrak(-ik))	at your service *(to man/ woman)*
الحِساب	(al-ḥisāb)	the bill

Exercise 3

Read the speech bubbles and think about which order they should be in:

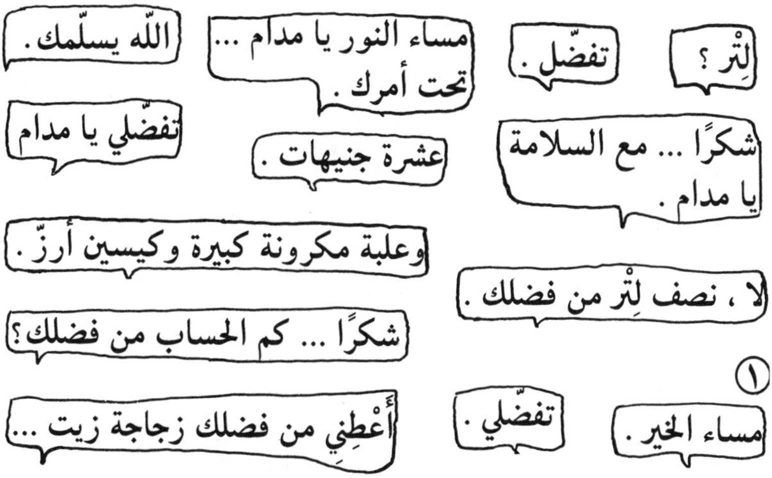

Now listen to the dialogue on the recording, and write numbers next to the bubbles in the correct order. The first is done for you.

In the restaurant

This newspaper advertisement appeared for the ليالينا (layālīna, 'Our nights') restaurant:

كامِل complete

خِدمة service

نُرَحِّب we welcome

شَهيّ delicious

فَقَط only

مَطعَم restaurant

Exercise 4

Look at the advertisement on page 229 and see how many of the details you can fill in on the form.

Tip: رَقم (raqm) = number as in 'figure' (e.g. telephone number);
عَدَد (ɛadad) = number as in 'quantity'

اِسم المطعم؟ .ليالينا.........................

اِسم الفندق؟ ....

المدينة؟ ....

عدد الأطباق؟ ....

رقم التليفون؟ ....

بكم العشاء؟..............................

بكم الخدمة؟...............................

Words for places

Many Arabic words for places begin with ma- (مـَ), for example مَطعَم (maṭɛam, restaurant). These words are called *nouns of place*. The root letters connected with a particular activity are put into the pattern مفعَل (mafɛal), or sometimes مفعلَة (mafɛala) or مفعِل (mafɛil), to mean the place where the activity happens. The root letters طعم (ṭ-ع-m) are connected with food, and so the noun of place, مطعم (maṭɛam, 'place of food'), has come to mean 'restaurant'.

Here are some more nouns of place you have already met:

مَدْرَسَة	'place of study', i.e. school, from root درس
مَكْتَب	'place of writing', i.e. office or desk, from root كتب
مَصْنَع	'place of manufacture', i.e. factory, from root صنع
مَتْحَف	'place for works of art', i.e. museum, from root تحف
مَجْلِس	'place of sitting', i.e. council, from root جلس

The plurals of nouns of place are predictable. Listen to these plurals and repeat the pattern.

مَدْرَسَة ← مَدَارِس

مَكْتَب ← مَكَاتِب

مَصْنَع ← مَصَانِع

مَتْحَف ← مَتَاحِف

مَجْلِس ← مَجَالِس

Exercise 5 Dictionary work

Using your existing knowledge and your dictionary, complete this table.

Plural	*Noun of place (meaning)*	*Verb (meaning)*
مَلاعِب	مَلعَب playing field/pitch/court	لَعِب/يَلْعَب to play
______	______ (______)	عرض/يعرِض (______)
______	مدخَل (______)	______ (______)
______	______ (______)	خرج/يخرُج (______)
______	مطعَم (______)	______ (______)
______	______ (______)	طبخ/يطبُخ (______)
______	______ (______)	غسل/يغسِل (______)
______	مسجِد (______)	______ (______)

Waiter! يا جرسون!

Listen to the dialogue between a customer and a waiter. The customer orders three courses and a drink.

Listen once without looking at the text. Can you make out some of the dishes the customer wants? Then listen again, following the Arabic.

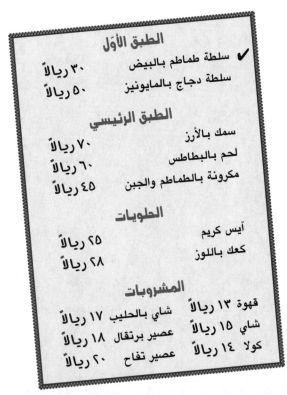

– يا جرسون! من فضلك!

– نعم!

– واحد سلطة طماطم بالبيض...

وبعد ذلك سمك بالأرز.

– تحت أمرك يا سيّدي. والمشروب؟

– آخذ عصير تفاح بارد من فضلك.

– تحت أمرك. هل تجرّب حلوياتنا الشهية بعد ذلك؟

– نعم. آخذ بعد ذلك آيس كريم بطعم الفانيليا.

– تحت أمرك.

Exercise 6

Put a tick next to the dishes the customer orders from the menu, as in the example.

الطبق الأوّل

✔ سلطة طماطم بالبيض ٣٠ ريالاً

سلطة دجاج بالمايونيز ٥٠ ريالاً

الطبق الرئيسي

سمك بالأرز ٧٠ ريالاً

لحم بالبطاطس ٦٠ ريالاً

مكرونة بالطماطم والجبن ٤٥ ريالاً

الحلويات

آيس كريم ٢٥ ريالاً

كعك باللوز ٢٨ ريالاً

المشروبات

قهوة ١٣ ريالاً

شاي ١٥ ريالاً

كولا ١٤ ريالاً

شاي بالحليب ١٧ ريالاً

عصير برتقال ١٨ ريالاً

عصير تفاح ٢٠ ريالاً

Exercise 7

Here is the customer's bill. Look at the menu and fill in the prices.

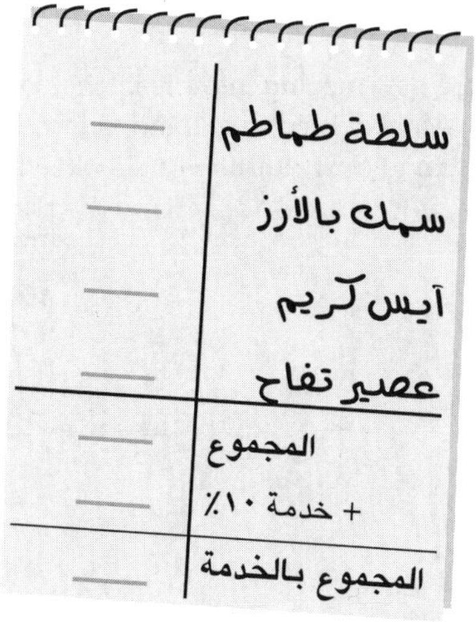

Exercise 8

Now imagine this is your bill, with some of the prices and dishes missing. Referring to the menu again, complete this bill:

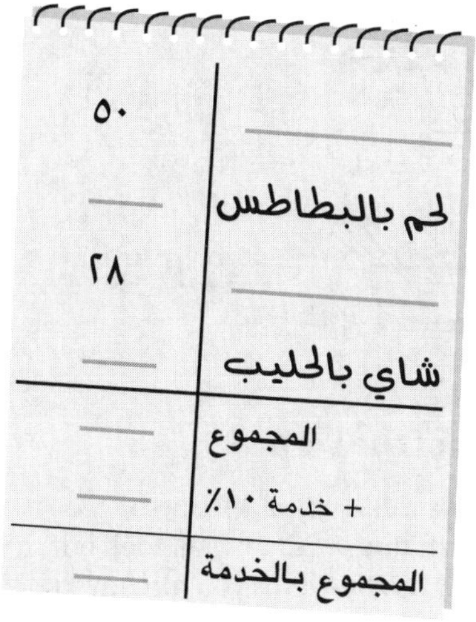

Conversation

At the restaurant

Use your completed bill from Exercise 8 and imagine that you are ordering this meal from the waiter. Prepare what you're going to say, using the dialogue on page 232 as a model, and then play the part of the customer on the recording.

In the kitchen في المَطبَخ

We are now moving into the kitchen of the restaurant to see what the cook, Ahmed, has been doing today.

Listen to the recording and look at the pictures.

أحمد طَبّاخ في مطعم . ماذا فعل اليوم ؟

غَسَلَ الأطباق .  سَخَّنَ الخبز . 

طَبَخَ اللحم .  أَخْرَجَ الزُبالة . 

نَظَّفَ المائدة . 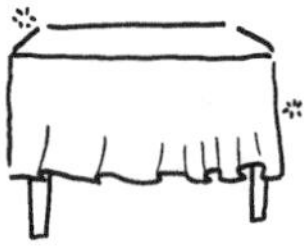 جَهَّزَ السلطة . 

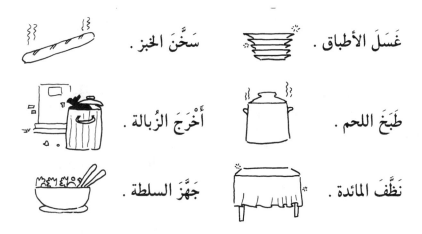

Forms of the verb

The verbs نظّف (naẓẓaf, cleaned), سخّن (sakhkhan, heated), جهّز (jahhaz, prepared) and أخرج (akhraj, took out) all follow a slightly different pattern from the verbs you already know. This is because they are *forms of the verb*.

In English you can sometimes find verbs which are derived from the same word, but which have slightly different endings which affect the meaning, for example:

liquefy
liquidate
liquidise

Arabic takes this concept of manipulation much further. The root letters of a verb can be put into a number of patterns to give different, but connected, meanings. These patterns are called *forms*.

There are ten forms altogether, but the ninth is rare. The basic form of the verb is *form I*. This is the form you already know. For example:

غَسَل/يَغْسِل (ghasal/yaghsil) to wash

دَرَس/يَدْرُس (daras/yadrus) to study

The other verb forms fall into three groups that share characteristics:

- Forms II, III and IV
- Forms V and VI
- Forms VII, VIII and X

The verbs نظّف (naẓẓaf), سخّن (sakhkhan), جهّز (jahhaz) and أخرج (akhraj) all fall into the first group of verb forms.

Forms II, III and IV

In the past tense forms II, III and IV are formed as follows:

- Form II: doubling the second root letter with a shadda (ـّ):

  فَعَل (faɛal) ⟵ (faɛɛal **فَعَّل**)

- Form III: adding a long ā *after the first root letter*:

  فَعَل (faɛal) ⟵ (fāɛal **فاعَل**)

- Form IV: adding a short a *before the first root letter* (and a sukūn over it):

  فَعَل (faɛal) ⟵ (afɛal **أَفْعَل**)

In the present tense, form II retains its shadda, form III its long ā and form IV its sukūn, but all three forms are vowelled with a ḍamma (ـُ) as the first vowel and a kasra (ـِ) as the last.

	Present, المُضارع	*Past,* الماضي
Form II	(yufaɛɛil) **يُفَعِّل**	(faɛɛal) **فَعَّل**
Form III	(yufāɛil) **يُفاعِل**	(fāɛal) **فاعَل**
Form IV	(yufɛil) **يُفْعِل**	(afɛal) **أَفْعَل**

The different forms have various general meaning patterns connected with them. For example, forms II and IV often make an action *transitive* (i.e. carrying out the action on someone/something else). So سخن (sakhan) means 'to be hot', but form II سخّن (sakhkhan) means 'to make hot' or 'to heat'. In a similar way, خرج (kharaj) means 'to go out', but form IV أخرج (akhraj) means 'to take out' or 'to eject'.

Form III can have the meaning pattern of doing something with someone else. For example, كتب (katab) means 'to write', but كاتب (kātab) means 'to write to someone else' or 'to correspond with'.

These meaning patterns are a guide which can help you expand your vocabulary through your knowledge of root letters. However, sometimes the reason why a particular form is used for a particular meaning is not obvious or has become altered over time, and you need to remember the individual verb.

The variations in the forms of the verb do not affect the endings and prefixes used to show the subject. These remain the same as those you have already learnt – see pages 156 and 218. The exception is that the first vowel of the present verb becomes 'u' in forms II, III and IV rather than 'a' in all the other forms:

هل سَخّنْتَ الخبز؟ (hal sakhkhanta l-khubz?)	Did you heat the bread? *(form II)*
سافرنا بالطائرة. (sāfarnā biṭ-ṭā'ira)	We travelled by plane. *(form III)*
كلّ يوم يُخْرِجون الزبالة. (kull yawm yukhrijūna z-zubāla)	Every day they take out the rubbish. *(form IV)*
أُنَظِّف المائدة بعد العشاء. (unaẓẓif al-mā'ida baɛda l-ɛashā')	I clean the table after dinner. *(form II)*

Forms of the verb in the dictionary

Very few root letters can be put into all the forms of the verb. Generally, most roots have *some* forms in common circulation.

If you look up a verb in Wehr's dictionary, you will find the forms referred to by Roman numerals. In the example entry for the root سخن on page 237, you can see that forms II and IV exist (although IV is not common). None of the other forms is used with this root.

سخن **sak̲una u, sak̲ana u** and **sak̲ina a** (سخونة **suk̲ūna,** سخانة **sak̲āna,** سخنة **suk̲na**) to be or become hot or warm; to warm (up); to be feverish **II** to make hot, to heat, warm (ه s.th.) **IV** = **II**

Exercise 9 Dictionary work

Using your existing knowledge and your dictionary, complete this table as in the example.

Meaning	*Present*	*Past*	*Form*	*Root*
to heat	يُسَخِّن	سَخَّن	II	سخن
______	______	______	III	سفر
______	______	______	II	صلح
______	______	______	IV	سلم
______	______	______	II	رتب
______	______	______	III	حدث
______	______	______	II	درس

Have you done it? هل فعلته؟

The owner of the restaurant is now checking that Ahmed has done everything he's supposed to:

Attached pronouns

In English we say '*our* house', putting the pronoun 'our' before the noun 'house'. However, with a verb we use a different pronoun and we put it *after* the verb: 'he saw *us*'. The same is true of '*their* dog' and 'I helped *them*', '*its* door' and 'she cleaned *it*', etc.

Arabic doesn't make this distinction. The same pronouns can be used with a verb or a noun, and they all come attached to the end of the word. For this reason, they are known as *attached pronouns*. You have already learnt these attached pronouns with nouns (see pages 60 and 127). Now you can also use them with verbs. The one small difference is that the attached pronoun -i (my) becomes -ni when used with a verb:

كتابي (kitābī) *my* book

استقبلني الوزير (istaqbala<u>nī</u> al-wazīr) the minister received *me*

Remember that non-human plurals are treated as *feminine singular*:

his/him, its/it *(masculine singular)* = ـهُ (-hu)

her, it/its *(feminine singular)* = ـها (-hā)

their/them *(human plurals)* = ـهُم (-hum)

their/them *(non-human plural)* = ـها (-hā) – same as *feminine singular*

Exercise 10

Look at the tasks on page 234 that Ahmed should have completed, and write three more questions and answers between the owner and Ahmed, following the examples on page 237.

Exercise 11

Now change these sentences to use attached pronouns, as in the example.

١ حَضر الوزير المعرض. حضره الوزير.

٢ استقبَلَت الرئيسة زعماء الأحزاب.

٣ استقبل الأمير وزير الخارجية.

٤ وجدت فاطمة الشباك المكسور.

٥ كل يوم يكتب محمود دروسه.

٦ عقد الرئيس جلسة عمل.

٧ شَرِبْتُ فنجان قهوة.

٨ كلّ يوم نطبخ العشاء مساءً.

He didn't do it لَم يَفْعَله

The next day the owner of the restaurant brings in Samir, a new cook, to replace Ahmed while he is on holiday. Look at the picture and listen to the recording:

لَمْ يَغْسِل الأطباق... لَمْ يَغْسِلها.

لَمْ يُنَظِّف المائدة... لَمْ يُنَظِّفها.

لم يطبخ اللحم... لم يطبخه.

Past negative

Remember that a present verb is made negative by putting لا (lā) in front, of the verb: لا أذهب بالسيارة (lā adhhab bis-sayyāra) I don't go by car/I'm not going by car.

There are *two* ways of making a past verb negative:

ما with *past verb*	ما غَسَلَ الأطباق	He didn't wash the dishes.
لَمْ with *present verb*	لَمْ يَغْسِل الأطباق	

لَمْ is more common in Modern Standard Arabic and ما is more common in spoken Arabic, but both are acceptable.

It can seem confusing that the *past* negative can be made with لَمْ and a *present* verb, but you can draw analogies to English – we say 'He *washed* the dishes' but 'he didn't *wash* the dishes'.

When لم is put in front of the present verb parts for أنتِ (anti, you *fem.*), أنتم (antum, you *pl.*) and هم (hum, they), the verb loses the nūn on the end. An extra, silent alif is written after the final wāw.

you *(fem.)* didn't mend	(lam tusalliḥī)	لم + تصلّحين = لم تصلّحي
you *(pl.)* didn't mend	(lam tusalliḥū)	لم + تصلّحون = لم تصلّحوا
they didn't mend	(lam yusalliḥū)	لم + يصلّحون = لم يصلّحوا

Exercise 12

Look back at the picture on page 239 and the sample sentences. Using the prompts below, make sentences about other tasks the replacement cook hasn't completed. You can use either لم or ما, as in the example.

١ أخرج/زُبالَة

لم يُخرِج الزُبالَة. لم يُخرِجها./ ما أخَرَجَ الزُبالَة. ما أخَرَجَها.

٢ نظّف/شبّاك

٣ سخن/خُبز

٤ صلّح/كرسيّ مكسور

٥ جهّز/سلطة

Exercise 13

The owner rings up Samir to find out what he's done. Make up a conversation between them. You could start like this:

– صباح الخير يا سمير. كيف المطعم؟ ماذا فعلتَ؟

– صباح النور. فعلتُ كلّ شيء.

– هل طبختَ اللحم؟

– ... لا، لم أطبخه.

Vocabulary in Unit 17

بَقّال (baqqāl) grocer

جُبْنَة (jubna) cheese

حَليب (ḥalīb) milk

بَيْض (bayḍ) eggs

زَيْت (zayt) oil

خُبْز (khubz) bread

عَصِير (ɛaṣīr) juice

أَرُزّ (aruzz) rice

سُكَّر (sukkar) sugar

مَكَرونَة (makarūna) macaroni

بَسْكَويت (baskawīt) biscuits

كَعْك (kaɛk) cake

مَسْحوق الغَسيل (masḥūq al-ghasīl) washing powder

مَعْجون الأَسْنان (maɛjūn al-asnān) toothpaste

صَابُون (ṣābūn) soap

شَامْبو (shāmbū) shampoo

أُنْبُوبَة (أَنابيب) (anbūba, anābīb) tube

قِطْعَة (قِطَع) (qiṭɛa, qiṭaɛ) piece

سَلَطَة (سَلَطَات) (salaṭa, salaṭāt) salad

آيس كِريم (āyis krīm) ice-cream

لَحْم (لُحوم) (laḥm, luḥūm) meat

جَرسون (garsūn) waiter

خِدْمَة (خِدْمَات) (khidma, khidmāt) service

كامِل (kāmil) complete

فَقَط (faqaṭ) only

شَهيّ (shahīy) delicious

طَبَّاخ (طَبَّاخون) (ṭabbākh, ṭabbākhūn) cook/chef

صباح / مَساء الخير (ṣabāḥ/masā' al-khayr) good morning/evening

صباح / مَساء النّور (ṣabāḥ/masā' an-nūr) *reply to above*

تَحت أمْرَك / أمْرِك (taḥt amrak/-ik) at your service *(to a man/woman)*

تَفَضَّل / تَفَضَّلي (tafaḍḍal/tafaḍḍalī) Here you are (take it, come in, etc.) *(to a man/woman)*

يا مَدام (yā madām) Madam

يا سَيِّدي (yā sayyidī) Sir

أَعْطِني (aɛṭinī) give me

معَ السَّلامَة (maɛa sālāma) goodbye

اللّه يسَلِّمك (allāh yusallimak/ik) *reply to a man/woman*

رَقْم (أَرْقام) (raqm, arqām) number *(numeral)*

عَدَد (أَعْداد) (ɛadad, aɛdād) number *(quantity)*

حِساب (حِسابات) (ḥisāb, ḥisābāt) bill

مَجْموع (majmūɛ) total

حَجَز / يحْجِز (ḥajaz/yaḥjiz) to book, reserve

لَعِب / يَلْعَب (laɛib/yalɛab) to play

عَرَض / يَعْرِض (ɛaraḍ/yaɛriḍ) to show/exhibit

طَبَخ / يَطْبُخ (ṭabakh/yaṭbukh) to cook

أَخَذ / يأخُذ (akhadh/ya'khudh) to take

صَلَّح / يُصَلِّح (ṣallaḥ/yuṣalliḥ) to mend

نَظَّف / يُنَظِّف (naẓẓaf/yunaẓẓif) to clean

سَخَّن / يُسَخِّن (sakhkhan/yusakhkhin) to heat

جَهَّز / يُجَهِّز (jahhaz/yujahhiz) to prepare

أَخْرَج / يُخْرِج (akhraj/yukhrij) to take out/eject

زُبالة (zubāla) rubbish

مَطْبَخ (مَطابِخ) (maṭbakh, maṭābikh) kitchen

مَلْعَب (مَلاعِب) (malɛab, malāɛib) playing field/pitch/court

مَدْخَل (مَداخِل) (madkhal, madhākhil) entrance

مَخْرَج (مَخارِج) (makhraj, makhārij) exit

مَسْجِد (مَساجِد) (masjid, masājid) mosque

مَغْسَلَة (مَغاسِل) (maghsala, maghāsil) laundry/launderette

unit 18 Comparing things

The biggest in the world الأكبَر في العالَم

Look at the pictures and listen to the recording:

هذا الولد طويل ...

ولكن هذه البنت أَطْوَل
من الولد . هي أَطْوَل بنت
في المدرسة .

هذا البيت قديم ...

ولكن هذا القصر أَقْدَم ...
هو أَقْدَم قصر في الدولة .

هذه السيّارة سَرِيعَة ...

ولكن هذه السيّارة
أَسْرَع ... هي أَسْرَع
سيّارة في العالَم .

البنت. (al-bint) the girl	من (min) than	أَطوَل (aṭwal) taller	هو (huwa) he/it (is)
القَصر. (al-qaṣr) the palace		أَقدَم (aqdam) older	هي (hiya) she/it (is)
هذه السيّارة (hādhihi s-sayyāra) this car		أَسرَع (asraع) faster	

المدرسة. (al-madrasa) the school	في (fī) in	أَطوَل ولد (aṭwal walad) the tallest boy	هو (huwa) he/it (is)
الدولة. (ad-dawla) the country		أَقدَم قَصر (aqdam qaṣr) oldest palace	هي (hiya) she/it (is)
العالَم (al-عālam) the world		أَسرَع سيّارة (asraع sayyāra) fastest car	

Comparatives and superlatives

Comparatives (taller, older, etc.) and *superlatives* (tallest, oldest, etc.) are formed in Arabic using the following pattern:

أَفعَل (afعal)

طويل tall/long → *root letters* **ط/و/ل** → **أَطوَل** taller/tallest

قديم old → *root letters* **ق/د/م** → **أَقدَم** older/oldest

سريع fast → *root letters* **س/ر/ع** → **أَسرَع** faster/fastest

Comparatives do not usually change according to whether they are describing something masculine, feminine or plural. The pattern remains the same:

هو أقدَم قصر في الدولة. (huwa aqdam qaṣr fī d-dawla)	It's the oldest palace in the country.
هي أطوَل بنت في المَدرَسة. (hiya aṭwal bint fī l-madrasa)	She's the tallest girl in the school.
هُم أسرَع من هؤلاء الأولاد. (hum asraع min hā'ulā'i l-awlād)	They're faster than these boys.

If the second and third root letters of an adjective are the same, they are written together with a shadda (ـّ) in the comparative. If the third root letter is wāw or yā', this changes to alif maqṣūra (see tip on page 77) in the comparative:

خَفيف light → *root letters* خ/ف/ف → أخَفّ lighter/lightest

حلِو sweet → *root letters* ح/ل/و → أحلَى sweeter/sweetest

Exercise 1

Make these adjectives into comparatives, as in the examples. The first nine adjectives should be familiar; the last six are new.

١ طويل – أطوَل (aṭwal)

٢ كبير – أكبَر (akbar)

٣ جميل

٤ قبيح

٥ صغير

٦ قديم

٧ جديد

٨ شديد

٩ سريع

١٠ رَخيص inexpensive/cheap

١١ كَثير a lot/many

١٢ فاضِل good

١٣ غَنيّ rich

١٤ فَقير poor

١٥ هامّ important

Exercise 2

Now choose one of the comparatives you formed in Exercise 1 to complete each sentence:

١ النيل (the Nile) ______ نهر في العالم.

٢ القاهرة ______ مدينة في أفريقيا.

٣ آسيا ______ قارّة (continent) في العالم.

٤ الفضّة ______ من الذهب.

٥ السيّارة ______ من الدرّاجة.

٦ اللوزة ______ من البطيخة.

At the car rental office عند مكتب استئجار السيّارات

Bashir wants to rent a car and has gone to the car rental office to enquire. Before you listen to his conversation, first decide what comparisons you might need to make between different cars available (for example, price). Then remind yourself of the Arabic adjectives and comparatives for these descriptions, for example, رخيص (rakhīṣ)/أرخص (arkhaṣ), inexpensive/more inexpensive.

Exercise 3

Listen once to the dialogue and see whether you can find out the following:

1 For how long does Bashir want the car?
2 When does he want the car rental to start?
3 Would he prefer a large or a small car?
4 What make and colour is the car he decides to rent?
5 How much is the rental per day?

Listen for a second time and fill in the chart below, comparing the three cars that Bashir is offered. Note: غالية (ghālya) = expensive *(fem.)*.

	Car 1	*Car 2*	*Car 3*
largest	✔		
smallest			
fastest			
newest			
cheapest			
most expensive			

Exercise 4

Put the phrases in the order you heard them in the dialogue between Bashir and the car rental assistant. Then listen to check your answer.

❑ عندنا هذه السيّارة الكبيرة الجميلة. ❑ بمائة وثمانين في اليوم.

❑ الحمراء أجدّ وأسرع سيّارة عندنا. ❑ نعم. هذا أفضل. آخذ البيضاء .

❑ الاسم، من فضلك... ❑ من متى يا سيّدي؟

❑ البيضاء أرخص وأصغر. ❑ بكم الحمراء؟

❑ من يوم السبت حتّى الخميس. ❑ غالية! هل هناك أرخص منها؟

[1] مساء الخير. أريد سيّارة لخمسة أيّام. ❑ ولكنّها قديمة. ممكن أجدّ منها؟

Comparing past and present

Fawzi and Fawzia have fallen on hard times. Look at the pictures of them now (الآن, al-ān) and twenty years ago (منذ عشرين سنة, mundhu ɛishrīn sana).

Now listen to the description and follow the text below.

مُنْذُ عِشرين سَنَة كان فَوْزي غَنِيًّا. كان أغْنَى رجُل في المَدينة...
ولَكنّه الآن فَقير وضَعيف.

في الماضي، كانَت زوجَتُه فَوْزيّة مُمَثِّلَة في الأفْلام السينمائيّة...
كان لَها أكبَر سيّارة في الشارِع... ولكِنَّها الآن فقيرة وليس لها
سيّارة، لها دَرَّاجة مكسورَة.

now, **الآن**	⟵ *the past,* **الماضي**
he is rich هو غَنيّ	he *was* rich كانَ غَنيًّا
she is an actress هي مُمَثِّلَة	she *was* an actress كانَت مُمَثِّلَة
she has a car لها سيّارة	she *had* a car كانَ لها سيّارة
له بيت جَميل he has a beautiful house	كانَ له بيت جَميل he *had* a beautiful house

Tip: Arabic expresses the concept of ‘ago’ using the word مُنذُ (mundhu) which literally means ‘since’: منذ عشرين سنة (mundhu ɛishrīn sana, twenty years ago), منذ يومين (mundhu yawmayn, two days ago), etc.

lākin + attached pronoun

If you want to follow the word لكن (lākin, but) with a pronoun (huwa, hiya, āna, etc.), then you must use the *attached pronouns* (see pages 60 and 127). In addition, the pronunciation before the pronoun will become lākinn(a). For example:

لكن (lākin) + **هو** (huwa) = **لكنّهُ** (lākinnahu)

لكن (lākin) + **هي** (hiya) = **لكنّها** (lākinnahā)

لكن (lākin) + **أنا** (āna) = **لكنّي** (lākinnī)

Exercise 5

Complete the following paragraphs about Fawzi and Fawzia, using the words in the box. (You may only use each word once.)

ولكنها	دجاجة	كان	جميلة	ليس
كانت	بيت	المدينة	أبيض	مُنذُ

_____ عِشرين سَنَة _____ فَوْزي غَنِيّاً. كان له _____

جميل وكبير في وسط _____ ، ولَكنّه الآن فقير و _____

له بيت.

في الماضي، _____ زوجَتُه فَوْزيّة غَنيَّة، وكان لها سيّارة

_____ وكبيرة وكلب _____ وصغير، _____ الآن فقيرة

وليس لها كلب، لها _____ .

Now listen to Fawzi telling us about how things used to be:

Was/were (kān)

Many sentences do not need the verb 'to be' in the present. However, it *is* required in the past. The verb كان (kān) is used.

kān is a little different from the other verbs you have met so far as it seems to have only two root letters. The root is actually ك/و/ن, but the wāw can change into a long or short vowel. In the past tense, the parts of the verb for huwa (he), hiya (she) and hum (they) have a long ā in the middle, but the other parts of the verb have a short u. However, the endings indicating the subject are still the same as other verbs:

I was	(أنا) كُنْتُ (kuntu)
you *(masc.)* were	(أنتَ) كُنْتَ (kunta)
you *(fem.)* were	(أنتِ) كُنْتِ (kunti)
he was	(هو) كانَ (kāna)
she was	(هي) كانَت (kānat)
we were	(نحن) كُنّا (kunnā)
you *(pl.)* were	(أنتم) كُنْتُم (kuntum)
they were	(هم) كانُوا (kānū)

Tip: kān is an important verb to learn. Try covering one of the two columns and testing yourself until you can remember all the different parts.

When the information that follows the verb kān (the *predicate*) is a noun or adjective *without* tā' marbūṭa, you need to add the additional alif tanwīn (اً), see page 144:

في الماضي كان فَوْزي غَنيًّا. (fī l-māḍī kāna fawzī ghanīyan)	In the past Fawzi was rich.
هل كُنتَ مدرّساً؟ (hal kunta mudarrisan)	Were you a teacher?

Exercise 6

Say and write the following in Arabic:

1 Ahmed was a teacher in the past.
2 The weather was hot yesterday.
3 I was in the office on Saturday.
4 The tree was taller than my house.
5 Where were you *(pl.)* at 9 o'clock?
6 We were in the centre of town.

Exercise 7

Fill in the gaps in the sentences using the correct form of kān, as in the example:

١ مُنْذُ عِشرين سَنَة كُنتُ غَنيًّا. الآن أنا فقير.

٢ منذ ثلاثين سَنَة ______ أحمد في الجيش. الآن هو محاسب في بنك.

٣ منذ نصف ساعة ______ في المدرسة. الآن هم في بيوتهم.

٤ منذ ستّين سَنَة ______ الرياض مدينة صغيرة. الآن هي أكبر مدينة في السعوديّة.

٥ في الماضي ______ مُدَرِّسًا. الآن أنتَ مُفَتِّش في وزارة التعليم.

٦ منذ دقيقتين ______ في البنك. الآن نحن عند البقّال.

Exercise 8

Now join the sentences in Exercise 7 using ولكن (wa-lākin), for example:

منذ عشرين سنة كُنتُ غنيًا ولكني الآن فقير.

Can you make two or three comparisons in Arabic like this about *your* life now and in the past?

Weak verbs

Verbs like kān that have either wāw (و) or yā' (ي) as one of the root letters are called *weak verbs*. This is because wāw and yā' are 'weak' letters that can be pronounced as consonants (w or y) or as vowels.

Most irregularities in Arabic verbs are due to wāw or yā' being one of the root letters, particularly the second or third root. The main consequence is that the root sound is often replaced by a long or short vowel, leaving only two obvious root consonants.

The precise rules as to how weak verbs behave take time and practice to absorb. However, it is possible to follow some general principles.

Hollow verbs

Weak verbs with wāw (و) or yā' (ي) as the *second* root letter are called *hollow verbs* since the middle root letter often disappears. kān is a hollow verb, as are many other common verbs. Their main charactistics are:

In the past:

- huwa, hiya and hum have a long ā in the middle (كانَت (kānat), she was; باعوا (bāεū), they sold)
- the other parts of the verb have a short vowel in the middle: u if the middle root letter is wāw (كُنتُ (kuntu), I was); and i if the middle root is yā' (بعنا (biεnā), we sold).

In the present:

- there is a long vowel in the middle: ī if the middle root letter is yā' (يزيد (yazīd), it increases); and usually ū if the middle root letter is wāw (أزور (azūr), I visit).

Defective verbs

Weak verbs with wāw (و) or yā' (ي) as the *third* root letter are called *defective verbs*. They are characterised by a long vowel at the end (مَشَى/يَمشي (mashā/yamshī), to walk; شكا/يشكو (shakā/yashkū, to complain).

In the past tense, this long vowel can change to ay or aw when an ending is added (مشَيت (mashaytu), I walked; شكَونا (shakawnā), we complained).

Weak verbs in the dictionary

You will need to look up weak verbs using the root letters, including wāw (و) or yā' (ي).

If you see the past of a hollow verb written like this – طار – or like this without vowels – طرت – you will not be able to tell whether the middle root letter is wāw or yā'. You may have to look in the dictionary under *both* roots. When you find the correct root you will see an entry like this:

> **(طير) طار *ṭāra* i (طيران *ṭayarān*) to fly; to fly away, fly off, take to the wing; to hasten, hurry, rush, fly (الى to); to be in a state of commotion, be jubilant, exult, rejoice; طار ب to snatch away,**

Exercise 9 Dictionary work

Here are some common weak verbs. Complete the table using your dictionary, as in the example:

المعنى *Meaning*	المصدر *Root*	المضارع *Present*	الماضي *Past*
to fly	ط/ي/ر	يَطير	طَارَ (طِرْتُ)
______	ز/و/ر	______	زَارَ ______
______	______	______	جرى ______
______	______	______	باع ______
______	______	يَعود	عاد ______
______	______	______	دعا ______
______	______	______	زاد ______
______	ق/و/ل	______	______ ______
______	ر/م/ي	______	______ ______

Forms of the verb: V and VI

The second group of verbal forms comprises forms V and VI.

In the past tense, forms V and VI look like forms II and III with تـ (ta-) added on the front:

Form V:

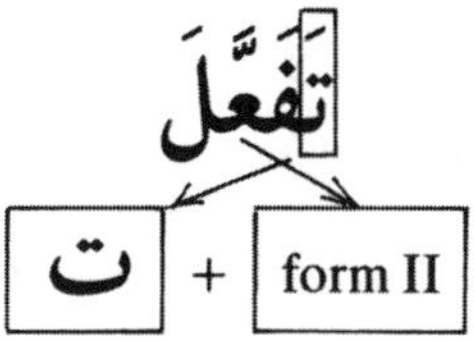

Form VI:

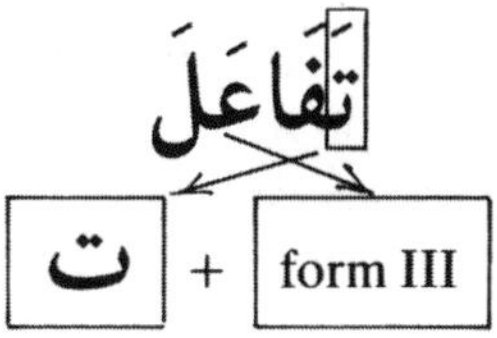

The present is similar to the past, with both tenses vowelled with fathas:

	Present المُضارع	*Past* الماضي
Form V	(yatafaععal) يَتَفَعَّل	(tafaععal) تَفَعَّل
Form VI	(yatafāعal) يَتَفاعَل	(tafāعal) تَفاعَل

Many common verbs are form V, and, like form I, the meaning is often *intransitive* (something you do yourself rather than an action performed on someone/something else). In contrast, form VI often carries the meaning of doing something together, or as a group.

to speak/talk (V)	(taḥaddath/yataḥaddath) تحدّث/يتحدّث
to learn (V)	(taعallam/yataعallam) تعلّم/يتعلّم
to remember (V)	(tadhakkar/yatadhakkar) تذكّر/يتذكّر
to cooperate (VI)	(taعāwan/yataعāwan) تعاون/يتعاون
to exchange (VI)	(tabādal/yatabādal) تبادل/يتبادل
to discuss/talk (VI)	(tanāqash/yatanāqash) تناقش/يتناقش

هل تتحدّث العربيّة؟ (hal tataḥaddath al-arabīyya)	Do you speak Arabic?
أين تعلّمتَها؟ (ayna taɛallamtahā)	Where did you learn it?
لا أتذكّر ابنك. (lā atadhakkar ibnak)	I don't remember your son.
نتعاون مع الوزارة. (nataɛāwan maɛa l-wizāra)	We are cooperating with the ministry.
تبادل الزعماء الأفكار وتناقشوا معًا. (tabādala zuɛamā' al-afkār wa-tanāqashū maɛan)	The leaders exchanged ideas and talked together.

Tip: Be careful not to confuse the additional تـ (ta-) of forms V and VI with the present tense تـ (ta-) prefix for 'you'. If appropriate you will need *both*, e.g. تتذكّر (tatadhakkar, *you* remember). In fact, the present tense of forms V and VI can generally be recognised by the distinctive opening sounds tata-, nata-, yata-, etc.

Exercise 10

Put these sentences into the past, as in the example.

١ نتعلّم الإنجليزيّة. - تعلّمنا الانجليزيّة.

٢ أتعلّم العربيّة.

٣ هل تتذكّر صَديقي مُنير؟

٤ تتعاون سميرة مع المدرّسين.

٥ نتناقش معًا.

٦ يتحدّث الوزراء عن المَعرَض ويتبادلون الأفكار.

Exercise 11

Write a short letter to a friend telling him or her about a day trip you took yesterday to an historic town near you. Look back at page 180 to remind yourself of some useful general phrases for letter writing. Follow this plan for your letter:

- open with some greetings
- tell your friend where you were yesterday
- ask your friend if he/she remembers this town
- you were with your friends, Nadia and Anwar
- you travelled by train because it's faster than the bus
- the weather was very cold, but the town was beautiful
- you visited the museum, but you didn't go to the market
- you learnt about the history of the town
- in the past, the museum was a palace (the oldest in the country)
- you didn't eat in a restaurant, you took sandwiches (سَندويتشات)

This exercise is a chance for you to create your own letter. There's no definitive correct answer, but it is a good idea to show your letter to a teacher or an Arabic-speaking friend if possible.

Vocabulary in Unit 18

العَالَم (al-ع‎ālam) the world

قَارَّة (قَارَّات) (qārra, qārrāt) continent

أَفريقيا (afrīqyā) Africa

آسيا (āsyā) Asia

النيل (an-nīl) the Nile

سَريع (sarīع‎) fast

حِلْو (ḥilw) sweet/beautiful

غَنيّ (ghanīy) rich

فَقير (faqīr) poor

هَامّ (hāmm) important

رَخيص (rakhīṣ) inexpensive/cheap

غالٍ، غالية (ghālin, ghālya) expensive *(masc., fem.)*

كَثير، أَكْثَر (kathīr, akthar) many/a lot, more/most

فاضِل، أَفْضَل (fāḍil, afḍal) good, better/best

استِئجار السيّارات (isti'jār as-sayyārāt) car rental

مُمَثِّل (مُمَثِّلون) (mumaththil, mumaththilūn) actor

مُمَثِّلة (مُمَثِّلات) (mumaththila, mumaththilāt) actress

الماضي (al-māḍī) the past

مُنْذُ (mundhu) since

سَنَة (سَنوات) (sana, sanawāt) year

مُنْذُ عشرين سنة (mundhu ɛishrīn sana) 20 years ago

الْيَوْم (al-yawm) today

الآن (al-ān) now

سَندويتش (سَندويتشات) (sandawītsh, sandawītshāt) sandwich

فِكْرَة (أَفكار) (fikra, afkār) idea/thought

كان / يكون (kān/yakūn) to be

طار / يطير (ṭār/yaṭīr) to fly

باع / يبيع (bāɛ, yabīɛ) to sell

قال / يقول (qāl/yaqūl) to say

زار / يزور (zār/yazūr) to visit

عاد / يَعود (ɛād/yaɛūd) to go back/return

زاد / يَزيد (zād/yazīd) to increase/go up (in price, etc.)

مَشى / يَمشي (mashā/yamshī) to walk

رَمى / يَرمي (ramā/yarmī) to throw

جَرى / يَجري (jarā/yajrī) to run

شَكا / يَشكو (shakā/yashku) to complain

دَعا / يَدعو (daɛā/yadɛu) to call

تَحَدَّث / يَتَحَدَّث (taḥaddath/yataḥaddath) to speak/talk

تَعَلَّم / يَتَعَلَّم (taɛallam/yataɛallam) to learn

تَذَكَّر / يَتَذَكَّر (tadhakkar/yatadhakkar) to remember

تَعاوَن / يَتَعاوَن (taɛāwan, yataɛāwan) to cooperate

تَبادَل / يَتَبادَل (tabādal, yatabādal) to exchange *(views, etc.)*

تَناقَش / يَتَناقَش (tanāqash, yatanāqash) to discuss

unit 19

Future plans

Months of the year أَشْهُر السَنَة

Look at the months and listen to the recording:

١ ينَايِر	٧ يُوليو
٢ فَبرايِر	٨ أَغُسْطُس
٣ مَارِس	٩ سِبتَمبَر
٤ أَبريل	١٠ أُكتُوبَر
٥ مايُو	١١ نوفَمبِر
٦ يونيو	١٢ ديسَمْبِر

Exercise 1

Write down the month *after* the one you hear on the recording. For example:

١ مارس

Now make sentences as follows:

١ شَهر مارس بعد فبراير وقبل ابريل.

The month of March is after February and before April.

If you look at the top of an Arabic newspaper or website, you may well see two dates. One refers to the Western calendar and one to the Muslim calendar. The most famous month of the Muslim calendar is Ramadan, the month of fasting. The Muslim date will have the letter hā' (هـ) after it, which stands for hijra (هجرة) or 'flight', as the calendar starts with the Prophet Muhammad's flight from Mecca to Medina in 622 AD. The Western date is followed by a mīm (م), which stands for mīlādīyya (ميلاديّة) or 'birth' (of Christ).

There are also alternative names for the months of the Western calendar, which are used in some Arab countries. The more international names are used here, but the alternatives and the months of the Muslim calendar appear in Appendix 3 for reference.

In the future
في المستقبل

Today is 22 February. Look at the Minister for Health's diary for this week and see whether you can work out what he is scheduled to do today.

اليوم

الظهر	الصباح	
	زيارة الكويت	فبراير ٢٠
٦,- نائب وزير الصحة	٩,٣٠ مؤتمر للممرضات في فندق ماريوت	فبراير ٢١
٥,- زيارة المستشفى الجديد	١٠,٣٠ اجتماع مع وزير الاقتصاد	فبراير ٢٢
٤,٤٥ جلسة عمل مع المساعدين في وزارة الصحّة	١١,- اجتماع مع رئيس الوزراء	فبراير ٢٣
	زيارة الأردنّ	فبراير ٢٤

 It's 11 o'clock in the morning. What's the Minister doing?

اليوم فِبرايِر ٢٢ والآن الساعة الحادية عشرة صباحًا.

الآن يحضُر وزير الصحّة اجتماعًا مع وزير الاقتصاد، وسيزور المستشفى الجديد الساعة الخامسة مساءً.

أمس، فِبرايِر ٢١ صباحًا، حضر الوزير مؤتمرًا للممرضات في فندق ماريوت، وبعد ذلك استقبل نائب وزارة الصحّة في مكتبه الساعة السادسة.

To express the future, you can simply add ‍سـ (sa-) in front of a present verb:

يحضُرُ الوزير اجتماعًا. (yaḥḍur al-wazīr ijtimāعan)	The minister is attending a meeting.
سيحضُرُ الوزير اجتماعًا. (sa-yaḥḍur al-wazīr ijtimāعan)	The minister will attend a meeting.
يزور المستشفى الجديد. (yazūr al-mustashfā l-jadīd)	He is visiting the new hospital.
سيزور المستشفى الجديد. (sa-yazūr al-mustashfā l-jadīd)	He will visit the new hospital.

Notice that all Arabic words, such as ‍سـ (sa-), which consist of only one letter with a short vowel are written together with the next word:

he will visit (sa-yazūr)	سيزُور	=	يَزُور	+	سَ
and a girl (wa-bint)	وبنت	=	بنت	+	وَ
Jihan has (li-jīhān)	لجيهان	=	جيهان	+	لِ
by car (bis-sayyāra)	بالسيّارة	=	السيّارة	+	بِ
so she returned (fa-rajaعat)	فَرَجَعَت	=	رَجَعَت	+	فَ

Exercise 2

غَدًا	(ghadan)	tomorrow
بَعدَ غد	(baɛda ghad)	the day after tomorrow
أمس	(ams)	yesterday
أوّل أمس	(awwal ams)	the day before yesterday

Using the diary on page 261, fill in the gaps in this description of the minister's schedule tomorrow, 23 February:

غَدًا، ٢٣ فبراير صباحًا، سيحضُر الوزير ______ مع ______

الوزراء الساعة الحادية ______ و ______ ذلك ______ جلسة

عمل مع ______ في وزارة ______ الساعة ______ إلا ربعًا.

Now write a similar description for his schedule on 20 and 24 February, taking care to use the correct tense.

Exercise 3

Think of something on your agenda today. It could be anything – going to school, university or work, going to a restaurant, attending a meeting or an exhibition, etc. In addition, think of something else that you did yesterday and the day before yesterday, and one thing that you will do tomorrow and likewise the day after tomorrow.

Firstly, try to write each event for the five days in note form in Arabic as if in a diary. Then write a description of your schedule for each day. For example, you could start something like this:

اليوم ١٤ أبريل والآن الساعة السادسة مساءً. سأذهب إلى وسط المدينة مع أمّي وسنأكل سمكًا في مطعم.

غدًا، ١٥ أبريل، سأحضر اجتماعًا في المكتب صباحًا.

An international tour

This is a newspaper article about an international tour due to be conducted by an American politician.

وزير الدفاع الأمريكي غدا في باريس ويزور الكويت ٦ ديسمبر

واشنطن : أعلن هنا أمس أن وزير الدفاع الأمريكي سيغادر واشنطن غدًا، الاثنين إلى باريس في جولة تشمل ٦ دول في أوروبا والخليج.

وسيغادر الوزير بروكسل إلى الخليج يوم الجمعة ويزور عُمان في الفترة من ٢ إلى ٤ ديسمبر والبحرين ٥ ديسمبر والسعودية يوم ٦ من الشهر ذاته ويزور الكويت في السابع من الشهر المذكور قبل أن يعود إلى واشنطن.

غادَر/يُغادِر	(ghādar/yughādir)	to leave
أوروبا	(ūrūbā)	Europe
الخَليج	(al-khalīj)	the Gulf
فِترة	(fitra)	period (of time)
المَذكور	(al-madhkūr)	the (above) mentioned

Exercise 4

Firstly, read the six questions below and give yourself *three minutes* to find as many of the answers as you can in the article.

1 What is the position of the minister in the American government?
2 How many countries will he visit on his tour?
3 Name three of the countries he will visit.
4 When is he starting his tour?
5 Where is he setting out from?
6 Where is he going first?

Exercise 5

Now match the cities with the countries in which they can be found:

واشِنطُن	فَرَنسا
بـاريس	البَحرين
بروكسل	عُمان
الرِّياض	أمريكا
المَنامَة	بَلجيكا
مَسْقَط	السَّعودية

Using the article and your answers above, plot on the map below the route the minister will be taking. The first leg has been done for you.

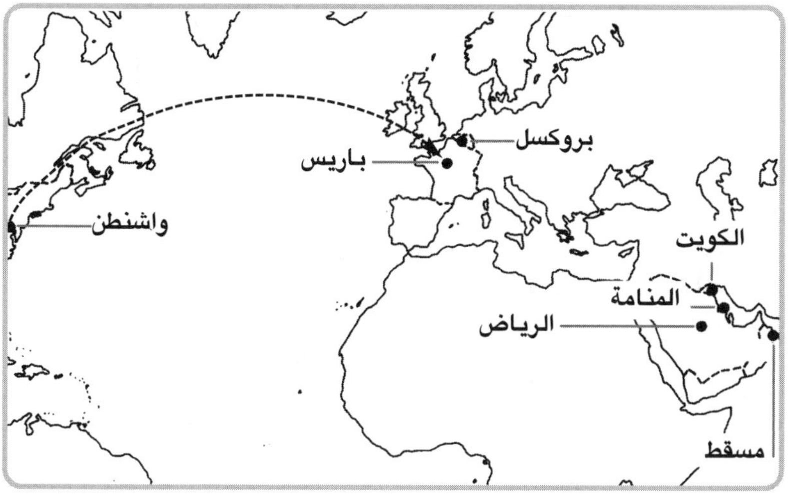

Exercise 6

Use your map and the article to fill in the missing information below.

يوم الاثنين ٢٨ نوفمبر: واشنطن إلى باريس

يوم الخميس ١ ديسمبر: باريس إلى ______

______ ______ ٢ ديسمبر: ______ إلى مسقط

يوم الأحد ٤ ______: مسقط إلى المنامة

يوم الاثنين __ ______: المنامة إلى ______

يوم الثلاثاء __ ______: ______ إلى الكويت

Exercise 7

Use the two tables below and the information in Exercise 6 to make sentences about the minister's tour, as in the examples:

	واشنطن		واشنطن		الاثنين	
	باريس		باريس		الثلاثاء	
	بروكسل		بروكسل		الأربعاء	— نوفمبر.
سَيُغَادِر	الكويت	إلى	الكويت	يوم	الخميس	
	مسقط		مسقط		الجمعة	— ديسمبر.
	البحرين		البحرين		السبت	
	الرياض		الرياض		الأحد	

	باريس				
	بروكسل	في الفَتْرَة من	— نوفمبر		— نوفمبر.
سَيَزُور	مسقط	(in the period		إلى	
	الكويت	from...)	— ديسمبر		— ديسمبر.
	البحرين				

سيغادر الوزير واشنطن إلى باريس يوم الاثنين ٢٨ نوفمبر.

The minister will leave Washington for Paris on Monday, 28 November.

سيزور باريس في الفترة من ٢٨ نوفمبر إلى ١ ديسمبر.

He will visit Paris in the period from 28 November to 1 December.

The flying bicycle الدرّاجة الطائرة

Mad Professor Filfil has invented a flying bicycle. He's testing his invention on a bystander. Listen to the story following the comic strip (from *right to left*).

Forms of the verb: VII, VIII and X

VII, VIII and X make up the final group of verbal forms. These three forms share characteristics:

- the *past* tense has an initial 'i' (اِ) but is otherwise vowelled with 'a'
- the *present* tense is the opposite – vowelled with 'a' except the final vowel, which is 'i'.

	Present المُضارع	*Past* الماضي
Form VII	(yanfaعil) **يَنفَعِل**	(infaعal) **اِنفَعَل**
Form VIII	(yaftعil) **يَفتَعِل**	(iftaعal) **اِفتَعَل**
Form X	(yastafعil) **يَستَفعِل**	(istafعal) **اِستَفعَل**

Examples

Form VII can be recognised by the nūn *before* the root letters. This form often has a passive meaning:

to be broken; to become broken	اِنْكَسَر / يَنْكَسِر
to be thrust forward; to move off	اِنْطَلَق / يَنْطَلِق

Form VIII is common and can be recognised by the tā' *between* the first and second root letters:

to come close (to); to approach	اِقْتَرَب / يَقْتَرِب
to meet; to gather together	اِجْتَمَع / يَجْتَمِع

Form X can be recognised by the sīn and tā' together ('st') *before* the root letters.

to receive (guests, etc.)	اِسْتَقْبَل / يَسْتَقْبِل
to take up (time); to last	اِسْتَغْرَق / يَسْتَغْرِق

Exercise 8

Here is some new vocabulary from the comic strip on page 269. Try to guess the words and phrases using the context and your existing knowledge, as in the example.

he fell	اِنتَبِه!
he took off	زُجاجة بَنزين
it seems that	اِقترِب!
it is necessary that	سَقَطَ
watch out!	قَبل أن تُحاول
the ground	يَبدو أن
a bottle of petrol (benzīn)	لا بُدّ أن
come closer!	بَعد قَليل
before you try	الأرض
in a little while	أقلَعَ

Check your answers in the answer section. Then listen again to the comic strip and see how much more you can understand.

Other features of verbs

You now have a good idea about how Arabic verbs work in general, including the past and present tenses, the future using sa- with the present tense, negative verbs, weak verbs, and forms of the verb.

There are other features of Arabic verbs which will help you to recognise vocabulary and manipulate roots. For example, verbs can be turned into nouns or participles to create related words. These often follow predictable patterns, particularly with the forms of the verb. Here are a few examples using familiar words:

مكسور (maksūr) broken, *passive part., form I* **كسر** (kasar) to break

اجتماع (ijtimāع) meeting, *noun, form VIII* **اجتمع** (ijtamaع) to meet

مدرّس (mudarris) teacher, *active part., form II* **درّس** (darras) to teach

اسلام/مُسلم (islām/muslim) Islam/Muslim, *noun/active part., form IV* **اسلم** (aslam) to surrender (to God)

دِفاع (difāع) defence, *noun, form III* **دافع** (dāfaع) to defend

We cannot cover all the different possibilities within the scope of this course, but you will find a summary in Appendix 2. This will be a useful reference when you want to identify the root letters in a word and look it up in the dictionary. With time and further study, you will learn to recognise these patterns and start to manipulate them yourself.

Exercise 9 Dictionary work

Using your dictionary, complete this table as in the example.

Meaning	*Present*	*Past*	*Form*	*Root*
to move off	يَنطَلِق	اِنطَلَق	VII	طلق
______	______	______	VIII	نبه
______	______	______	X	علم
______	______	______	VIII	شغل
______	______	______	X	خدم
______	______	______	VIII	سمع
______	______	______	VII	قلب

Vocabulary in Unit 19

شَهْر (أَشْهُر) (shahr, ash-hur) month

يَنَاير (yanāyir) January

فِبرايِر (fibrāyir) February

مَارِس (māris) March

أَبريل (abrīl) April

مايُو (māyū) May

يونيو (yūniyū) June

يُوليو (yūliyū) July

أَغُسْطُس (aghustus) August

سِبتَمبِر (sibtambir) September

أُكتُوبَر (uktūbir) October

نوفَمبِر (nūfambir) November

ديسَمْبِر (dīsambir) December

المُسْتَقْبَل (al-mustaqbal) the future

غَداً (ghadan) tomorrow

بَعْدَ غد (baعda ghad) the day after tomorrow

أَوَّل أَمْس (awwal ams) the day before yesterday

أوروبا (ūrūbā) Europe

الخَليج (al-khalīj) the Gulf

فَتْرَة (فَتْرَات) (fatra, fatrāt) period (of time)

مذكور (madhkūr) (above) mentioned

الأرض (al-arḍ) the ground

سَقَط/يَسقُط (saqaṭ/yasquṭ) to fall

حَاوَل / يُحاوِل (ḥāwal/yuḥāwil) to try, to attempt

غَادَر / يُغادِر (ghādar/yughādir) to leave, to depart

أَقْلَع / يُقْلِع (aqlaع/yuqliع) to take off (aeroplane, etc.)

اِنْطَلَق / يَنْطَلِق (inṭalaq/yanṭaliq) to move off, to set out

اِنْتَبَه / يَنْتَبِه (intabah/yantabih) to take care, to watch out

اِقْتَرَب / يَقْتَرِب (من) (iqtarab/yaqtarib) to come close (to), to approach

اِجْتَمَع / يَجْتَمِع (ijtamaع/yajtamiع) to meet, to gather together

اِسْتَغْرَق / يَسْتَغْرِق (istaghraq/yastaghriq) to take up (time), to last

لابُدَّ أن (lā budd an) It is necessary that ...

يَبْدُو أن (yabdū an) It seems/appears that ...

unit 20

Review and advice on further study

Review

Exercise 1

Fill in the missing words in the shopping phrases, and then put the conversation in the correct order:

❑ ونصف ــــــ جبنة بيضاء من فضلِك. كم ــــــ؟

❑ صباح النور يا سيّدي.

❑ تحت ــــــ ... تَفَضّل.

❑ أعطني ــــــ فضلِك كيس سُكَّر وــــــ عصير تُفّاح.

❑ صباح ــــــ.

❑ اللّه يسلِّمَك.

❑ ١٣ جنيه من ــــــ.

❑ تفضّلي. ــــــ السَلامَة.

Exercise 2

Listen to Salwa and Ahmad in a restaurant. Fill in the chart below according to what they decide to order, as in the example.

الحلويات	الطبق الرئيسي	الطبق الأوّل	المشروبات	
			عصير منجة	سلوى
				أحمد

Exercise 3

Look back at the menu on page 232 and choose a meal for a vegetarian customer.

Then make up a conversation similar to that on page 232 between the waiter and the (male) customer ordering the vegetarian meal.

Finally, complete the bill below for your vegetarian customer.

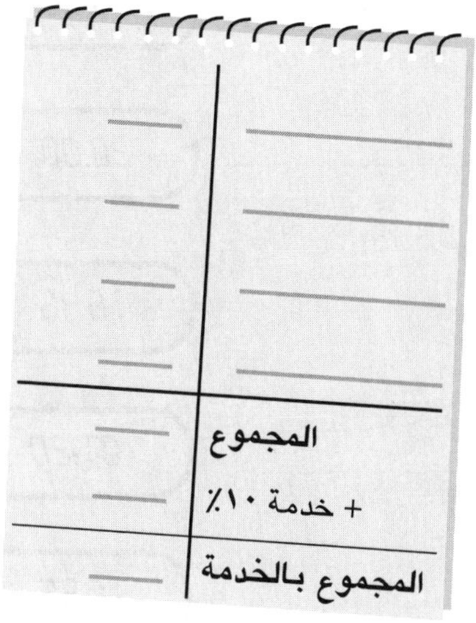

Exercise 4

Write the plural of these words, as in the example:

١ بَيْت – بُيُوت
٢ شَيخ
٣ وَكيل
٤ كِتاب
٥ وَزير
٦ مَكتَب
٧ قِطار
٨ مُمَثِّلَة
٩ مَدينَة
١٠ مُساعِد
١١ دَرس
١٢ سَنة
١٣ مَتْحَف
١٤ طَبَق
١٥ أَمير

Try to make sentences containing each of the plurals, e.g.:

هناك بيوت جميلة في المدينة القديمة.

There are beautiful houses in the old town.

Exercise 5

Look at the clocks and give the time and date in Arabic, as in the example.

١ 

الساعة الثانية ظهرًا، يوم ١٤ يناير

٢ 

____

٣ 

____

٤ 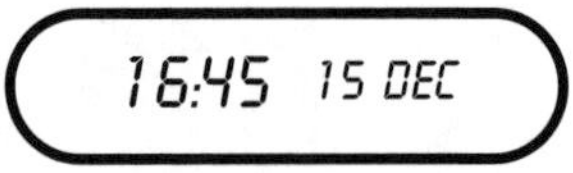

____

٥ 

____

٦ 

____

Exercise 6

Last year, Fatima went on a seven-month tour of the world. Listen to her talking about where she went, and write the countries next to the months in which she visited them.

March	France/Belgium
April	________
May	________
June	________
July	________
August	________
September	________

Exercise 7

How many of these verbs can you remember? Fill in the chart below, as in the example.

Meaning	*Form*	*Present*	*Past*
to approach	VIII	يَقتَرِب	اِقتَرَب
______	______	______	أَخْرَج
______	______	يَغْسِل	______
______	______	يَنْطَلِق	______
to mend/fix	II	______	______
______	______	______	اِجتَمَع
______	______	______	عَقَد
to try/attempt	III	______	______
______	______	يُرَتِّب	______
to clean	______	______	______
______	______	______	زار
______	______	يَتَعاوَن	______
______	______	______	تَذَكَّر
______	______	يَسْتَغْرِق	______

Exercise 8

Re-write these sentences, starting with the phrase in brackets, as in the example.

> *Remember:*
>
> | *Present negative* | *Past negative* |
> |---|---|
> | **لا** + *present verb* | **ما** + *past verb* or |
> | | **لَمْ** + *present* (without final ن if applicable) |

١ **عقد الوزير أمس جلسة عمل.** (كلّ يوم...)

كلّ يوم يعقد الوزير جلسة عمل.

٢ **ذهبَت زينب أمس إلى البنك.** (كلّ يوم...)

٣ **زُرْنا أوَّل أمس المتحف في وسط المدينة.** (غداً...)

٤ **كل يوم ينظِّفون الأطباق.** (أمس...)

٥ **لا نتذكّر اسم المدرسة.** (أمس...)

٦ **ينطلق الأصدقاء الآن إلى المدينة.** (منذ ٣ ساعات...)

٧ **اجتمع وزراء الاقتصاد في عَمَّان وتبادلوا الأفكار.** (اليوم...)

٨ **في السنوات الماضية لم تَتَعاوَن دُوَل العالم الثالث.** (الآن...)

Exercise 9

Look at the list on page 277 of things Nadia has to do today. It is now the afternoon and she has ticked off what she has done so far.

Using the verbs in the box and looking at the list, make sentences about what Nadia has done today, as in the example.

غسل / يغسل	ذهب / يذهب	رتَّب / يرتِّب	طبَخ / يطبُخ
نظَّف / ينظِّف	أخرج / يُخرِج	كتَب / يكتُب	صلّح / يُصلِّح

لم تُصَلِّح درّاجتها المكسورة.

لم تُصَلِّحها.

She didn't mend her bicycle.

She didn't mend it.

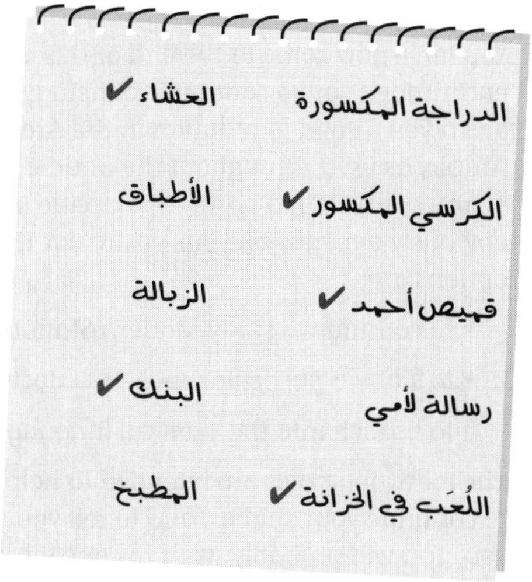

Conversation

Review

In your final review, you're going to tell us about yourself, your job or studies, and what you did for your holiday last year.

Firstly, prepare the following information in Arabic. Look back at the relevant units if you need to remind yourself of the language you'll need.

- your name
- where you're from
- your occupation (job/student – look in a dictionary if necessary)
- where you went for your holiday last year
- what month it was
- how you travelled
- what the weather was like
- one thing you did on holiday and one thing you ate
- one thing you *didn't* do

Now join in the conversations on the recording. You'll be asked questions which will prompt the information you have prepared. There is no single correct answer – the reply is up to you. Replay the conversation as many times as you like, making up different answers every time.

Good luck! حَظّ سَعيد!

Advice on further study

You have now come to the end of this course and we hope that it has encouraged you to continue your study of Arabic. *Mastering Arabic* has given you a solid foundation in the Arabic script and informal standard Arabic, as used throughout the Middle East.

You are now in a position to decide in which direction to go, and this obviously depends on your particular needs and interests. Your main options are:

- to continue to study Modern Standard Arabic in more depth
- to study a particular spoken dialect
- to branch into the classical language.

The following notes are intended to help you decide how you would like to continue your studies, and to tell you what material is available to you. You will probably want to concentrate on one of the above options, but they are not mutually exclusive and you may like to sample them all.

Modern Standard Arabic

If you have an interest in understanding Arabic in the form of TV and radio programmes, newspapers, comics, books, signs, advertisements, correspondence, conference proceedings, formal speeches, etc., then you should continue to expand your knowledge of Modern Standard Arabic (MSA).

Course books

There are a number of programmes for MSA which will take you beyond the scope of *Mastering Arabic*. Most have accompanying audio and some have video, although this can be expensive. Make sure you choose one that matches your needs. Some, for example, are designed for use in a classroom and are difficult to follow if you're working by yourself. Others may be traditional and not contain a variety of activities and exercises. Try to find one which suits your style of learning. You could classify your level now as 'early intermediate'.

If you are interested in continuing to study MSA, you should also make sure you have good dictionaries and reference books for grammar, verbs and vocabulary. Again, choose carefully. It's better to take your time and browse than to choose a title blind and find that it doesn't suit your style of learning or your level. If possible, try to find some reference titles that include an element of practice (not just the translation of unconnected sentences).

Arabic media

There is a wealth of other material for you to use to improve your knowledge of Modern Standard Arabic. The growth of Arabic TV satellite stations and internet sites has triggered a renaissance and revitalisation of 'standard' Arabic. Pan Arab communication has suddenly become much more common and immediate than it was before. Politicians, leading personalities and members of the public from different parts of the Middle East now routinely take part in interviews and chat shows intended for a pan Arab audience. It is possible to hear a wide range of Arabic accents and levels of formality all within the same programme, and sometimes within the same sentence! Arabic-speakers from all walks of life are also growing more used to adjusting their language to make themselves understood outside their local area.

Many of these satellite stations are available outside the Middle East, as are Arabic newspapers, magazines and comics. You can sometimes also find short comic strips and cartoons on Arabic websites.

Literature

In 1988 Naguib Mahfouz, an Egyptian writer, won the Nobel prize for literature. He died in 2006 at the age of 94. The prize created international interest in modern Arabic literature. Mahfouz himself has written many novels which can be found outside the Arab World both in the original Arabic and in translation. However, Mahfouz's Arabic style is difficult for a beginner and it would be better to start with graded extracts from literature and then progress to authors such as Taha Hussein or Jibran Khalil Jibran, who use a simpler style. Children's books and fables are also a good way of introducing yourself to Arabic stories.

Look around you

If you go to a part of town where there are a lot of Arabic-speakers, you can look at the signs, posters, labels on imported food, etc. A word of warning: other languages are also written in Arabic script (for example, Farsi and Urdu), so do not panic if you come across material in which all the words look totally unfamiliar and the script has some strange additions. You will also find ingredients and instructions written in Arabic on many food packages and household products.

Spoken dialects

Native speakers are not as aware as learners of the differences between spoken dialects and Modern Standard, and will slip in and out of them quite easily. In informal talk and chat you will find conversations difficult to follow if you cannot understand the dialect.

If your main interest is in talking to Arabic-speakers in everyday informal situations, therefore, you should acquire a knowledge of the appropriate spoken dialect. These vary from region to region but are all more or less related to MSA, so your knowledge will be very useful. In this course, we have tried to point out where there are variations from MSA which are common to many spoken dialects, but to gain fluency you will need either access to native speakers or a course in your chosen dialect, or ideally both.

There are many programmes designed to teach you the dialect of a particular country or region. If possible, choose one that includes Arabic script as well as transliteration (English letters). Having mastered the script, you will find it useful to be able to compare dialect written in Arabic as well as transliteration. If you are unsure about which dialect to learn, then it is best to opt for either *Egyptian* or *Levant* (Syria, Jordan, etc.), as these are the most widely understood.

Classical Arabic

Classical Arabic, as used in the Qur'an and other religious and classical literature, is structurally not that different from MSA. It is the use of vocabulary and the style of the language that varies, just as Shakespearian English is different from English in *The Times* newspaper.

There are specialist dictionaries and reference books for classical Arabic. They are not always very user-friendly, however, and may be old and difficult to follow. You may find it easier to continue to study Modern Standard and to combine this with reading classical texts which have translations alongside the Arabic, so that you acquire a feel for the style.

It only remains to wish you luck, and to hope that this book has given you the foundation you need to continue to master Arabic.

part 2

Reference material

Appendixes

Appendix 1: The Arabic alphabet

Final	*Medial*	*Initial*	*Isolated*	*Letter*
ـا	ـا	ا	ا	ألف (alif)
ـب	ـبـ	بـ	ب	باء (bā′)
ـت	ـتـ	تـ	ت	تاء (tā′)
ـث	ـثـ	ثـ	ث	ثاء (thā′)
ـج	ـجـ	جـ	ج	جيم (jīm)
ـح	ـحـ	حـ	ح	حاء (ḥā′)
ـخ	ـخـ	خـ	خ	خاء (khā′)
ـد	ـد	د	د	دال (dāl)
ـذ	ـذ	ذ	ذ	ذال (dhāl)
ـر	ـر	ر	ر	راء (rā′)
ـز	ـز	ز	ز	زاي (zāy)
ـس	ـسـ	سـ	س	سين (sīn)
ـش	ـشـ	شـ	ش	شين (shīn)

Final	*Medial*	*Initial*	*Isolated*	*Letter*
ـص	ـصـ	صـ	ص	صاد (ṣād)
ـض	ـضـ	ضـ	ض	ضاد (ḍād)
ـط	ـطـ	طـ	ط	طاء (ṭā’)
ـظ	ـظـ	ظـ	ظ	ظاء (ẓā’)
ـع	ـعـ	عـ	ع	عين (ع‎ayn)
ـغ	ـغـ	غـ	غ	غين (ghayn)
ـف	ـفـ	فـ	ف	فاء (fā’)
ـق	ـقـ	قـ	ق	قاف (qāf)
ـك	ـكـ	كـ	ك	كاف (kāf)
ـل	ـلـ	لـ	ل	لم (lām)
ـم	ـمـ	مـ	م	ميم (mīm)
ـن	ـنـ	نـ	ن	نون (nūn)
ـه	ـهـ	هـ	ه	هاء (hā’)
ـو	ـو	و	و	واو (wāw)
ـي	ـيـ	يـ	ي	ياء (yā’)

فتحة (fatḥa) — a dash above the letter, pronounced as a short ‘a’ after the letter, e.g. ...بَـ (ba)

ضمّة (ḍamma) — a comma-shape above, pronounced as a short ‘u’ after the letter, e.g. ...بُـ (bu)

كسرة (kasra) — a dash below, pronounced as a short ‘i’ after the letter, e.g. ...بِـ (bi)

سكون (sukūn) — a small circle above, showing that *no vowel* follows the letter, e.g. بِنْت (bint, girl)

شدّة (shadda) — a small ‘w’ shape, above showing that the letter is *doubled*, e.g. بُنّ (bunn, coffee beans)

مدّة (madda) — a wavy symbol written over an alif and pronounced ā, e.g. آنسة (ānisa, young woman)

(Note: These symbols are not generally included in modern written Arabic. This book uses them where necessary for clarity.)

Appendix 2: The Arabic verb

Tenses

Past tense

The feminine plural verbs are relatively uncommon and so have not been taught. They are included here for your reference.

Example	*Ending*	
I opened (fataḥtu) فَتَحتُ	(-tu) تُ	أنا I
you *(m.)* opened (fataḥta) فَتَحتَ	(-ta) تَ	you *(m.)* أنتَ
you *(f.)* opened (fataḥti) فَتَحتِ	(-ti) تِ	you *(f.)* أنتِ
he/it opened (fataḥa) فَتَحَ	(-a) ـَ	he/it هو
she/it opened (fataḥat) فَتَحَت	(-at) ـَت	she/it هي
we opened (fataḥnā) فَتَحنا	(-nā) نا	we نَحنُ
you *(m. pl.)* opened (fataḥtum) فَتَحتُم	(-tum) تُم	you *(m. pl.)* أنتُم
you *(f. pl.)* opened (fataḥtunna) فَتَحتُنَّ	(-tunna) تُنَّ	you *(f. pl.)* أنتُنَّ
they *(m.)* opened (fataḥū) فَتَحوا	(-ū) وا	they *(m.)* هُم
they *(f.)* opened (fataḥna) فَتَحنَ	(-na) نَ	they *(f.)* هُنَّ

Present/future tense

The feminine plural verbs are also included for your reference.

Example	*Ending*	*Prefix*	
I open (aftaḥ[u*]) أفتَح		(a-) أَ	أنا
you *(m.)* open (taftaḥ[u*]) تَفتَح		(ta-) تَـ	أنتَ
you *(f.)* open (taftaḥīna) تَفتَحينَ	(-īna) ينَ	(ta-) تَـ	أنتِ
he/it opens (yaftaḥ[u*]) يَفتَح		(ya-) يَـ	هو
she/it opens (taftaḥ[u*]) تَفتَح		(ta-) تَـ	هي
we open (naftaḥ[u*]) نَفتَح		(na-) نَـ	نَحنُ

you *(m. pl.)* open (taftaḥūna) تَفتَحونَ	(-ūna) ونَ	(ta-) تَـ	أنتُم
you *(f. pl.)* open (taftaḥna) تَفتَحنَ	(-na) نَ	(ta-) تَـ	أنتُنَّ
they *(m.)* open (yaftaḥūna) يَفتَحونَ	(-ūna) ونَ	(ya-) يَـ	هُم
they *(f.)* open (yaftaḥna) يَفتَحنَ	(-na) نَ	(ya-) يَـ	هُنَّ

* *The full pronunciation includes a final u, but this is not heard except in formal contexts.*

There are also special verb endings for 'they' and 'you' when the subject is dual. ا (-ā) is added to past verbs and ان (-ān) to present verbs:

they both attended حَضَرا (ḥaḍarā)

you both drank شَرِبتُما (sharibtumā)

they both travel يُسافران (yusāfirān)

you both cooperated يَتَعاوَنان (yataعāwanān)

Forms of the verb

	Present المُضارع	*Past* الماضي
Form II	(yufaععil) يُفَعِّل	(faععal) فَعَّل
Form III	(yufāعil) يُفاعِل	(fāعal) فاعَل
Form IV	(yufعil) يُفعِل	(afعal) أفْعَل
Form V	(yatafaععal) يَتَفَعَّل	(tafaععal) تَفَعَّل
Form VI	(yatafāعal) يَتَفاعَل	(tafāعal) تَفاعَل
Form VII	(yanfaعil) يَنفَعِل	(infaعal) اِنفَعَل
Form VIII	(yaftعil) يَفتَعِل	(iftaعal) اِفتَعَل
Form X	(yastafعil) يَستَفعِل	(istafعal) اِستفعل

Verbal nouns from forms of the verb

The following table shows you the verbal nouns for the different forms. Some of the examples may already be familiar and these can help you to remember the patterns.

Example	*Verbal noun*	*Verb*	*Form*
preparation (tajhīz) تَجهيز	(tafعīl) تَفعيل	فَعَّل/يُفَعِّل	II
/ dispute (khilāf) خِلاف conversation (muḥādatha) مُحادثة	/ (fiعāl) فِعال (mufāعala) مُفاعلة	فاعَل/يُفاعل	III
information (iعlām) إعلام	(ifعāl) إفعال	أفعَل/يُفعِل	IV
progression (taqaddum) تَقَدُّم	(tafaععul) تَفَعُّل	تفعَّل/يتفعَّل	V
cooperation (taعāwun) تَعاوُن	(tafāعul) تَفاعُل	تَفاعَل/يتَفاعَل	VI
withdrawal (insiḥāb) اِنسحاب	(infiعāl) اِنفعال	اِنفَعَل/يَنفَعِل	VII
meeting (ijtimā)ع اِجتِماع	(iftiعāl) اِفتعال	اِفتَعَل/يَفتَعِل	VIII
use/usage (istikhdām) اِستِخدام	(istifعāl) اِستفعال	اِستَفعَل/يَستَفعِل	X

Active and passive participles

You can form active and passive participles from verbs. An *active participle* will show the 'doer', or subject, of the action; a *passive participle* will show the 'receiver', or object, of the action.

Basic verbs

Active participles are formed using the pattern فاعل (fāعil):

player/(someone) playing (lāعib) لاعِب ← to play لَعِبَ/يلعَب

Passive participles are formed using the pattern مَفعول (mafعūl):

(something) broken (maksūr) مكسور ← to break كَسَرَ/يَكسِر

These participles can be used as either nouns or adjectives, for example مكسور (maksūr) can mean 'broken' or 'a broken item'.

Forms of the verb

Active and passive participles are formed from forms of the verb by taking the present verb and:

- replacing the initial يُـ (yu-) or يَـ (ya-) with مُـ (mu-)
- vowelling with a final kasra (i) for the active participle and a final fatḥa (a) for the passive participle:

trainer (mudarrib) مُدَرِّب ← trains (yudarrib) يُدرِّب

trained (person) (mudarrab) مُدَرَّب

user (mustakhdim) مُستَخدِم ← uses (yastakhdim) يستخدم

used (item) (mustakhdam) مُستَخدَم

Appendix 3: Months of the year

Islamic lunar calendar

١ المُحَرَّم	٥ جَمادَى الأولى	٩ رَمَضان
٢ صَفَر	٦ جَمادَى الآخِرة	١٠ شَوّال
٣ رَبيع الأول	٧ رَجَب	١١ ذُو القِعْدَة
٤ رَبيع الثاني	٨ شَعْبان	١٢ ذُو الحِجَّة

Alternative names for Western months

January كانُون الثّاني	May آيّار	September أيلول
February شُباط	June حَزيران	October تِشرين الأوّل
March آذار	July تَمّوز	November تِشرين الثّاني
April نيسان	August آب	December كانُون الأوّل

Appendix 4: Broken plurals

Plural pattern	*Example*
فِعال (fiɛāl)	كَلب (kalb) dog → كِلاب (kilāb)
أَفعال (afɛāl)	صاحِب (ṣāḥib) friend/owner → أصحاب (aṣḥāb)
فُعَل (fuɛal)	عُلبة (ɛulba) box/packet → عُلَب (ɛulab)
فُعول (fuɛūl)	بيت (bayt) house → بُيوت (buyūt)
فُعُل (fuɛul)	كِتاب (kitāb) book → كُتُب (kutub)
أَفعُل (afɛul)	شَهر (shahr) month → أشهُر (ash-hur)
فَواعِل (fawāɛil)	شارِع (shāriɛ) street → شَوارِع (shawāriɛ)
فُعَلاء (fuɛalā')	وَزير (wazīr) minister → وُزَراء (wuzarā')
فُعلان (fuɛlān)	قَميص (qamīṣ) shirt → قُمصان (qumṣān)
فَعائِل (fuɛā'il)	رِسالة (risāla) message → رَسائِل (rasā'il)
فَعالِل (faɛālil)	مَكتَب (maktab) office → مَكاتِب (makātib)
فَعاليل (faɛālīl)	مِفتاح (miftāḥ) key → مَفاتيح (mafātīḥ)

Answers to exercises

UNIT 1

Exercise 1

See the table of printed and handwritten letters on page 3.

Exercise 2

1 بَ	4 تِ	7 بُ
2 تُ	5 يَ	8 ثَ
3 ثِ	6 نِ	

Exercise 3

1 bi	4 tu	7 nu
2 na	5 ba	8 thu
3 ya	6 ti	

Exercise 4

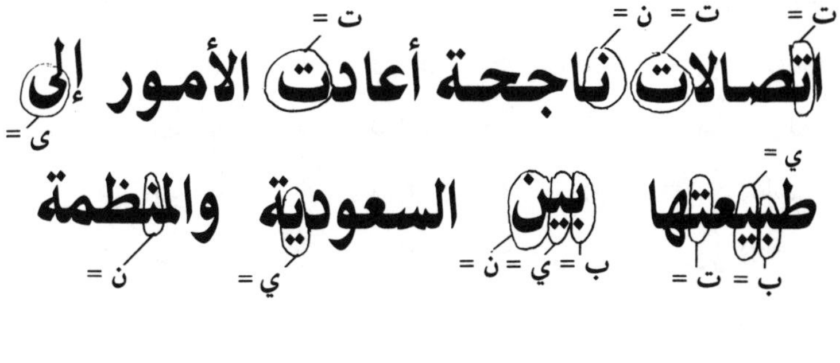

Exercise 5

1 ت + ي + ن = **تين**

2 ن + ي = **ني**

3 ت + ب + ن = **تبن**

4 ن + ب + ت = **نبت**

5 ي + ب + ن + ي = **يبني**

6 ب + ي + ت + ي = **بيتي**

Exercise 6

1 بَيْت

2 ثَبَتَت

3 تِبْن

4 ثَبَتَ

5 يَثِب

6 ثُبَن

Exercise 7

1 بَ + ت + ت = بَتّ (batt)

2 بَ + ي + يِ + ن = بَيِّن (bayyin)

3 تُ + ن + ن = تُنّ (tunn)

4 نَ + ي + ي = نَيّ (nayy)

Exercise 8

A4 (tibn) **B3** (bayt) **C1** (bint) **D2** (bunn) **E5** (bayna)

UNIT 2

Exercise 1

See the table on page 13.

Exercise 2

1	بَ (ba)	+	ر (r)	+	د (d)	=	بَرْد (bard)
2	وَ (wa)	+	ر (r)	+	د (d)	=	وَرْد (ward)
3	رَ (ra)	+	ب (b)	+	و (w)	=	رَبْو (rabw)
4	بَ (ba)	+	ذ (dh)	+	ر (r)	=	بَذْر (badhr)
5	بِ (bi)	+	ر (r)	+	ر (r)	=	بِرّ (birr)
6	بُ (bu)	+	ر (r)	+	ر (r)	=	بُرّ (burr)
7	ثَ (tha)	+	و (w)	+	ب (b)	=	ثَوْب (thawb)
8	دَ (da)	+	رَ (ra)	+	ز (z)	=	دَرَز (daraz)

Exercise 3

1 وَزِير
2 دِين
3 دَيْن
4 بَيْت
5 يُرِيد
6 بَرِيد
7 بَيْن
8 بَيِّن
9 زَيْن
10 وَارِد

Exercise 4

1 بَدْر
2 نُور
3 رَدّ
4 نَادِر
5 نَار
6 دَار
7 بَرْد
8 يَزِيد

Exercise 5

1 (zayn)
2 (dīnā)
3 (zayd)
4 (zaynab)
5 (nādir)
6 (badr)

A4 B3 C1 D3

Exercise 6

1 أنا زينب.
2 أنا زين.
3 أنا دينا.
4 أنا بدر.

Exercise 7

1 أنا زينب وأنتَ؟
أنا نادر.

2 أنا زين وأنتِ؟
أنا دينا.

UNIT 3

Exercise 1

1 خ (ح) ه
2 (خ) ح ه
3 خ (ح) ه
4 خ ح (ه)
5 (خ) ح ه
6 خ ح (ه)
7 خ ح (ه)
8 (خ) ح ه
9 خ (ح) ه
10 خ ح (ه)

Exercise 2

1G (aḥmad)
2D (najjār)
3F (baḥḥār)
4C (mawj)
5A (midḥat)
6H (ukht)
7B (akh)
8E (najāḥ)

Exercise 3

1 ن + ح + ت = نحت
2 ب + ه + م = بهم
3 ج + م + د = جمد
4 ي + ت + ي + ه = يتيم
5 ب + ح + ر = بحر
6 أ + م + ه = أمه
7 ه + ا + م + د = هامد
8 ن + ج + ز = نجز

Exercise 4

1 feminine
2 feminine
3 masculine
4 feminine
5 feminine
6 feminine
7 masculine
8 masculine

Exercise 5

1 هذا حمار.
2 هذه دجاجة.
3 هذا نهر.
4 هذه خيمة.
5 هذه زجاجة.
6 هذه بنت.

Exercise 6

sister	أُخت
daughter	بِنْت
mother	أُمّ
husband	زَوْج
brother	أَخ
wife	زَوْجَة
son	ابْن
father	أَب

Exercise 7

1 مدحت هو ابن أحمد.
2 وردة هي أخت مدحت.
3 أحمد هو زوج جيهان.
4 وردة هي بنت جيهان.
5 جيهان هي أمّ وردة.
6 جيهان هي زوجة أحمد.

Exercise 8

There are many possibilities for different sentences using this family tree. Use Exercise 7 as a guide.

Tip: Take care with أب (ab, father) and أخ (akh, brother). When they are put in front of another name, a long ū is added, making abū and akhū:

أنور هو أبو زينب. (anwar huwa abū zaynab) Anwar is Zaynab's father.

بدر هو أخو زينب. (badr huwa akhū zaynab) Badr is Zaynab's brother.

UNIT 4

Exercise 1

1 **س** ص
2 د **ض**
3 ه **ح**
4 **د** ض
5 س **ص**
6 **ه** ح
7 د **ض**
8 **د** ض
9 **س** ص
10 س **ص**
11 ه **ح**
12 **س** ص

Exercise 2

1C 2A 3F 4B 5D 6E

Exercise 3

1 هي ممرّضة.
2 هو مهندس.
3 هي خبّازة.
4 هو محاسب.
5 هو نجّار.
6 هي مهندسة.

Exercise 4

Masculine plural	*Feminine plural*
خبّازون	خبّازات
محاسبون	محاسبات
ممرّضون	ممرّضات
مهندسون	مهندسات
نجّارون	نجّارات

Exercise 5

1 نحن ممرّضات.
هنّ ممرّضات.

2 نحن مهندسون.
هم مهندسون.

3 نحن مراسلات.
هنّ مراسلات.

4 نحن محاسبون.
هم محاسبون.

5 نحن مهندسون.
هم مهندسون.

6 نحن نجّارون.
هم نجّارون.

Optional exercise (Structure notes)

1 هي ممرّضةٌ (mumarridatun).

2 هو مهندسٌ (muhandisun).

3 هي خبّازةٌ (khabbāzatun).

4 هو محاسبٌ (muḥāsibun).

5 هو نجّارٌ (najjārun).

6 هي مهندسةٌ (muhandisatun).

UNIT 5

Exercise 1

1	same	5	different
2	same	6	different
3	different	7	same
4	same	8	different

Exercise 2

كلمات رئيس مصر الصادقة
تعكس عمق علاقات الشعبين الشقيقين

Exercise 3

1 هذا كتاب.

2 هذا مفتاح.

3 هذا قلم.

4 هذه حقيبة.

5 هذا قميص.

6 هذا كلب.

7 هذه درّاجة.

8 هذه سيّارة.

9 هذا خاتم.

Exercise 4

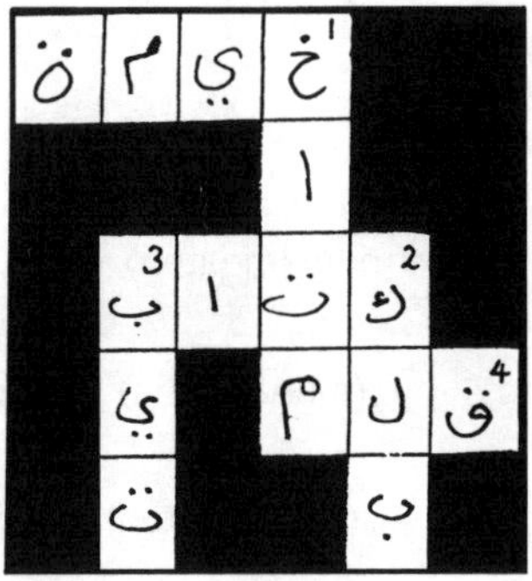

Exercise 5

جميل ... قبيح

ثقيل ... خفيف

أبيض ... أسود

مكسور ... سليم

جديد ... قديم

Exercise 6

1 هذا القميص أبيض.

2 وهذا القميص أسود.

3 هذه البنت جميلة.

4 وهذه البنت قبيحة.

5 هذه السيّارة قديمة.

6 وهذه السيّارة جديدة.

Exercise 7

هذا قلمكَ. شكرًا.

هذا قلم الولد وقلمهُ جديد وأبيض.

وهذه حقيبة المدرّسة وحقيبتها قديمة.

Exercise 8

(Model answers: yours may vary slightly.)

هذا مفتاح محمّد وهو أسود.

هذه درّاجة محمّد وهي مكسورة وقديمة.

هذا قميص محمّد وهو أبيض. قميصه قديم.

هذا كلب محمّد وهو أسود. كلبه جميل وخفيف.

هذا قلم محمّد وهو أبيض. قلمه جديد.

هذا مفتاح جيهان وهو أبيض.

هذه سيّارة جيهان. سيّارتها جديدة وجميلة.

هذه حقيبة جيهان وهي ثقيلة.

هذا خاتم جيهان وهو جميل.

Exercise 9

Try to check your descriptions with an Arabic-speaker.

UNIT 6

Exercise 1

1	ط	5	ص
2	ت	6	س
3	ظ	7	ض
4	ذ	8	د

Exercise 2

1 ✔	3 ✘	5 ✔	7 ✘
2 ✘	4 ✔	6 ✘	8 ✔

Exercise 3

See alphabet in Appendix 1, pages 281–2.

Exercise 4

1D 2B 3A 4C

Exercise 5

1 ع + ل + ي = **علي**

2 ج + م + ع = **جمع**

3 غ + ط + س = **غطس**

4 ظ + ل + م = **ظلم**

5 ط + ي + ن = **طين**

6 ن + ع + م = **نعم**

Exercise 6

Word	*Initial letter*	*Sun letter?*
البنت	ب	✗
التبن	ت	✔
الثوب	ث	✔
النهر	ن	✔
الياسمين	ي	✗
الدجاجة	د	✔
الذباب	ذ	✔
الراديو	ر	✔
الزجاجة	ز	✔
الولد	و	✗
الفيلم	ف	✗
القميص	ق	✗
الكتاب	ك	✗
الليمون	ل	✔
الطين	ط	✔
الظاهر	ظ	✔
العرب	ع	✗
الغرب	غ	✗

Exercise 7

1 هذا كرسي. d
2 هذه خزانة. c
3 هذه مائدة. f
4 هذا باب. h
5 هذا شبّاك. b
6 هذا تليفزيون. g
7 هذا سرير. a
8 هذه صورة. e

Exercise 8

1 هل هذه خزانة؟
لا هي مائدة.
2 هل هذا كتاب؟
لا، هو قلم.
3 هل هذا مفتاح؟
لا، هو خاتم.
4 هل هذا كلب؟
نعم، هو كلب.
5 هل هذه درّاجة؟
لا، هي سيّارة.
6 هل هذا شبّاك؟
نعم، هو شبّاك.

Exercise 9

1 الزجاجة تحت المائدة.
2 الجريدة على الكرسي.
3 الحمار بين الخيمة والسيّارة.
4 الصورة بجانب الشبّاك.
5 الكلب في الحقيبة.
6 الصورة فوق التليفزيون.

Exercise 10

1 نعم، هو بجانب المائدة.

2 التليفزيون على المائدة.

3 المائدة بين الخزانة والكرسي.

4 نعم، هي بجانب الشبّاك.

5 الخزانة بجانب الباب.

6 لا، هو على المائدة.

7 السرير تحت الشبّاك.

8 لا، هو بجانب الخزانة.

9 هي على الخزانة.

10 نعم، هي بين الكرسي والخزانة.

UNIT 7

Exercise 1

1C 2A 3D 4B

1 بدر محاسب وهو في البنك.

2 زينب ممرّضة وهي في المستشفى.

3 زين مدرّسة وهي في المدرسة.

4 أحمد مهندس وهو في المصنع.

Exercise 2

1 ✔	6 ✘
2 ✔	7 ✔
3 ✘	8 ✘
4 ✔	9 ✔
5 ✘	10 ✘

Exercise 3

1 هناك تليفزيون على المائدة ولكن ليس هناك زجاجة.

2 هناك سيّارة في الشارع ولكن ليس هناك درّاجة.

3 هناك ولد بجانب الكرسي ولكن ليس هناك بنت.

4 هناك كلب تحت الشجرة ولكن ليس هناك حمار.

Exercise 4

1 تِينة	3 حَمامة	5 لَوْزة
2 وَرْدة	4 ذُبابة	6 بَطِّيخة

Exercise 5

1 هناك سيّارة جديدة أمام المصنع.

2 هناك قلم مكسور على المائدة.

3 أنا في سيّارتي الجديدة الجميلة.

4 ليس هناك شجر بجانب المستشفى.

5 هناك مدرّس جديد في المدرسة.

6 أحمد محاسب في البنك الجديد.

Exercise 6

1 هي كبيرة.
2 هو طويل.
3 هي صغيرة.
4 هي قويّة.
5 هو ضعيف.
6 هي قصيرة.

Exercise 7

Your drawing should feature the following:

- a street
- a hospital in the middle of the picture, with a tall nurse standing by the door
- a new white factory on the right of the hospital, with big beautiful trees in front of it
- an ugly black dog under the trees and some pigeons above it
- a small school to the left of the hospital, with an old bicycle next to the gate/door.

UNIT 8

Exercise 1

1 م + ص + ر = مِصْر
2 ع + م + ا + ن = عُمان
3 د + م + ش + ق = دِمَشْق
4 م + س + ق + ط = مَسْقَط
5 ل + ب + ن + ا + ن = لُبْنان
6 ب + ي + ر + و + ت = بَيروت
7 ب + غ + د + ا + د = بَغْداد

Exercise 2

	word with ال	*sun letter*	*first letter*	*word*
(al-bayt)	اَلْبَيْت	no	ب	بيت
(an-nahr)	اَلنَّهْر	yes	ن	نهر
(al-khayma)	اَلْخَيْمَة	no	خ	خيمة
(adh-dhubāb)	اَلذُّبَاب	yes	ذ	ذباب
(az-zujāja)	اَلزُّجَاجَة	yes	ز	زجاجة
(al-warda)	اَلْوَرْدَة	no	و	وردة
(al-maṣnaع)	اَلْمَصْنَع	no	م	مصنع
(al-kitāb)	اَلْكِتَاب	no	ك	كتاب
(as-sayyāra)	اَلسَّيَّارَة	yes	س	سيّارة
(ad-darrāja)	اَلدَّرَاجَة	yes	د	درّاجة
(al-qamīs)	اَلْقَمِيص	no	ق	قميص
(al-ḥaqība)	اَلْحَقِيبَة	no	ح	حقيبة
(ash-shubbāk)	اَلشُّبَّاك	yes	ش	شبّاك
(aṣ-ṣūra)	اَلصُّورَة	yes	ص	صورة

Exercise 3

male زيد/أنور/حسين/أحمد/محمّد/مدحت/بدر

female جيهان/دينا/زينب

both زين/نور

Exercise 4

father حسين mother جيهان

son أحمد elder daughter زينب younger daughter دينا

Exercise 5

ق	ا	ف	و	ن
م	ث	ظ	م	ي
م	ص	ش	ه	ح
ر	ا	ج	ن	س
ض	ذ	ض	د	ق
ة	م	ت	س	ش
ي	د	خ	ط	ر
و	ر	ب	ه	ن
ب	س	ا	ح	م
ا	ل	ز	ج	و
خ	ط	ت	م	ش

Masculine sing.	*Masculine pl.*	*Feminine sing.*	*Feminine pl.*
مدرّس	مدرّسون	مدرّسة	مدرّسات
مهندس	مهندسون	مهندسة	مهندسات
نجّار	نجّارون	نجّارة	نجّارات
خبّاز	خبّازون	خبّازة	خبّازات
ممرّض	ممرّضون	ممرّضة	ممرّضات
محاسب	محاسبون	محاسبة	محاسبات

Exercise 6

1 جريدة
2 هل
3 زينب
4 هناك
5 مصنع
6 ذباب
7 كتاب
8 باب

Exercise 7

1 هذه سيّارة.
2 هذا مفتاح.
3 هذا كتاب.
4 هذه درّاجة.
5 هذا سرير.
6 هذا باب.
7 هذا تليفزيون.
8 هذا شبّاك.
9 هذه حقيبة.
10 هذا كرسيّ.
11 هذا كلب.
12 هذا قلم.

Exercise 8

The answer to this depends on where you put the objects. Try to check your answer with an Arabic-speaker.

Exercise 9

مكسور ... سليم　　جديد ... قديم　　كبير ... صغير

طويل ... قصير　　قويّ ... ضعيف　　أسود ... أبيض

قبيح ... جميل　　ثقيل ... خفيف

(Model answer: yours may vary slightly.)

هذه صورة بيت جميل، وعلى يمين البيت هناك شجرة طويلة . لَون هذا البيت الجميل أبيض، ولكن الباب أسود. أمام البيت هناك سيّارة جديدة ولكن على يسار السيّارة هناك درّاجة مكسورة، والدرّاجة أمام الشجرة الطويلة. وهناك دجاجة صغيرة تحت السيّارة. على يمين الصورة هناك حمار جميل، وبين الحمار الجميل والسيارة هناك كلب أبيض وقبيح .

Exercise 10

1 هل الحمار قبيح؟ لا، هو جميل.

2 هل السيّارة أمام البيت؟ نعم، هي أمام البيت.

3 هل الكلب جميل؟ لا، هو قبيح.

4 هل الدرّاجة سليمة؟ لا، هي مكسورة.

5 هل الدجاجة على السيّارة؟ لا، هي تحت السيّارة.

6 هل باب البيت أبيض؟ لا، هو أسود.

7 هل الشجرة طويلة؟ نعم، هي طويلة.

8 هل الكلب بين الحمار والسيّارة؟ نعم، هو بين الحمار والسيّارة.

Exercise 11

1 هذا قلمي.
هذا قلم زينب. هذا قلمها.

2 هذا بيتي.
هذا بيت نادر. هذا بيته.

3 هذه درّاجتي.
هذه درّاجة زين. هذه درّاجتها.

4 هذه سيّارتي.
هذه سيّارة زيد. هذه سيّارته.

UNIT 9

Exercise 1

ب	ث	م	ا	ه	ر	ض	ن	ف	ت
ا	ق	ص	ل	ظ	و	س	ل	ش	ز
ه	ز	ر	س	ر	ض	ص	ي	ي	ن
ق	ا	ر	ع	ل	ا	ز	ب	ذ	ت
ش	ب	خ	و	ا	ن	م	ي	ل	ا
س	ح	ن	د	ر	ا	ل	ا	ب	ج
غ	ع	ا	ي	ث	ت	ج	ل	ن	ف
ي	و	غ	ة	ي	ح	و	س	ا	ن
ف	ت	ث	م	ه	ض	ش	و	ن	ز
ا	ي	ر	و	س	ز	ت	د	ذ	ز
س	ع	ن	ب	ا	خ	ن	ا	م	ع
ق	ش	ث	ذ	ز	غ	ج	ن	م	ر

Exercise 2

1 لا، هي في مصر.

2 لا، هي في العراق.

3 نعم، هي في السعوديّة.

4 هي في الأردنّ.

5 نعم، هي بين السعوديّة وسوريا.

6 هي في عُمان.

7 نعم، هي تحت السعوديّة.

8 لا، هي بجانب سوريا.

Exercise 3

1 القاهرة في مصر وهي عاصمة مصر.

2 الخرطوم في السودان وهي عاصمة السودان.

3 طرابلس في ليبيا وهي عاصمة ليبيا.

4 عمّان في الأردنّ وهي عاصمة الأردنّ.

5 بيروت في لبنان وهي عاصمة لبنان.

6 دمشق في سوريا وهي عاصمة سوريا.

7 بغداد في العراق وهي عاصمة العراق.

8 الرياض في السعوديّة وهي عاصمة السعوديّة.

9 مسقط في عُمان وهي عاصمة عُمان.

10 صنعاء في اليمن وهي عاصمة اليمن.

Exercise 4

1 أسوان في جنوب مصر.

2 سيوة في غرب مصر.

3 الإسكندرية في شمال مصر.

4 بور سعيد في شرق مصر.

Exercise 5

1C 2A 3F 4E 5G 6H 7I 8B 9D

Exercise 6

Country الدَّوْلَة	Nationality الجِنْسِيَّة
الأردن	أردنيّ
العِراق	عِراقيّ
اليابان	يابانيّ
أمريكا	أمريكيّ
أسبانيا	أسبانيّ
رُوسيا	رُوسيّ
الصّين	صينيّ
عُمان	عُمانيّ
إيطاليا	إيطاليّ
سوريا	سوريّ
لُبنان	لُبنانيّ
مِصْر	مِصْريّ
ليبيا	ليبيّ
فرنسا	فرنسيّ
ألمانيا	ألمانيّ
إنجلترا	إنجليزي

Exercise 7

1 هو من الأردنّ. هو أردنيّ.

2 هو من روسيا. هو روسيّ.

3 هي من مصر. هي مصريّة.

4 هي من إيطاليا. هي إيطاليّة.

5 هو من السعوديّة. هو سعوديّ.

6 هي من لبنان. هي لبنانيّة.

7 هو من أمريكا. هو أمريكيّ.

8 هي من ليبيا. هي ليبيّة.

Exercise 8

1 هو من أمريكا. هو أمريكيّ.

2 هي من اليابان. هي يابانيّة.

3 هم من السعوديّة. هم سعوديّون.

4 هم من روسيا. هم روس.

5 هنّ من أسبانيا. هنّ أسبانيّات.

Exercise 9

1 هم يمنيّون.

2 هنّ ألمانيّات.

3 هم إنجليز.

4 هنّ لبنانيّات.

5 هل هنّ سعوديّات؟

6 هل هم روس؟

Exercise 10

الإسم ...... أحمد حسين ....

الجنسيّة .. سعودي ....

المهنة .... مهندس (في الرياض) ....

اسم الزوجة .. دينا حسين ....

جنسية الزوجة .. مصرية ....

مهنة الزوجة .. مدرّسة ....

(Model description: yours may vary slightly.)

محمد نور محاسب في دمشق. محمد سوري، ولكن زوجته زينب يمنيّة. زينب ممرّضة في دمشق.

UNIT 10

Exercise 1
See pages 115–16.

Exercise 2

1	film	6	kilo
2	telephone	7	democracy
3	tomatoes	8	parliament
4	potatoes	9	medal
5	cigarette	10	million

Exercise 3

١ تليفونات ٣ برلمانات

٢ ديموقراطيّات ٤ ميداليات

Exercise 4

١ كتابان/كتابَين ٤ نهران/نهرَين

٢ مفتاحان/مفتاحَين ٥ جريدتان/جريدتَين

٣ مدرستان/مدرستَين ٦ دولتان/دولتَين

Exercise 5

١ أربعة جنيهات ٤ ستّ ميداليات

٢ خمسة تليفونات ٥ عشر ممرّضات

٣ خبّازان/خبّازَين ٦ كلبان/كلبين

Exercise 6

١ هناك كم سيّارة في الصورة؟ هناك خمس سيّارات.

٢ هناك كم شجرة في الصورة؟ هناك ستّ شجرات.

٣ هناك كم ممرّضة في الصورة؟ هناك ثلاث ممرّضات.

٤ هناك كم كلبًا في الصورة؟ هناك كلبان.

٥ هناك كم مهندسًا في الصورة؟ هناك أربعة مهندسين.

٦ هناك كم زجاجة في الصورة؟ هناك زجاجتان.

Exercise 7

– بكم كيلو التفاح من فضلك؟ كيلو التفاح بثمانية جنيهات.

– بكم كيلو البطاطس من فضلك؟ كيلو البطاطس بثلاثة جنيهات.

– بكم كيلو البرتقال من فضلك؟ كيلو البرتقال بستّة جنيهات.

– بكم كيلو الطماطم من فضلك؟ كيلو الطماطم بأربعة جنيهات.

Exercise 8

– بكم الصندل من فضلك؟

– بكم السلّة من فضلك؟

– بكم الطبلة من فضلك؟

– بكم التي-شيرت من فضلك؟

– بكم القلادة من فضلك؟

– بكم الطبق من فضلك؟

Exercise 9

I'd like a gold/silver necklace, please.	أريد قلادة ذهب/فضّة من فضلك.
I'd like a gold/silver ring, please.	أريد خاتم ذهب/فضّة من فضلك.
I'd like some leather sandals, please.	أريد صندل جلد من فضلك.
I'd like a cotton T-shirt, please.	أريد تي-شيرت قطن من فضلك.
I'd like a silk/cotton shirt, please.	أريد قميص حرير/قطن من فضلك.
I'd like a glass bottle, please.	أريد زجاجة زجاج من فضلك.
I'd like a wooden chair, please.	أريد كرسي خشب من فضلك.
I'd like a leather bag, please.	أريد حقيبة جلد من فضلك.
I'd like a copper/silver plate, please.	أريد طبق نحاس/فضّة من فضلك.

UNIT 11

Exercise 1

General meaning	*Root*	*Word*
calculating	ح/س/ب	محاسب
bigness	ك/ب/ر	كبير
carving (wood)	ن/ج/ر	نجّار
opening	ف/ت/ح	مفتاح
sealing (a letter)	خ/ت/م	خاتم
moving along	د/ر/ج	درّاجة
producing	ص/ن/ع	مصنع
falling sick	م/ر/ض	ممرّضة
studying	د/ر/س	مُدرِّس + مَدْرَسة

Exercise 2

بَيْت	بُيُوت	pattern 2
قَلَم	أَقْلام	pattern 1
بَنْك	بُنُوك	pattern 2
فِيلْم	أَفْلام	pattern 1
وَلَد	أَوْلاد	pattern 1

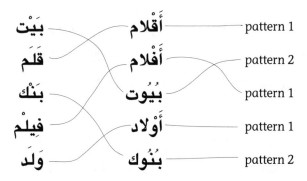

Exercise 3

ألوان	لَوْن (lawn) colour
أطباق	طَبَق (ṭabaq) plate
أصحاب	صَاحِب (ṣāḥib) friend/owner
أشكال	شَكل (shakl) shape
أوقات	وَقْت (waqt) time
أسواق	سُوق (sūq) market
أكواب	كُوب (kūb) cup
سُيوف	سَيْف (sayf) sword
قُلوب	قَلْب (qalb) heart
مُلوك	مَلِك (malik) king
شُموع	شَمعة (shamعa) candle
شُيوخ	شَيْخ (shaykh) sheikh

Exercise 4

١ هذه قلوب. هي قلوب.

٢ هذه بيوت. هي بيوت.

٣ هؤلاء أولاد. هم أولاد.

٤ هذه أطباق. هي أطباق.

٥ هذه أشكال. هي أشكال.

٦ هؤلاء شيوخ. هم شيوخ.

Exercise 5

١ هذه بيوت.

٢ هؤلاء أولاد.

٣ السيوف جميلة.

٤ هذه الأكواب مكسورة.

٥ أين البنوك؟ هي هناك.

٦ الدرّاجات خفيفة.

٧ هل هؤلاء مدرّسون؟

٨ لا، هم محاسبون.

Exercise 6

أريد ستّة أطباق ورق، من فضلك.

أريد عشرة أكواب بلاستيك، من فضلك.

أريد ستّ قبّعات، من فضلك.

أريد سبع زجاجات كولا، من فضلك.

أريد خمس شموع، من فضلك.

أريد تسعة أكياس بلاستيك، من فضلك.

Exercise 7

Meaning	*Feminine (& non-human plurals)*	*Masculine*
green	خَضْراء	أخضَر
blue	زَرْقاء	أزرَق
black	سَوْداء	أسوَد
yellow	صَفْراء	أصفَر

Exercise 8

١ قميص أحْمَر

٢ سيّارة حَمْراء

٣ أطباق بَيْضاء

٤ زجاجات خَضْراء

٥ أكياس صَفْراء

٦ الكلب الأسْوَد

٧ الدرّاجة الزَرْقاء

٨ الشُموع الصَفراء

UNIT 12

Exercise 1

thief	لصّ
investigation	تَحْقيق
yesterday	أَمْس
theft/robbery	سَرِقة
with	مَعَ

1 In Amman (Jordan).
2 A million dollars.
3 Yesterday.
4 The Kuwaiti bank.
5 Two.

Exercise 2

١ هل كَتَبْتَ خِطابات في مكتبك؟ نعم، كَتَبْتُ خِطابات في مكتبي.

٢ هل ذهبتَ إلى مطعم أمريكيّ؟ لا، ذهبتُ إلى مطعم عربيّ.

٣ هل أكلتَ سمكًا في المطعم؟ نعم، أكلتُ سمكًا في المطعم.

٤ هل رجعتَ إلى البيت (بيتك) مساءً؟ نعم، رجعتُ إلى البيت (بيتي) مساءً.

٥ هل سمعتَ عن السرقة في الراديو؟ لا، سمعتُ عن السرقة في التليفزيون.

Exercise 3

١ أنا زينب شَوْقي وبيتي في وسط مدينة عمّان.

٢ أمس ... ذهبتُ إلى البنك صباحًا ...

٣ وشربتُ فنجان شاي.

٤ فتحتُ الخزانة ...

٥ وجلستُ على مكتبي.

٦ ذهبتُ إلى مطعم صيني...

٧ وفي المطعم سمعتُ عن السرقة في الراديو.

٨ رجعتُ من المطعم إلى البنك ...

٩ وجدتُ الشبّاك المكسور.

Exercise 4

١ ماذا شَرِبْتَ؟

٢ أين شَرِبْتَ القهوة؟

٣ هل ذهبتَ إلى مطعم عربي؟

٤ ماذا أكلتَ في المطعم؟

٥ ماذا فعَلتَ في مكتبك؟

٦ ما اسمك؟

٧ متى سَمَعتَ عن السرقة؟

Exercise 5

١ أمس، خرَجْتُ من البيت صباحًا.

٢ ذَهَبَتْ إلى البنك.

٣ هل أَكَلْتَ التُفَّاحة؟

٤ أوّلاً، كتب خطابات.

٥ أين سَمِعْتِ عن السرقة؟

٦ ذَهَبْتُ إلى البيت وجَلَسْتُ على كرسيّ.

٧ شَرِبَتْ فنجان قهوة مع صاحبتها.

٨ ماذا فَعَلْتَ أمس؟

Exercise 6

اسمها زينب شوقي وبيتها في وسط مدينة عمّان .
أمس ذهبَت إلى البنك الكويتي صباحًا .
أوّلاً شربَت فنجان شاي . . .وفتحت الخزانة .
ثمّ جلسَت على مكتبها وبعد ذلك ذهبَت إلى
المطعم وسمعَت عن السرقة في الراديو .

Exercise 7

أكلتُ سمكًا في المطعم أمس.

شَرِبَت دينا زجاجة كولا.

وَجَدْتُ ولدًا صغيرًا بجانب باب المدرسة.

أولاً، فتحت زينب خزانة البنك الكويتي صباحًا.

جلَسَت على كرسيّ خشبيّ.

أخيرًا، رَجَعتُ إلى بيتي مساءً.

Exercise 8

٢ ذهب إلى مصنع السيّارات في جنوب المدينة.

٥ ذهب إلى مدرسة كبيرة في وسط المدينة.

٣ شرب فنجان قهوة مع المهندسين في المصنع.

١ خرج من القصر الملكي.

٧ رجع إلى القصر الملكي.

٦ جلس مع الأولاد والبنات والمدرّسين.

٤ سمع من المهندسين عن السيّارة الجديدة.

Exercise 9

Word الكَلِمة	Root المَصدَر	Meaning المَعنى
وَزير	و ز ر	minister
سَفير	س ف ر	ambassador
وِزارة	و ز ر	ministry
مَعْرَض	ع ر ض	exhibition/show
رِسَالَة	ر س ل	letter/message
عِلاقَة	ع ل ق	relation/link

UNIT 13

Exercise 1

	Singular	*Pattern*	*Plural*
mountain	جَبَل	فِعال	جِبال
camel	جَمَل	فِعال	جِمال
toy	لُعْبَة	فُعَل	لُعَب
sea	بَحْر	فِعال	بِحار
masterpiece/artefact	تُحْفَة	فُعَل	تُحَف
state/nation	دَوْلَة	فُعَل	دُوَل
wind	ريح	فِعال	رِياح

Exercise 2

١ كم كلبًا في الصورة؟ هناك أربعة كِلاب.

٢ كم جملاً في الصورة؟ هناك خمسة جِمال.

٣ كم لُعبة في الصورة؟ هناك تسع لُعَب.

٤ كم جبلاً في الصورة؟ هناك ستّة جِبال.

٥ كم رجلاً في الصورة؟ هناك سبعة رِجال.

٦ كم عُلبة في الصورة؟ هناك ثماني عُلَب.

Exercise 3

See page 169.

Exercise 4

See page 169.

Exercise 5

١	٤٦	٣	٣٥	٥	٩٣	٧	١٨٥
٢	٨١	٤	١٢٤	٦	٧٢	٨	١٥٧

Exercise 6

٦١ رجلاً (wāḥid wa-sittīn rajulan)

٢٣ سيفًا (thalātha wa-ɛishrīn sayfan)

٧٢ قلمًا (ithnān wa-sabɛīn qalaman)

٥٨ كلبًا (thamānya wa-khamsīn kalban)

٤٩ صورة (tisɛ wa-arbaɛīn Sūra)

٢٨ مفتاحًا (thamānya wa-ɛishrīn miftāḥan)

١٦ زجاجة (sitt ɛashar zujāja)

١٨ جملاً (thamanyat ɛashar jamalan)

٩٣ خيمة (thalāth wa-tisɛīn khayma)

Exercise 7

١ ما هي دَرَجَة الحَرارة؟ دَرَجَة الحرارة ١٥. الطَّقس بارد.
٢ ما هي دَرَجَة الحَرارة؟ دَرَجَة الحرارة ٤٠. الطَّقس حارّ.
٣ ما هي دَرَجَة الحَرارة؟ دَرَجَة الحرارة ٣٠. الطَّقس مُعْتَدِل.
٤ ما هي دَرَجَة الحَرارة؟ دَرَجَة الحرارة ١٠. الطَّقس بارد.
٥ ما هي دَرَجَة الحَرارة؟ دَرَجَة الحرارة ٥٠. الطَّقس حارّ جدًّا.
٦ ما هي دَرَجَة الحَرارة؟ دَرَجَة الحرارة ٢٥. الطَّقس مُعْتَدِل.

Exercise 8

١ دَرَجَة الحَرارة ١٨.
٢ دَرَجَة الحَرارة ٢٩.
٣ الطَّقس غائم وبارد.
٤ الطَّقس صحو و ومعتدل.
٥ لا، الطَّقس صحو.
٦ لا، الطَّقس معتدل.
٧ نعم.
٨ لا، درجة الحرارة الصغرى ٢٠.
٩ هناك ٤٠ مدينة.
١٠ لا، الطَّقس صحو في ٢٥ مدينة.

Exercise 9

1 Ahmad.
2 London.
3 Cold and cloudy.
4 Centre of town.
5 Japanese.
6 To the museum.
7 Went back to the hotel.
8 Have you written a letter to me?

Exercise 10

عزيزتي سارة،

كيف حالِك؟ نحن في باريس والطقس حارّ وصحو. ذهبنا أمس صباحًا إلى متحف كبير وأكلنا في مطعم فرنسي في وسط المدينة. بعد ذلك أنا ذهبت إلى البنك ولكن نادر والأولاد ذهبوا إلى المتحف. وأنتِ؟ هل كتبتِ لي خطابًا؟

مع تحياتي زينب

UNIT 14

Exercise 1

See page 169.

Exercise 2

يوم الجمعة قبل يوم السبت.

يوم الخميس بعد يوم الأربعاء.

يوم الأحد قبل يوم الاثنين.

يوم الثلاثاء قبل يوم الأربعاء.

يوم السبت بعد يوم الجمعة.

Exercise 3

algebra	الجَبْر
emir (prince)	أَمير
saffron	زَعْفَران
alkali	القِلي
vizier (minister)	وَزير
tamarind	تَمْر هِنْدي
alcohol	الكُحول

Exercise 4

سُفَراء	ambassadors
رُؤَساء	presidents/chairmen
زُعَماء	leaders
وُكَلاء	agents

Exercise 5

سَفيرات	*(female)* ambassadors
رَئيسات	*(female)* presidents/chairwomen
زَعيمات	*(female)* leaders
وَكيلات	*(female)* agents

Exercise 6

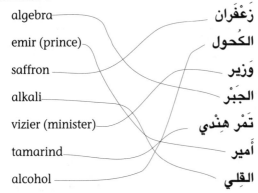

Meaning	*General noun*	*Root letters*
ministry	وِزارة	و ز ر
embassy	سِفارة	س ف ر

emirate	إِمارة	ء م ر
agency	وِكالة	و ك ل
leadership	زِعامة	ز ع م
presidency/chairmanship	رِئاسة	ر ء س

Exercise 7

ماذا فعل الرئيس يوم الاثنين؟

حضر افتتاح المصنع الجديد صباحًا،

وعقد اجتماعًا مع السفيرة الإيطاليّة ظهرًا.

ماذا فعل الرئيس يوم الثلاثاء؟

استقبل الرئيس الأمير في مكتبه صباحًا، وبعد ذلك عقد جلسة

مع زعماء الأحزاب ظهرًا.

Exercise 8

١ Prince Abdullah/the ambassador of Pakistan

استقبل الأمير عبد الله سفير باكستان.

Prince Abdullah received the ambassador of Pakistan.

٢ the Egyptian President/a Saudi princess

استقبل الرئيس المصري أميرة سعودية.

The Egyptian President received a Saudi princess.

٣ the *(female)* Minister of Education/teachers' leaders

حضرت وزيرة التعليم اجتماعًا مع زعماء المدرّسين.

The *(female)* Minister of Education attended a meeting with teachers' leaders.

٤ the Minister of Agriculture/the German President

كتب الرئيس الألمانيّ رسالة إلى وزير الزراعة.
The German President wrote a message to the Minister of Agriculture.

٥ Prince Sulaiman/the British ambassador

حضر الأمير سليمان اجتماعًا مع السفير البريطانيّ.
Prince Sulaiman attended a meeting with the British ambassador.

٦ the Syrian President/the Deputy Foreign Minister

استقبل الرئيس السوري نائب وزير الخارجية.
The Syrian President received the Deputy Foreign Minister.

٧ the Minister of Justice/the Iraqi president

كتب وزير العدل رسالة إلى الرئيس العراقيّ.
The Minister of Justice wrote a message to the Iraqi President.

٨ the Emir of Kuwait/the ambassadors of Europe

كتب أمير الكويت رسالة إلى سفراء أوروبا.
The Emir of Kuwait wrote a message to the ambassadors of Europe.

Exercise 9

١ ذهب وزير الدفاع البريطانيّ إلى الرياض. ✔
٢ استقبل الأمير حسن الوزير البريطاني. ✔
٣ استقبل الأمير الوزير في مكتبه ظهر أمس. ✘
٤ الأمير حسن هو رئيس الوزراء. ✘
٥ بعد الاستقبال رجع الوزير البريطاني إلى لندن. ✘
٦ الأمير حسن هو وزير الدفاع السعودي. ✘
٧ الأمير أشرف هو نائب وزير الدفاع. ✔
٨ حضر الجلسة من جانب السعودي أميران ومساعد. ✔

Exercise 10

١ خرج السفراء من السفارة وذهبوا إلى القصر الملكيّ.

٢ عقد الوزير جلسة عمل مع السفير اليمنيّ.

٣ ذهب الزعماء إلى المصنع وسمعوا عن السيارة الجديدة.

٤ جلسَت الرئيسة على مكتبها وكتبَت رسالة إلى وزير الدفاع.

٥ أكل الرجال سمكًا في المطعم، وبعد ذلك شربوا زجاجات كولا.

٦ حضرَت وزيرة الاقتصاد افتتاح بنك جديد.

٧ ذهبَت زينب إلى البنك ووجدَت الشبّاك المكسور.

٨ ماذا فعلَت الرئيسة يوم الثلاثاء؟

UNIT 15

Exercise 1

وَاحِد	١	أحد عشر	١١	ثلاثين	٣٠
اِثْنَان	٢	اثنا عشر	١٢	أربعين	٤٠
ثَلاثَة	٣	ثَلاثَة عشر	١٣	خمسين	٥٠
أَرْبَعة	٤	أَرْبَعة عشر	١٤	سِتّين	٦٠
خَمْسَة	٥	خَمْسَة عشر	١٥	سَبعين	٧٠
سِتّة	٦	سِتّة عشر	١٦	ثَمانين	٨٠
سَبْعة	٧	سَبْعة عشر	١٧	تِسعين	٩٠
ثَمَانية	٨	ثَمَانية عشر	١٨	خَمْسَة وتسعين	٩٥
تِسْعة	٩	تسعة عشر	١٩	ثَلاثة وأربعين	٤٣
عَشرَة	١٠	عشرين	٢٠	أرْبَعة وثلاثين	٣٤

Exercise 2

١ ٩٤ ٣ ١٩ ٥ ٦١ ٧ ٤٣ ٩ ٣٨

٢ ٥٦ ٤ ٧٠ ٦ ٨٨ ٨ ١٤ ١٠ ٢٩

Exercise 3

٢ ٤ ٦ ٨ ١٠ ١٢ ١٤ ١٦ ١٨ ٢٠ ٢٢

٣ ٦ ٩ ١٢ ١٥ ١٨ ٢١ ٢٤ ٢٧ ٣٠ ٣٣

١١ ٢٢ ٣٣ ٤٤ ٥٥ ٦٦ ٧٧ ٨٨ ٩٩ ١١٠ ١٢١

٧ ١٤ ٢١ ٢٨ ٣٥ ٤٢ ٤٩ ٥٦ ٦٣ ٧٠ ٧٧

١ ١ ٢ ٣ ٥ ٨ ١٣ ٢١ ٣٤ ٥٥ ٨٩

(add together the previous two numbers)

Exercise 4

1 Khartoum.
2 113.
3 2291.
4 Saudi Arabia.
5 Belgium.
6 Ash-sharq Al-Awsat.

١ ١٥ دولة

٢ لا

٣ لا (مصر بين السعودية والكويت)

٤ ٥١ طائرة

٥ خمس طائرات

٦ نعم

٧ طائرتان

٨ لا (لمصر ١٣ طائرة)

٩ نعم

١٠ لا

Exercise 5

ون/ين	ات	أفعال	فُعول	فِعال	فُعَل	فُعَلاء
مُساعِدون	أميرات	أولاد	شموع	رجال	تُحَف	زعماء
	جُنَيهات	أسواق	شؤون	جبال	عُلَب	سفراء
	سيّارات	أحزاب	لصوص	جمال	لُعَب	وكلاء
	كُرات	أفلام	سيوف	بحار	صُوَر	رؤساء
	دَرّاجات	أكياس	بنوك			
	تِليفونات	أكواب	قلوب			
	سِفارات	أطباق	شيوخ			
			ملوك			

Exercise 6

١ كم كلبًا في الصورة؟ هناك ثلاثة كلاب في الصورة.

٢ كم جملاً في الصورة؟ هناك أربعة جمال في الصورة.

٣ كم سيّارة في الصورة؟ هناك عشر سيّارات في الصورة.

٤ كم صورة في الصورة؟ هناك خمس صُوَر في الصورة.

٥ كم درّاجة في الصورة؟ هناك سبع درّاجات في الصورة.

٦ كم رجلاً في الصورة؟ هناك ستّة رجال في الصورة.

٧ كم علبة في الصورة؟ هناك ثلاث عُلَب في الصورة.

٨ كم لعبة في الصورة؟ هناك ثماني لُعَب في الصورة.

Exercise 7

ذَهب	مائدة
قُطْن	قلادة
خَشَب	حقيبة
جلد	شِبّاك
زُجاج	قَميص

أريد مائدة خشب من فضلك.

أريد قلادة ذَهب من فضلك.

أريد حقيبة جلد من فضلك.

أريد شبّاك زُجاج من فضلك.

أريد قَميص قُطْن من فضلك.

Exercise 8

Meaning	*Feminine*	*Masculine*
green	خَضْراء	أَخْضَر
blue	زَرْقاء	أَزْرَق
white	بَيْضاء	أَبْيَض
black	سَوْداء	أَسْوَد
yellow	صَفْراء	أَصْفَر
red	حَمْراء	أَحْمَر

١ باب بيتي [add colour of your door *(masc.)*].

٢ سيّارتي [add colour of your car *(fem.)*].

٣ البحر الأحمر في شرق مصر.

٤ وجدتُ طماطم حمراء في السوق.

٥ راية مصر بيضاء وسوداء وحمراء.

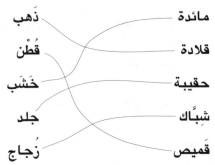

Exercise 9

في الأسبوع الماضي، ذهب أحمد وفاطمة وصاحبهما الألماني هَانْز إلى القاهرة ووصلوا هناك يوم السبت مساءً.

يوم الأحد خرج الأصحاب صباحًا وذهبوا إلى المتحف المصري في وسط المدينة، ووجدوا هناك معرضًا لتُحَف فرعونيّة. بعد ذلك ذهبوا إلى مطعم بجانب المتحف وأكل أحمد وفاطمة سمكًا من البحر الأحمر، ولكن هانز أكل بورجر.

يوم الاثنين حضر أحمد وهانز مؤتمرًا ثقافيًّا، ولكن فاطمة جلسَت في البلكون وكتبَت خطابًا لأمها. أخيرًا، رجع الأصحاب يوم الثلاثاء.

Exercise 10

	الصباح	الظهر
الأحد	افتتاح البنك الياباني الجديد	جلسة عمل مع المفتّش العامّ
الاثنين	/	السفير السوداني في مكتبي
الثلاثاء	مؤتمر وزراء الاقتصاد العرب	اجتماع مع وزير العدل
الأربعاء	معرض البنوك الإسلامية	الأمير أحمد في القصر الملكيّ
الخميس	وزير الاقتصاد العراقي في الوزارة	/

There are many possible questions. Try to check yours with an Arabic-speaker.

UNIT 16

Exercise 1

١ كم الساعة؟ الساعة الخامسة.

٢ كم الساعة؟ الساعة التاسعة.

٣ كم الساعة؟ الساعة الثامنة.

٤ كم الساعة؟ الساعة الثانية.

٥ كم الساعة؟ الساعة الحادية عشرة.

Exercise 2

١ كم الساعة؟ الساعة العاشرة والثُلث.

٢ كم الساعة؟ الساعة الثامنة والرُبع.

٣ كم الساعة؟ الساعة الثانية والنِصف.

٤ كم الساعة؟ الساعة العاشرة إلا ثُلثًا.

٥ كم الساعة؟ الساعة السادسة إلا عشر دَقائِق.

٦ كم الساعة؟ الساعة الحادية عشرة إلا خمس دَقائِق.

Exercise 3

	Arabic film	*American film*	*French film*
Thursday showing times	1.30pm		3pm
Friday showing times	1.30pm	9pm	6pm
Saturday showing times	4.45pm		

Exercise 4

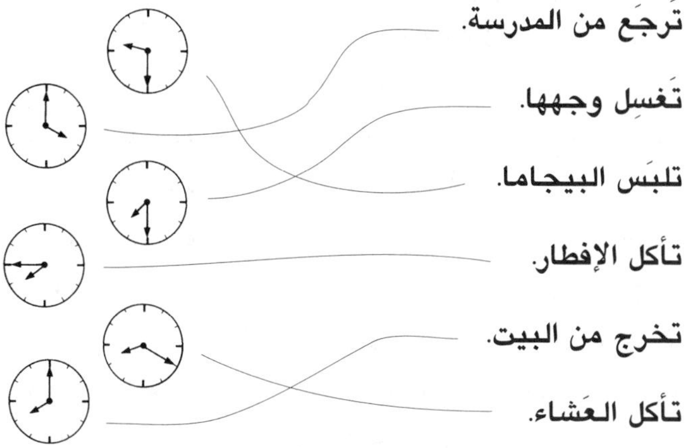
تَرجَع من المدرسة.
تَغسِل وجهها.
تلبَس البيجاما.
تأكل الإفطار.
تخرج من البيت.
تأكل العَشاء.

Try to check your paragraph with an Arabic-speaker.

Exercise 5

(These are model answers: yours may vary slightly.)

١ لا تذهب فاطمة إلى المدرسة بالحمار، تذهب بالدراجة.

٢ لا يذهب محمود إلى المدرسة الساعة السابعة والنصف، يذهب الساعة الثامنة.

٣ لا يشرب محمود فنجان شاي، يشرب زجاجة كولا.

٤ لا تغسل فاطمة وجهها الساعة الواحدة والثلث، تغسل وجهها الساعة السابعة والنصف.

Exercise 6 & Exercise 7

Try to check your answers with an Arabic-speaker.

Exercise 8

١ ماذا تدرسون يوم الثلاثاء ظهرًا؟ ندرس الموسيقى من الساعة الواحدة والنصف حتّى الساعة الثالثة.

٢ ماذا تدرسون يوم الثلاثاء صباحًا؟ ندرس الرياضيّات من الساعة الثامنة والنصف حتّى الساعة العاشرة وبعد ذلك ندرس الانجليزية حتّى الساعة الثانية عشرة.

٣ ماذا تدرسون يوم الاثنين ظهرًا؟ ندرس الرسم من الساعة الواحدة والنصف حتّى الساعة الثالثة.

٤ ماذا تدرسون يوم الخميس صباحًا؟ ندرس الكيمياء من الساعة الثامنة والنصف حتّى الساعة العاشرة وبعد ذلك ندرس الرياضيّات حتّى الساعة الثانية عشرة.

٥ ماذا تدرسون يوم السبت ظهرًا؟ ندرس الجغرافيا من الساعة الواحدة والنصف حتّى الساعة الثالثة.

٦ ماذا تدرسون يوم الأحد ظهرًا؟ ندرس الرياضة من الساعة الواحدة والنصف حتّى الساعة الثالثة.

٨ ماذا تدرسون يوم الاثنين صباحًا؟ ندرس التربية الدينية من الساعة الثامنة والنصف حتّى الساعة العاشرة وبعد ذلك ندرس الرياضيّات حتّى الساعة الثانية عشرة.

Exercise 9

كلّ يوم يخرج الأولاد من بيوتهم الساعة الثامنة إلا ربعًا ويذهبون إلى المدرسة بالأوتوبيس. يدرسون حتّى الساعة الثانية عشرة وبعد ذلك يأكلون الغداء.

بعد الغداء يدرسون من الساعة الواحدة والنصف حتّى الساعة الثالثة ثم يرجعون من المدرسة إلى بيوتهم.

Exercise 10

• Damascus University • medicine • lectures on Sunday/Tuesday/Thursday
• eggs/tea for breakfast • leaves house 10am • university by train
• attends lectures/sits in library until 4pm • returns home
• Friday goes to cinema with friends • eats in falafel restaurant

UNIT 17

Exercise 1

biscuits	بَسْكَوِيت
shampoo	شَامْبو
rice	أَرُزّ
cake	كَعْك
sugar	سُكَّر
macaroni	مَكَرونَة

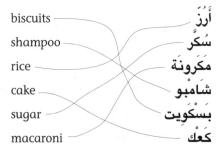

Exercise 2

زجاجة	علبة	كيس	قطعة	أنبوبة
عصير برتقال	حليب	أرز	كعك	معجون الطماطم
كولا	شاى	سكّر	جبنة	
عصير تفاح	مسحوق الغسيل			
ماء	مكرونة			
حليب	قهوة			
	طماطم			
	معجون الطماطم			

Exercise 3

– مساء الخير.
– مساء النور يا مدام ... تحت أمرك.
– أعطني من فضلك زجاجة زيت ...
– لتر؟
– لا نصف لتر من فضلك.
– تفضّلي.
– وعلبة مكرونة كبيرة وكيسين أرزّ.
– تفضّلي يا مدام.
– شكرًا ... كم الحساب من فضلك؟
– عشرة جنيهات.
– تفضّل.
– شكرًا ... مع السلامة يا مدام.
– الله يسلّمك.

Exercise 4

اِسم المطعم؟ ..ليالينا..........................

اِسم الفندق؟ ..ماريوت..........................

المدينة؟ ...جدّة..............................

عدد الأطباق؟ ...أربعة..........................

رقم التليفون؟ ......٦٧١٤٠٠٠.....................

بكم العشاء؟....٨٠ ريالا..........................

بكم الخدمة؟....٨ ريالا (١٠٪)...................

Exercise 5

Plural	*Noun of place (meaning)*	*Verb (meaning)*
مَلاعِب	مَلعَب playing field/pitch/court	لَعِب/يَلْعَب to play
مَعارِض	مَعرَض exhibition/show	عرض/يعرِض to exhibit/show
مَداخِل	مَدخَل entrance	دخل/يدخُل to enter
مَخارِج	مَخرَج exit	خرج/يخرُج to exit/go out
مَطاعِم	مَطعَم restaurant	طعم/يطعَم to taste
مَطابِخ	مَطبَخ kitchen	طبخ/يطبُخ to cook
مَغاسِل	مَغسَلة launderette	غسل/يغسِل to wash
مَساجِد	مَسجِد mosque	سجد/يسجُد to bow in worship

Exercise 6

الطبق الأوّل

✔ سلطة طماطم بالبيض	٣٠ ريالاً
سلطة دجاج بالمايونيز	٥٠ ريالاً

الطبق الرئيسي

✔ سمك بالأرز	٧٠ ريالاً
لحم بالبطاطس	٦٠ ريالاً
مكرونة بالطماطم والجبن	٤٥ ريالاً

الحلويات

✔ آيس كريم	٢٥ ريالاً
كعك باللوز	٢٨ ريالاً

المشروبات

قهوة	١٣ ريالاً	شاي بالحليب	١٧ ريالاً
شاي	١٥ ريالاً	عصير برتقال	١٨ ريالاً
كولا	١٤ ريالاً	✔عصير تفاح	٢٠ ريالاً

Exercise 7

سلطة طماطم	٣٠
سمك بالأرز	٧٠
آيس كريم	٢٥
عصير تفاح	٢٠
المجموع	١٤٥
+ خدمة ١٠٪	١٤.٥٠
المجموع بالخدمة	١٥٩.٥٠

Exercise 8

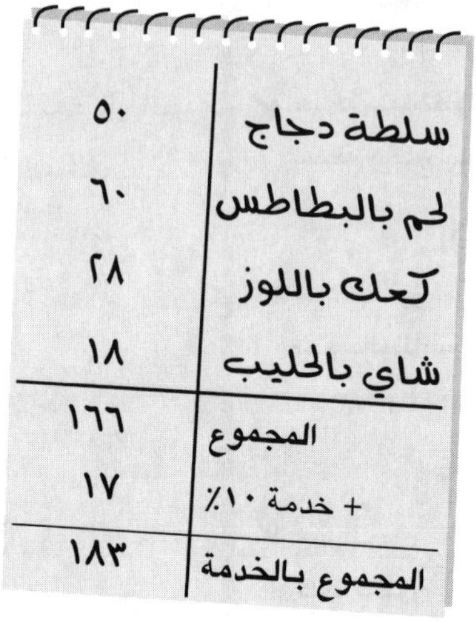

سلطة دجاج	٥٠
لحم بالبطاطس	٦٠
كعك باللوز	٢٨
شاي بالحليب	١٨
المجموع	١٦٦
+ خدمة ١٠٪	١٧
المجموع بالخدمة	١٨٣

Exercise 9

Meaning	*Present*	*Past*	*Form*	*Root*
to heat	يُسَخِّن	سَخَّن	II	سخن
to travel	يُسافِر	سافَر	III	سفر
to mend/fix	يُصَلِّح	صَلَّح	II	صلح
to embrace Islam	يُسلِم	أسلَم	IV	سلم
to tidy/arrange	يُرَتِّب	رَتَّب	II	رتب
to talk/discuss	يُحادِث	حادَث	III	حدث
to teach	يُدَرِّس	دَرَّس	II	درس

Exercise 10

١ هل سخّنْتَ الخبز؟ نعم، سخّنْتُه.

٢ هل أخرَجْتَ الزبالة؟ نعم، أخرَجْتُها.

٣ هل جهّزتَ السلطة؟ نعم، جهّزتُها.

Exercise 11

١ حضره الوزير.
٢ استقبلَتهم الرئيسة.
٣ استقبله الأمير.
٤ وجدته فاطمة.
٥ كل يوم يكتبها محمود.
٦ عقدها الرئيس.
٧ شَرِبْتُه.
٨ كلّ يوم نطبخه مساءً.

Exercise 12

١ لم يُخرِج الزُبالَة. لم يُخرِجها. / ما أخْرَجَ الزُبالَة. ما أخْرَجَها.
٢ لم يُنَظِّف الشبّاك. لم يُنظّفه. / ما نَظَّفَ الشبّاك. ما نَظَّفَه.
٣ لم يُسَخِّن الخُبز. لم يُسَخِّنه. / ما سَخَّنَ الخُبز. ما سَخَّنَه.
٤ لم يُصَلِّح الكرسيّ المكسور. لم يُصَلِّحه. / ما صَلَّحَ الكرسيّ المكسور. ما صَلَّحَه
٥ لم يُجَهِّز السلطة. لم يُجَهِّزها. / ما جَهَّزَ السلطة. ما جَهَّزَها.

Exercise 13
Try to check your conversation with an Arabic-speaker.

UNIT 18

Exercise 1

١ طويل أطوَل (aṭwal)
٢ كبير أكبَر (akbar)
٣ جميل أجمَل (ajmal)
٤ قبيح أقبَح (aqbaḥ)
٥ صغير أصغَر (aṣghar)
٦ قديم أقدَم (aqdam)
٧ جديد أجَدّ (ajadd)
٨ شديد أشَدّ (ashadd)
٩ سريع أسرَع (asraع)
١٠ رَخيص أرخَص (arkhaṣ)
١١ كَثير أكثَر (akthar)
١٢ فاضِل أفضَل (afḍal)
١٣ غَنيّ أغنى (aghnā)
١٤ فَقير أفقَر (afqar)
١٥ هامّ أهَمّ (ahamm)

Exercise 2

١ النيل أطول نهر في العالم.
٢ القاهرة أكبر مدينة في أفريقيا.
٣ آسيا أكبر قارّة في العالم.
٤ الفضَّة أرخص من الذهب.
٥ السيّارة أسرع من الدرّاجة.
٦ اللوزة أصغر من البطيخة.

Exercise 3

	Car 1	*Car 2*	*Car 3*
largest	✔		
smallest			✔
fastest		✔	
newest		✔	
cheapest			✔
most expensive		✔	

Exercise 4

٤ عندنا هذه السيّارة الكبيرة الجميلة.
٨ بمائة وثمانين في اليوم.

٦ الحمراء أجدّ وأسرع سيّارة عندنا.
١١ نعم. هذا أفضل. آخذ البيضاء .

١٢ الاسم، من فضلك...
٢ من متى يا سيّدي؟

١٠ البيضاء أرخص وأصغر.
٧ بكم الحمراء؟

٣ من يوم السبت حتّى الخميس.
٩ غالية! هل هناك أرخص منها؟

١ مساء الخير. أريد سيّارة لخمسة أيّام.
٥ ولكنّها قديمة. ممكن أجدّ منها؟

Exercise 5

مُنذُ عِشرين سَنَة كان فَوْزي غَنِيًّا. كان له بيت جميل وكبير في وسط المدينة، ولَكنّه الآن فَقير وليس له بيت.

في الماضي، كانَت زوجَتُه فَوْزيّة غَنيَّة، وكان لها سيّارة جديدة وكبيرة وكلب جميل وصغير، ولَكنّها الآن فقيرة وليس لها كلب، لها دجاجة.

Exercise 6

١ كان أحمد مدرّسًا في الماضي.

٢ الطقس كان حارًّا أمس.

٣ كُنتُ في المكتب يوم السبت.

٤ كانت الشجرة أطوَل من بيتي.

٥ أين كُنتُم الساعة التاسعة؟

٦ كُنّا في وسط المدينة.

Exercise 7 & Exercise 8 *(in brackets)*

١ مُنْذُ عِشرين سَنَة كُنتُ غَنيًا. الآن أنا (ولكنّي الآن) فقير.

٢ منذ ثلاثين سَنَة كان أحمد في الجيش. الآن هو (ولكنّه الآن) محاسب في بنك.

٣ منذ نصف ساعة كانوا في المدرسة. الآن هم (ولكنّهم الآن) في بيوتهم.

٤ منذ ستّين سَنَة كانَت الرياض مدينة صغيرة. الآن هي (ولكنّها الآن) أكبر مدينة في السعوديّة.

٥ في الماضي كُنتَ مدرّسًا. الآن أنتَ (ولكنّك الآن) مُفَتّش في وزارة التعليم.

٦ منذ دقيقتين كُنّا في البنك. الآن نحن (ولكنّا الآن) عند البقّال.

Exercise 9

الماضي *Past*	المضارع *Present*	المصدر *Root*	المعنى *Meaning*
طَارَ (طِرْت)	يَطير	ط/ي/ر	to fly
زَارَ (زُرْت)	يَزور	ز/و/ر	to visit
جرى (جَرَيْت)	يَجْري	ج/ر/ي	to run
باع (بِعْت)	يَبيع	ب/ي/ع	to sell
عاد (عُدْت)	يَعود	ع/و/د	to return
دعا (دَعَوْت)	يَدْعو	د/ع/و	to call
زاد (زِدْت)	يَزيد	ز/ي/د	to increase
قال (قُلْت)	يَقول	ق/و/ل	to say
رمى (رَمَيْت)	يَرْمي	ر/م/ي	to throw

Exercise 10

١ تعلّمنا الإنجليزيّة.
٢ تعلّمتُ العربيّة.
٣ هل تذكّرتَ صَديقي مُنير؟
٤ تعاونَت سميرة مع المدرّسين.
٥ تناقشنا معًا.
٦ تحدّث الوزراء عن المَعرَض وتبادلوا الأفكار.

Exercise 11
Try to check your conversation with an Arabic-speaker.

UNIT 19

Exercise 1

١ مارس	شهر مارس بعد فبراير وقبل أبريل.
٢ يونيو	شهر يونيو بعد مايو وقبل يوليو.
٣ سبتمبر	شهر سبتمبر بعد أغسطس وقبل أكتوبر.
٤ أغسطس	شهر أغسطس بعد يوليو وقبل سبتمبر.
٥ يناير	شهر مايو بعد ديسمبر وقبل فبراير.
٦ مايو	شهر مايو بعد أبريل وقبل يونيو.
٧ أكتوبر	شهر أكتوبر بعد سبتمبر وقبل نوفمبر.
٨ أبريل	شهر أبريل بعد مارس وقبل مايو.

Exercise 2

غداً، ٢٣ فبراير صباحًا، سيحضُر الوزير اجتماعًا مع رئيس الوزراء الساعة الحادية عشرة وبعد ذلك سَيَعْقُد جلسة عمل مع المساعدين في وزارة الصحّة الساعة الخامسة إلا ربعًا.

أوّل أمس، ٢٠ فبراير، زار الوزير الكويت.

بعد غد، ٢٤ فبراير، سَيَزور الوزير الأردنّ.

Exercise 3
Try to check your diary and description with an Arabic-speaker.

Exercise 4

1 Minister of Defence.
2 Six.
3 *Any three from* France, Belgium, Oman, Bahrain, Saudi, Kuwait.
4 Tomorrow.
5 Washington.
6 Paris.

Exercise 5

واشِنطُن/أمريكا	الرِّياض/السَّعودية
باريس/فَرَنسا	المَنامَة/البَحرين
بروكسل/بلَجيكا	مَسْقَط/عُمان

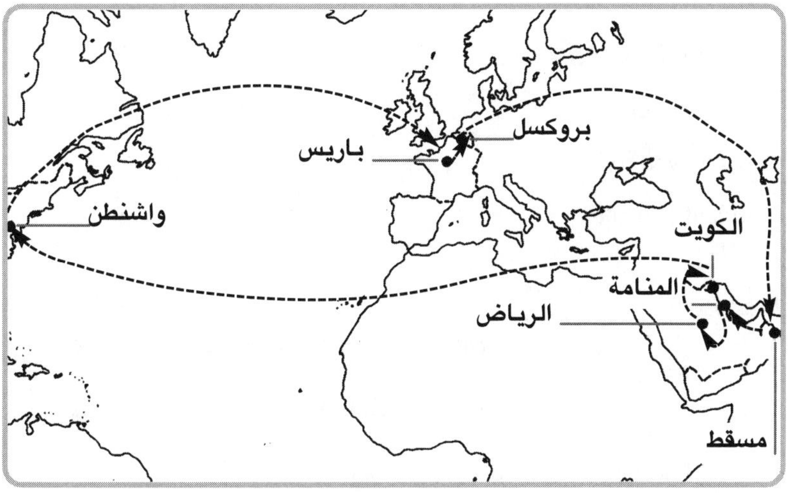

Exercise 6

يوم الاثنين	٢٨ نوفمبر:	واشنطن إلى باريس
يوم الخميس	١ ديسمبر:	باريس إلى بروكسل
يوم السبت	٢ ديسمبر:	بروكسل إلى مسقط
يوم الأحد	٤ ديسمبر:	مسقط إلى المنامة
يوم الاثنين	٥ ديسمبر:	المنامة إلى الرياض
يوم الثلاثاء	٦ ديسمبر:	الرياض إلى الكويت

Exercise 7

There are many possible sentences. Try to check yours with an Arabic-speaker.

Exercise 8

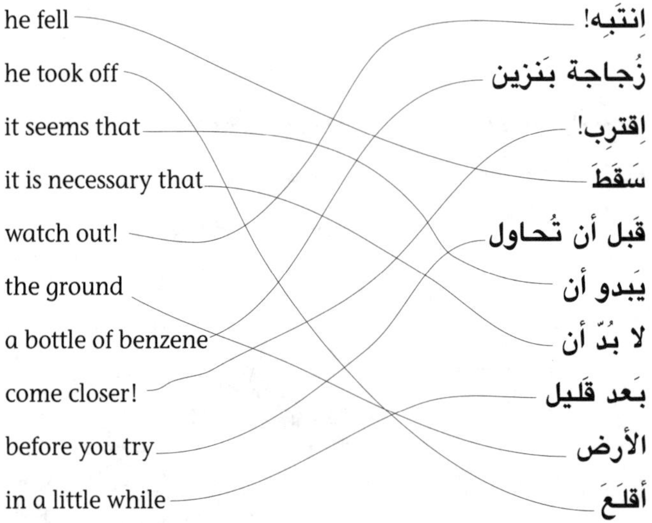
he fell
he took off
it seems that
it is necessary that
watch out!
the ground
a bottle of benzene
come closer!
before you try
in a little while
اِنتَبِه!
زُجاجة بَنزين
اِقترِب!
سَقَطَ
قَبل أن تُحاوِل
يَبدو أن
لا بُدّ أن
بَعد قَليل
الأرض
أقلَعَ

Exercise 9

Meaning	*Present*	*Past*	*Form*	*Root*
to move off	يَنطَلِق	اِنطَلَق	VII	طلق
to take care	يَنتَبِه	اِنتَبَه	VIII	نبه
to enquire	يَستَعلِم	اِستَعلَم	X	علم
to work	يَشتَغِل	اِشتَغَل	VIII	شغل
to use/employ	يَستَخدِم	اِستَخدَم	X	خدم
to listen	يَستَمِع	اِستَمَع	VIII	سمع
to overturn	يَنقَلِب	اِنقَلَب	VII	قلب

UNIT 20

Exercise 1

٥ ونصف كيلو جبنة بيضاء من فضلِك. كم الحساب؟

٢ صباح النور يا سيّدي.

٤ تحت أمرك ... تَفَضّل.

٣ أعطني من فضلِك كيس سُكّر وزجاجة (عُلبة) عصير تُفّاح.

١ صباح الخير.

٨ اللّه يسلِّمَك.

٦ ١٣ جنيه من فضلك.

٧ تفَضّلي. مع السَلامَة.

Exercise 2

	المشروبات	الطبق الأوّل	الطبق الرئيسي	الحلويات
سلوى	عصير منجة	سلطة	دجاج بالبطاطس	كعك
أحمد	كولا	مكرونة	سمك بالرزّ	-----

Exercise 3

You should have chosen the tomato salad and the macaroni with tomato. The final bill and conversation will depend on your choice of dessert and drink. Try to check them with an Arabic-speaker.

Exercise 4

١ بَيْت بُيُوت
٢ شَيخ شُيوخ
٣ وَكيل وُكَلاء
٤ كِتاب كُتُب
٥ وَزير وُزَراء
٦ مَكتَب مَكاتِب
٧ قِطار قِطارات
٨ مُمَثِّلَة مُمَثِّلات
٩ مَدينَة مُدُن
١٠ مُساعد مُساعِدون/ين
١١ دَرْس دُروس
١٢ سَنة سَنَوات
١٣ مَتْحَف مَتاحِف
١٤ طَبَق أطباق
١٥ أَمير أُمَراء

Exercise 5

١ الساعة الثانية ظهرًا، يوم ١٤ يناير

٢ الساعة السادسة والنصف صباحًا، يوم ٢٤ أكتوبر

٣ الساعة الثامنة مساءً، يوم ١٠ يوليو

٤ الساعة الخامسة إلا ربعًا، يوم ١٥ ديسمبر

٥ الساعة السابعة والثلث صباحًا، يوم ٦ مارس

٦ الساعة الحادية عشرة إلا خمس دقائق صباحًا، يوم ١ أبريل

Exercise 6

March	France/Belgium
April	Germany
May	England
June	America
July	America
August	Canada
September	Mexico

Exercise 7

Meaning	*Form*	*Present*	*Past*
to approach	VIII	يَقتَرِب	اِقتَرَب
to take out	IV	يُخرِج	أَخْرَج
to wash	I	يَغْسِل	غَسَل
to set off	VII	يَنْطَلِق	اِنْطَلَق
to mend/fix	II	يُصَلِّح	صَلَّح

اِجتَمَع	يَجتَمِع	VIII	to meet
عَقَد	يَعقُد	I	to hold/convene
حاوَل	يُحاوِل	III	to try/attempt
رَتَّب	يُرَتِّب	II	to tidy/arrange
نَظَّف	يُنَظِّف	II	to clean
زار	يَزور	I	to visit
تَعاوَن	يَتَعاوَن	VI	to cooperate
تَذَكَّر	يَتَذَكَّر	V	to remember
اِستَغرَق	يَسْتَغْرِق	X	to take up (time)

Exercise 8

١ كلّ يوم يعقد الوزير جلسة عمل.

٢ كلّ يوم تذهب زينب إلى البنك.

٣ غدًا سَنزور المتحف في وسط المدينة.

٤ نَظَّفوا الأطباق أمس.

٥ لم نتذكّر (ما تذكّرنا) اسم المدرسة أمس.

٦ منذ ٣ ساعات اِنطلق الأصدقاء إلى المدينة.

٧ اليوم يجتمع وزراء الاقتصاد في عَمَّان ويتبادلون الأفكار.

٨ الآن لا تَتَعاوَن دُوَل العالم الثالث.

Exercise 9

١ لم تُصَلِّح دراجتها المكسورة. لم تصلِّحها.

٢ صَلَّحَت الكرسي المكسور. صلَّحَته.

٣ غَسَلَت قميص أحمد. غسلَته.

٤ لم تَكتُب رسالة لأمّها. لم تكتُبها.

٥ رَتَّبَت اللعب في الخزانة. رتَّبَتها.

٦ طَبَخَت العشاء. طبخَته.

٧ لم تُنَظِّف الأطباق. لم تنظِّفها.

٨ لم تُخرِج الزبالة. لم تُخرِجها.

٩ ذَهَبَت إلى البنك. ذهبت إليه.

١٠ لم تُنَظِّف المطبخ. لم تنظِّفه.

English–Arabic glossary

The following glossary contains the key words presented in *Mastering Arabic*.

The meanings given are as used in this book. There may be alternative English or Arabic meanings. For these, you will need to use a dictionary.

Plurals are given in brackets after the singular.

Verbs are followed by *(v.)* in the English. (If a word is not followed by *(v.)*, you can presume that it is not a verb.) Both the past and present tenses are given in Arabic.

A	about *(a subject, etc.)*	عَنْ
	above	فَوْقَ
	accountant	مُحاسِب
	actor	مُمَثِّل (ون/ين)
	actress	مُمَثِّلة (ات)
	aeroplane	طائِرة (ات)
	affair	شَأْن (شُئون)
	Africa	أفْريقيا
	after	بَعْدَ
	after that	بَعْدَ ذلِك
	afternoon	بَعْدَ الظُّهْر
	agency	وِكالة (ات)
	agent	وَكيل (وُكَلاء)

ago: ... ago	مُنذُ ...
agriculture	زِراعة (ات)
aid *(e.g. foreign aid)*	مَعونة (ات)
aide	مُساعِد (ون/ين)
all	كُلّ
all right	حَسَنًا
almonds	لَوْز
ambassador	سَفير (سُفَراء)
America	أمْريكا
American	أمْريكيّ (ون/ين)
and so	فَـ
appears: it appears that	يَبدو أَن
apples	تُفّاح
approach *(v.)*	اِقْتَرَب / يَقْتَرِب
April	أبْريل
Arab/Arabic	عَرَبيّ (عَرَب)
Arabic *(language)*	العَرَبيّة
arrive *(v.)*	وَصَل / يَصِل
artefact	تُحْفة (تُحَف)
Asia	آسْيا
assistant	مُساعِد (ون/ين)
at *(used to talk about possession)*	عِنْدَ
attempt *(v.)*	حاوَل / يُحاوِل
attend *(v.)*	حَضَر / يَحضَر
August	أغُسطُس

B	bag/case	حَقيبة (حَقائِب)
	bag *(plastic, etc.)*	كِيس (أكْياس)
	baker	خَبّاز (ون/ين)
	ball	كُرَة (ات)
	banana(s)	مَوْز
	bank	بَنْك (بُنوك)
	banner	راية (رايات)
	basket	سَلّة (سِلال)
	be *(v.)*	كان / يكون
	beautiful	جَميل، حُلْو
	bed	سَرير (أَسِرَّة)
	before	قَبْلَ
	before that	قَبْلَ ذلِك
	begin *(v.)*	بَدَأ / يَبْدأ
	below	تَحْتَ
	beside	بِجانِب
	better, best	أَفْضَل
	Best wishes *(close of letter, etc.)*	مَعَ تَحِيّاتي
	between	بَيْنَ
	bicycle	دَرّاجة (ات)
	big	كَبير
	bill	حِساب (ات)
	biscuits	بَسكَويت
	black *(masc./fem.)*	أَسْوَد / سَوْدَاء
	blue *(masc./fem.)*	أَزْرَق / زَرْقَاء

	book	كِتاب (كُتُب)
	book *(v.)*	حَجَز / يَحْجِز
	bookshop	مَكتَبة (ات)
	bottle	زُجَاجة (ات)
	box	عُلْبة (عُلَب)
	boy	وَلَد (أوْلاد)
	bread	خُبْز
	breakfast	إفْطار
	broken	مَكْسور
	brother	أَخ (إِخوَة)
	burger	بورجَر
	bus	باص (ات) / أُتوبيس (ات)
	but	لكِن
C	cabinet *(of ministers)*	مَجْلِس (مَجالِس)
	cake	كَعْك
	call *(v.)*	دَعا / يَدعو
	camel	جَمَل (جِمال)
	can I have? *(possible?)*	مُمكِن؟
	candle	شَمعة (شُموع)
	capital *(city)*	عاصِمة (عَواصِم)
	car	سَيّارة (ات)
	carpenter	نَجّار (ون/ين)
	carry *(v.)*	حَمَل / يَحمِل
	carton	عُلْبة (عُلَب)
	certainly	حاضِر

chair	كُرْسيّ (كَراسي)
chairman, leader	رَئيس (رُؤَساء)
chairmanship	رِئاسة (ات)
cheap	رَخيص
cheese	جُبْنة
chef	طَبَّاخ (ون/ين)
chemistry	الكيمياء
chicken	دَجَاجة (دَجَاج)
China	الصِّين
Chinese	صِينيّ
cigarette	سيجارَة (سَجَائِر)
cinema	سينِما
city	مَدينة (مُدُن)
class, lesson	دَرْس (دُروس)
clean *(v.)*	نَظَّف / يُنَظِّف
clear *(weather)*	صَحْو
clock	ساعة (ات)
cloudy	غَائِم
coffee	قَهْوَة
coffee beans	بُنّ
cola	كولا
cold	بـارِد
colour	لَوْن (أَلْوان)
come close *(v.)*	اِقْتَرَب / يَقْتَرِب
complain	شَكا / يَشْكو

concerning	عَنْ
condition	حَال (أَحوال)
conference	مُؤْتَمَر (ات)
continent	قَارّة (ات)
convene (v.)	عَقَد / يَعْقِد
cook (person)	طَبّاخ (ون/ين)
cook (v.)	طَبَخ / يَطْبُخ
cooperate (v.)	تَعَاوَن / يَتَعَاوَن
cotton	قُطْن
country	دَوْلة (دُوَل)
course (of a meal)	طَبَق (أَطْباق)
court (tennis, etc.)	مَلْعَب (مَلاعِب)
cultivate (v.)	زَرَع / يَزْرَع
culture	ثَقَافة (ات)
cup	فِنْجان (فَناجين)
cupboard	خَزانة (ات)
D daughter	بِنْت (بَنات)
day	يَوْم (أَيّام)
day after tomorrow	بَعْدَ غَد
day before yesterday	أَوَّل أَمْس
dear (opening of letter; masc./fem.)	عَزيزي / عَزيزَتي
December	ديسَمبِر
defence	دِفاع
defend (v.)	دافَع / يُدافِع
degree (temperature, etc.)	دَرَجة (ات)

	delicious	شَهيّ
	democracy	الديموقْراطيّة
	depart *(v.)*	غادَر / يُغادِر
	deputy	نائِب (نُوّاب)
	desk	مكتَب (مَكاتِب)
	desserts	حلَويّات
	Dinar	دينار (دَنانير)
	dinner	عَشَاء
	Dirhem	دِرْهَم (دَراهِم)
	discuss *(v.)*	تَناقَش / يَتَناقَش
	do *(v.)*	فَعَل / يَفْعَل
	dog	كَلْب (كِلاب)
	donkey	حِمار (حَمير)
	door	باب (أبْواب)
	drawing	رَسْم (رُسوم)
	drink *(v.)*	شَرِب / يَشْرَب
	drum	طَبْلة (طُبول)
E	east	شَرْق
	eat *(v.)*	أَكَل / يأكُل
	economy	اِقْتِصاد
	education	تَعْليم
	eggs	بَيْض
	Egypt	مِصْر
	Egyptian	مِصْريّ
	eight	ثَمانِية

	eighteen	ثَمانِيَة عَشَر
	eighty	ثَمانين
	eleven	أَحَد عَشَر
	embassy	سِفارَة (ات)
	emir	أَمير (أُمَراء)
	emirate	إمارَة (ات)
	engineer	مُهَنْدِس (ون/ين)
	engineering	الهَنْدَسة
	England	اِنْجِلترا
	English *(adj.)*	اِنجِليزيّ (إنجِليز)
	English *(language)*	الاِنجِليزيّة
	entrance	مَدْخَل (مَداخِل)
	Europe	أوروبا
	evening	مَساء
	every	كُلّ
	every day	كُلّ يَوْم
	exchange *(views, etc.)* *(v.)*	تَبادَل / يتَبادَل
	exhibit *(v.)*	عَرَض / يعْرِض
	exhibition	مَعْرَض (مَعارِض)
	exit	مَخْرَج (مَخارِج)
	exit *(v.)*	خَرَج / يَخْرُج
	exterior	خارِجيَّة
F	face	وَجْه (وُجوُه)
	factory	مَصْنَع (مَصانِع)
	faculty *(university)*	كُلِّية (ات)

fall *(v.)*	سَقَط / يَسْقُط
fast	سَريع
father	أَب (آباء)
February	فَبراير
fifteen	خَمْسة عَشَر
fifty	خَمْسين
figs	تين
film	فيلْم (أفلام)
finally	أَخيراً
find *(v.)*	وَجَد / يَجِد
fine *(weather)*	صَحْو
firstly	أَوَّلاً
fish	سَمَك
five	خَمْسة
flag	راية (رايات)
flies	ذُباب
fly *(v.)*	طَار / يَطير
for	لِـ...
forty	أَرْبَعين
four	أَرْبَعة
fourteen	أَرْبَعة عَشَر
France	فَرَنْسا
French	فَرَنْسيّ (ون/ين)
Friday	يَوم الجُمعة
friend	صَاحِب (أَصْحاب)

	from	مِنْ
	future	مُسْتَقْبَل
G	game	لُعْبة (لُعَب)
	general *(adj.)*	عَامّ
	geography	الجُغْرافيا
	German	أَلْماني
	Germany	أَلْمانيا
	girl	بِنْت (بَنات)
	give me	أَعْطِني
	glass *(material)*	زُجاج
	go *(v.)*	ذَهَب / يَذْهَب
	go back *(v.)*	رَجَع / يَرْجَع، عاد / يَعود
	go out *(v.)*	خَرَج / يَخرُج
	gold	ذَهَب
	good evening/afternoon	مَساء الخَيْر، مَساء النُّور
	good morning	صَباح الخَيْر، صَباح النُّور
	goodbye	مَعَ السَّلامة
	green *(masc./fem.)*	أَخْضَر / خَضْراء
	greeting	تَحِيَّة (ات)
	grocer	بَقّال (ون/ين)
	ground	أَرْض
	Gulf (the)	الخَليج
H	half	نِصْف
	hat	قُبَّعة (ات)
	he	هُوَ

head *(of organisation, etc.)*	رَئيس (رُؤَساء)
health	صِحَّة
hear *(v.)*	سَمِع / يَسْمَع
heart	قَلْب (قُلوب)
heat	حَرارَة
heat *(v.)*	سَخَّن / يُسَخِّن
heavy	ثَقيل
hello	أَهلاً
help	مُساعَدة (ات)
helper	مُساعِد (ون/ين)
hen	دَجاجة (دَجاج)
her	...ـها
here you are *(masc./fem./plural)*	تَفَضَّل / تَفَضَّلي / تَفَضَّلوا
his	...ـهُ
history	تاريخ
hold *(a meeting, etc.) (v.)*	عَقَد / يَعْقِد
home	بَيْت (بُيوت)
hospital	مُسْتَشْفى (مُسْتَشْفيات)
hot	حارّ
hotel	فُنْدُق (فَنادِق)
hour	سَاعة (ات)
house	بَيْت (بُيوت)
how?	كَيْفَ ؟
how are you?	كَيْفَ الحال/كَيفَ حالك؟
how many?	كَم؟

	how much?	بِكَم؟
	hundred	مائة (مئات)
	husband	زَوْج (أزْواج)
I	I	أَنا
	I'd like...	أُريد...
	ice-cream	آيس كريم
	idea	فِكْرَة (أَفْكار)
	important	هَامّ
	in	في
	in front of	أَمام
	in the middle of	في وَسَط
	increase *(v.)*	زاد / يَزيد
	industry	صِناعة (ات)
	inexpensive	رَخيص
	inspector	مُفَتِّش (ون/ين)
	interior	داخِليّة
	investigation	تَحقيق (ات)
	Iraq	العِراق
	Iraqi	عِراقيّ
	it *(masc./fem.)*	هُوَ / هِيَ
	Italian	اِيطاليّ
	Italy	اِيطاليا
J	January	يَنايِر
	Japan	اليابان
	Japanese	يابانيّ

	Jordan	الأُرْدُنّ
	Jordanian	أُرْدُنّي
	juice	عَصير
	July	يوليو
	June	يونيو
	justice	عَدْل
K	key	مِفْتاح (مَفَاتيح)
	kilo	كيلو
	king	مَلِك (مُلوك)
	kitchen	مَطْبَخ (مَطابِخ)
L	laundry, launderette	مَغْسَلة (مَغاسِل)
	law *(study)*	الحُقوق
	lead *(v.)*	قاد / يَقود
	leader	زَعيم (زُعَماء)
	leadership	زِعامة (ات)
	learn *(v.)*	تَعَلَّم / يَتَعَلَّم
	leather	جِلد
	leave *(v.)*	غادَر / يُغادِر
	Lebanese	لُبْنانيّ
	Lebanon	لُبْنان
	lecture	مُحاضَرة (ات)
	left *(direction)*	يَسار
	lesson	دَرْس (دُروس)
	letter *(mail)*	خِطاب (ات)، رِسالة (رَسائِل)
	library	مَكتَبة (ات)

	Libya	ليبْيا
	Libyan	لِيبْيّ (ون/ين)
	light *(weight)*	خَفيف
	like: I'd like	أُريد
	Lira *(money)*	ليرَة (ات)
	long	طَويل
	lunch	غَدَاء
M	macaroni	مكَرونة
	madam	مَدام
	man	رَجُل (رِجال)
	mangoes	مَنجة
	many	كَثير
	March	مارِس
	market	سوق (أسواق)
	masterpiece	تُحْفة (تُحَف)
	mathematics	الرياضِيّات
	matter	شَأْن (شُئون)
	May	مايو
	me	...ـني
	meat	لَحْم
	medal	ميدالية (ات)
	medicine *(study)*	الطِّبّ
	meet *(v.)*	اِجْتَمَع / يَجْتَمِع، تَقابَل / يَتَقابَل
	meeting	اِجْتِمَاع (ات)
	mend *(v.)*	صَلَّح / يُصلِّح

	mentioned: above mentioned	مَذكور
	middle	وَسَط
	Middle East	الشَّرق الأوْسَط
	mild	مُعْتَدِل
	military	عَسْكَريّ
	milk	حَليب
	million	مَلْيون (ملايين)
	minister	وَزير (وُزَراء)
	ministry	وِزارَة (ات)
	minute	دَقيقة (دَقائِق)
	moderate	مُعْتَدِل
	Monday	يَوم الاِثْنَين
	month	شَهْر (شُهور)
	more, most	أَكْثَر
	morning	صَباح
	mosque	مَسْجِد (مَساجِد)
	mother	أُمّ (أُمَّهات)
	mountain	جَبَل (جِبال)
	move off *(v.)*	اِنْطَلَق / يَنْطَلِق
	museum	مَتْحَف (مَتاحِف)
	music	موسيقى
	my	...ـي
N	name	اِسْم (أَسْماء)
	nation	دَولة (دُوَل)
	nationality	جِنْسيَّة (ات)

	necessary: it is necessary that	لا بُدَّ أَن
	necklace	قِلادة (قَلائِد)
	new	جَديد
	newspaper	جَريدَة (جَرائِد)
	nine	تِسْعة
	nineteen	تِسْعة عَشَر
	ninety	تِسْعين
	no	لا
	noon	ظُهْر
	north	شَمال
	November	نُوفَمبِر
	now	اَلآن
	number *(numeral)*	رَقْم (أَرْقام)
	number *(quantity)*	عَدَد (أَعْداد)
	nurse	مُمَرِّضة (ات)
O	October	أُكْتوبَر
	office	مَكْتَب (مَكاتِب)
	oil	زَيت (زُيوت)
	old *(of objects)*	قَديم
	old *(of people)*	كَبير السِّن
	Oman	عُمان
	Omani	عُمانيّ (ون/ين)
	on	عَلَى
	on the left of	عَلَى يَسار
	on the right of	عَلَى يَمين

	one	واحِد
	only	فَقَط
	open *(v.)*	فَتَح / يَفْتَح
	opening ceremony	اِفْتِتاح (ات)
	oranges	بُرْتُقال
	our	...نا
	overcast *(weather)*	غائِم
P	packet	عُلْبة (عُلَب)
	palace	قَصْر (قُصور)
	parliament	بَرْلَمان (ات)
	party *(celebration)*	حَفْلة (ات)
	party *(political)*	حِزب (أَحْزاب)
	past: the past	الماضي
	pen	قَلَم (أَقْلام)
	period *(of time)*	فَتْرَة (فَتَرات)
	pharaonic	فِرعونيّ
	picture	صورَة (صُوَر)
	piece	قِطْعة (قِطَع)
	pigeons	حَمام
	pitch *(football, etc.)*	مَلْعَب (مَلاعِب)
	pizza	بيتزا
	plane	طائِرة (ات)
	plastic	بلاستيك
	plate	طَبَق (أَطْباق)
	play *(v.)*	لَعِب / يَلْعَب

	playing field	مَلْعَب (مَلاعِب)
	please *(masc./fem.)*	مِن فَضْلَك / مِن فَضلِك
	poor	فَقير (فُقَراء)
	potatoes	بَطاطِس
	Pound *(money)*	جُنَيه (ات)
	prefer *(v.)*	فَضَّل / يُفَضِّل
	prepare *(v.)*	جَهَّز / يُجَهِّز
	presidency	رِئاسة
	president	رَئيس (رُؤَساء)
	price	سِعْر (أَسْعار)
	prince	أَمير (أُمَراء)
	princess	أَميرة (ات)
	profession	مِهْنة (مِهَن)
	professor	أُسْتاذ (أساتِذة)
	pupil *(school)*	تِلميذ (تلامِذة)
	put on *(for clothes, etc.) (v.)*	لَبِس / يَلْبَس
	put out *(rubbish, etc.) (v.)*	أَخْرَج / يُخْرِج
Q	quarter	رُبْع (أَرباع)
R	receive *(guests, etc.) (v.)*	اِسْتَقْبَل / يَسْتَقبِل
	red *(masc./fem.)*	أَحْمَر / حَمْراء
	religious education	التَّربية الدينيّة
	remember *(v.)*	تَذَكَّر / يَتَذَكَّر
	reserve *(v.)*	حَجَز / يَحْجِز
	restaurant	مَطْعَم (مَطاعِم)
	return *(v.)*	رَجَع / يَرجِع، عاد / يَعود

rice	أَرُز
rich	غَنيّ
right *(direction)*	يَمين
ring	خاتِم (خَواتِم)
river	نَهْر (أنْهار)
Riyal	ريال (ات)
robbery	سَرِقة (ات)
rose	وَرْدَة (وَرْد)
royal	مَلَكيّ
rubbish	زُبالة
run *(v.)*	جَرَى/يَجْري
Russia	روسيا
Russian	روسيّ (روس)

S

salad	سَلَطة (ات)
sandals	صَندَل
sandwich	سَنْدويتش
Saturday	يوم السَّبْت
Saudi *(country)*	السَّعوديّة
Saudi *(nationality)*	سَعوديّ (ون/ين)
say *(v.)*	قال / يَقول
school	مَدْرَسة (مَدارِس)
sea	بَحْر (بِحار)
seems: it seems that	يَبْدو أَن
sell *(v.)*	باع / يَبيع
September	سِبتَمبِر

service	خِدْمة (ات)
at your service	تَحْت أَمْرَك
session	جَلْسة (ات)
set out *(v.)*	اِنْطَلَق / يَنْطَلِق
seven	سَبْعة
seventeen	سَبْعة عَشَر
seventy	سَبْعين
shampoo	شَامبو
shape	شَكْل (أشْكال)
she	هِيَ
sheikh	شَيْخ (شُيوخ)
shirt	قَميص (قُمْصان)
short	قَصير
shorts	شورت
show *(v.)*	عَرَض / يَعْرِض
silk	حَرير
silver	فِضّة
since *(e.g. 'since 1982')*	مُنْذُ
sir	سَيِّدي
sister	أُخْت (أَخَوات)
sit down *(v.)*	جلَس / يَجْلِس
six	سِتّة
sixteen	سِتّة عَشَر
sixty	سِتّين
small	صَغير

	so	فَـ...
	soap	صابون
	son	اِبْن (أبْنـاء)
	south	جَنوب
	Spain	اِسْبـانيـا
	Spanish	اِسْبـانيّ (ون/ين)
	speak *(v.)*	تَكَلَّم / يَتَكَلَّم
	sport	رِيـاضة (ات)
	state *(condition)*	حـال (أحْوال)
	state *(country)*	دَولـة (دُوَل)
	street	شارِع (شَوارِع)
	strong	قَوِيّ
	student	طالِب (طَلَبة)
	study *(v.)*	دَرَس / يَدْرُس
	Sudan	السودان
	Sudanese	سودانيّ (ون/ين)
	sugar	سُكَّر
	Sunday	يوم الأحَد
	supper	عَشاء
	sweet	حُلْو
	sword	سَيف (سُيوف)
	Syria	سوريـا / سوريـة
	Syrian	سوريّ (ون/ين)
T	table	مائِدَة (مَوائِد)
	take *(v.)*	أخَذ / يأخُذ

take off *(plane, etc.) (v.)*	أَقْلَع / يُقْلِع
take out *(rubbish, etc.) (v.)*	أَخْرَج / يُخْرِج
take up *(of time, etc.) (v.)*	اِستَغْرَق / يَسْتَغْرِق
talk *(v.)*	تَكَلَّم / يَتَكَلَّم
tall *(for people)*	طَويل
tea	شاي
teacher	مُدَرِّس (ون/ين)
telephone	تليفون (ات)
television	تليفزيون (ات)
temperature	دَرَجة الحَرارَة
ten	عَشَرة
tennis	تَنِس
tent	خَيمة (خِيام)
thank you	شُكْراً
theft	سَرِقة (ات)
their *(masc./fem.)*	...ـهُم / ...ـهُنَّ
then	ثُمَّ
there is/are	هُناك
there is not/are not	لَيْسَ هُناك
these *(people)*	هؤُلاءِ
these *(non-humans)*	هذِهِ
they *(masc.)*	هُم
they *(fem.)*	هُنَّ
thief	لِصّ (لُصوص)
third	ثُلْث (أَثْلاث)

thirteen	ثَلاثة عَشَر
thirty	ثَلاثين
this *(masc.)*	هذا
this *(fem.)*	هذِهِ
thought	فِكرَة (أفكار)
three	ثَلاثة
throw *(v.)*	رَمَى / يَرمي
Thursday	يوم الخَميس
time	وَقْت (أَوقات)
tin *(of beans, etc.)*	عُلبة (عُلَب)
to *(for)*	لِـ...
to *(towards)*	إلَى
today	اليَوم
tomatoes	طَماطِم
tomorrow	غَدًا
toothpaste	مَعْجون الأسنان
total	مَجْموع
towards	إلَى
town	مَدينة (مُدُن)
toy	لُعْبة (لُعَب)
train	قِطار (ات)
tree	شَجَرة (شَجَر)
try *(v.)*	حاوَل / يُحاوِل
tube	أُنبوبة (أنابيب)
Tuesday	يوم الثُلاثَاء

	twelve	اِثنا عَشَر
	twenty	عِشْرين
	two	اِثنان
U	ugly	قَبيح
	university	جامِعة (ات)
	until	حَتَّى
V	visit *(v.)*	زار / يَزور
W	waiter	جَرسون
	walk *(v.)*	مَشى / يَمْشي
	wash *(v.)*	غَسَل / يَغْسِل
	washing powder	مَسْحوق الغَسيل
	watch *(wrist)*	سَاعة (ات)
	watch out *(v.)*	اِنْتَبَه / يَنْتَبِه
	water	مَاء
	watermelons	بَطِّيخ
	we	نَحْنُ
	weak	ضَعيف
	wear *(v.)*	لَبِس / يَلبَس
	weather	طَقْس
	Wednesday	يوم الأربعاء
	week	أُسبوع (أَسابيع)
	weight	وَزن (أوزان)
	west	غَرب
	what *(+ noun)*?	ما؟
	what's your name?	ما اِسْمك؟

	what (+ verb)?	ماذا؟
	when?	مَتَى؟
	where?	أَيْنَ؟
	which?	أَيّ؟
	white (masc./fem.)	أَبيَض / بَيضاء
	whole, unbroken	سَليم
	why?	لِماذا؟
	wife	زَوجة (ات)
	wind (fem.)	ريح (رِياح)
	window	شُبّاك (شَبابيك)
	with	مَعَ، بِ...
	wood	خَشَب
	working session, workshop	جَلْسة عَمَل
	world (the)	العالَم
	write (v.)	كَتَب / يَكتُب
Y	year	سَنة (سَنوات / سِنون)
	yellow (masc./fem.)	أَصْفَر / صَفْراء
	Yemen	اليَمَن
	Yemeni	يَمَنيّ
	yes	نَعْم
	yesterday	أمْس
	you (masc./fem./plural)	أَنتَ / أَنتِ / أَنتُم
	young	صَغير السِنّ
	your (masc./fem./plural)	...كَ / ...كِ / ...كُم
Z	zero	صِفْر

Grammar index

The following index contains the key Arabic structures and grammar in *Mastering Arabic*, referenced by page number.

accusative case 144
active participles 285
adjectives 56, 86
adverbial phrases 144
agreement of adjectives 58
alif
  as first letter of word 20
  alif maqṣūra 77
  alif tanwīn 144, 252
assimilation 72
attached pronouns
  with noun 60, 127
  with verb 238
  with lākin (but) 250
bi + transportation 214
case endings 48
collective nouns 85
colours 142
comparatives 245
ḍamma 5
defective verbs 253
definite article (al-) 57
definite case ending 62
dual
  noun 119, 163
  verb 284
elision of al- 62
fatḥa 5
feminine
  noun 30, 42
  plural verb 283
forms of the verb 234
  forms II, III and IV 235
  forms V and VI 255
  forms VII, VIII and X 268
future with sa-/sawfa 262
gender 23, 30
genitive case 80
hamza 20, 184
hollow verbs 253
iḍāfa 33, 83, 195, 227
  genitive with iḍāfa 88
kam + singular 121
kasra 5
masculine nouns 30, 42
moon letters 72

negative 83, 216, 239
nisba adjective 107, 110
nominal sentences 22
nominative case 48
non-human plural 138
nouns of place 230
numbers 115, 169, 171
passive participles 285
past tense 156, 283
past tense negative 239
  with lam 239
  with mā 239
plural
  sound feminine 45, 86, 164
  sound masculine 45, 86, 163
  broken plural 135, 167, 286
  plural with numbers 120, 172
possession
  with ع inda 126
  with li 126
  with maع a 126
possessive constructions 33
present tense 218, 223, 283
present tense negative 216
question marker (hal) 75
root letters (al-maṣdar) 131
shadda 9
singular verb with plural 193
sukūn 8
sun letters 72
superlatives 245
syntax 188
tā' marbūṭa 30, 227
time 208
verb 283
verbal nouns 284
vowels
  short vowels 5
  long vowels 17
was/were (kān) 251
weak verbs 253
word order 188

Also available . . .

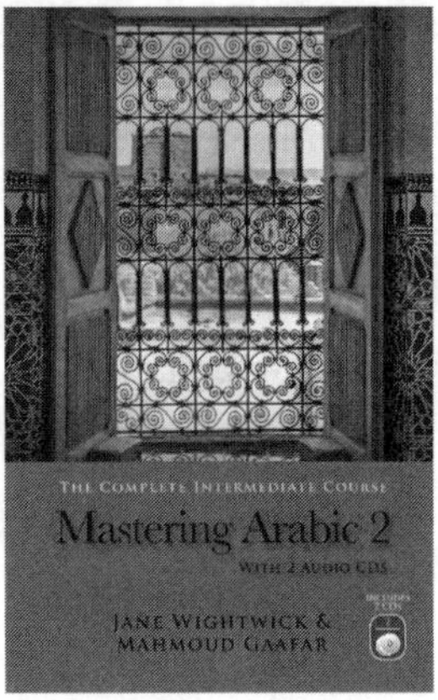

Mastering Arabic 2

With 2 Audio CDs: The Complete Intermediate Course

Mastering Arabic 2 is a modern, engaging, intermediate Arabic course offering lively dialogues, varied texts and exercises, and fascinating cultural insights. The course builds upon lessons from the best-selling *Mastering Arabic 1* but is suitable for any learner with some prior knowledge of Arabic.

- Teaches Modern Standard Arabic, the universal language of the Arab world, understood by all Arabic speakers
- Includes 14 carefully paced language lessons with cartoon illustrations, engaging exercises, and conversation sections
- Covers a wide variety of topics relevant to the Arab world, including house and home, work and routine, travel and tourism, food and cooking, news and media, and arts and cinema
- Based on a tested methodology proven to work for self-study or classroom use
- Focuses on the geography, culture, and dialects of major Arab countries
- Two audio CDs feature correct pronunciation by native speakers and help learners start speaking Arabic right away

ISBN 978-0-7818-1254-2
$29.95 paperback